African Women

Christine Obbo

To Aidan, Erifazi and Yayeri for providing the emotional and intellectual sustenance that enabled me to grow.

African Women
Their Struggle for Economic Independence

Christine Obbo

'Town Migration is not for Women'
— This book is African women's reply

Zed Press, 57 Caledonian Road, London N1 9DN

African Women: Their Struggle for Economic Independence was first published by Zed Press, 57 Caledonian Road, London N1 9DN in July 1980.

Copyright © Christine Obbo, 1980

ISBN 0 905762 33 9

Designed by Mayblin/Shaw
Copy-edited by Bev Brown
Typeset by Donald Typesetting
Proofread by Penelope Fryxell
Cover design by Jacque Solomons
Printed by Redwood Burns, Esher and
    Trowbridge

Contents

List of Tables

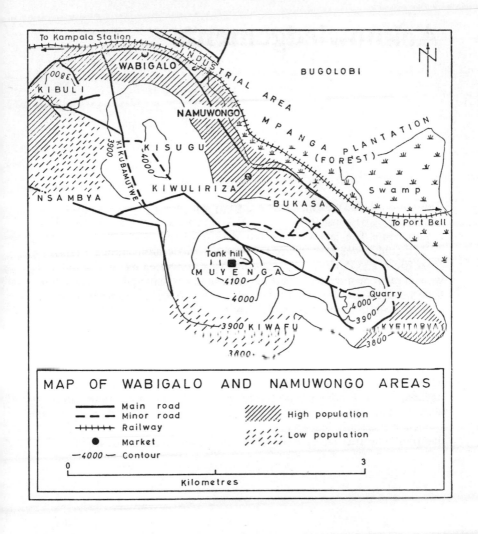

Map of Wabigalo and Namuwongo

Acknowledgements

This book is based on a much revised study which was presented at the University of Wisconsin (Madison, U.S.A.) as partial fulfillment of the Ph.D. requirements. The data was collected in 1971-73 and 1974.

This study owes its existence to the initial encouragement of Professor Peter Rigby and Professor A.W. Southall who convinced me that studying women or women-related problems was a valid academic pursuit. The latter lived also through the tortuous process of my writing up this study as well.

I am grateful, in addition, to Jan Vansina, David Parkin and John Middleton for sparing time to read and offer useful comments.

I should also like to thank Frances Lindner whose secretarial skills managed to turn my scribbles into a readable manuscript.

Lastly, I will always remember with love and appreciation the people who shared their homes and lives with me in ways I still find difficult to understand. Their privacy is protected through the use of fictitious names derived from their ethnic groups. Such was the enthusiasm and courage of the women in this study that I will continue to be interested in the 'woman question' long after it may cease to be fashionable in certain quarters.

A Fable by way of Preface

Once upon a time very long ago, God needed someone to help him with something he wanted done. He turned to the women, who already had their hands full even in those days. Just then they were making milk jugs and water basins and mats to cover the huts. God summoned them: 'Come here: I shall send you out on an important mission.' The women replied: 'Yes, we are coming but wait a moment, we shall finish our work here.' After a while, God summoned them again, and the women responded once more: 'Wait a moment, we are nearly done. Let us finish our mats and jugs.'

Men at that time did not have to milk the cows, build houses, fetch wood and water as the women did; their only duty was now and again to put up a fence to protect the livestock. So, since at that moment they had nothing else to do, they came running at God's call and said, 'Send us instead, Father.'

Then God turned to the women and said: 'Hereafter, women, your chores will never be done; when one is completed, the next one will be waiting for you. Hence the men may rest since they came at once when I called, but you, women, will have to work and toil with neither pause nor rest till the day you die.' And so it has been ever since.[1]

Time passed. Then one day some strangers came with books, seeds and guns. The men who had been resting embraced the strangers amidst protests from the women that the newcomers were going to harm the land and its people. Certainly their political and economic ideas soon divided the men into two groups — leaders and toilers. The latter had to be taught the dignity of labour by being required to pay taxes. As for the women, they just worked away unnoticed by anyone.

In the end, the women appealed to the good sense of their sons, brothers and husbands to compensate and reward them for their labour. But the men reminded them that God had condemned them to be the servants of the human species. They claimed that even the books of the strangers confirmed that women's place was indeed under men. Some of the women grumbled that 'the hardest of penalties is to be poor and also a woman.'[2] Others searched around for alternatives that would open up some kind of remedy for them. It was not long before the women realized that society depended upon them for its perpetuation and sustenance, and they became determined to bargain with these discoveries to acquire a share in the decisions regarding their labour and sexuality. The women's strongest assets were their hands — which, in some cases, enabled them to accumulate property in the form of land. But this made the men furious for it was now evident that property represented relationships between people and not between people and things.[3]

The men accused the women of getting out of control. And the women escaped to the cities determined to support themselves by hard work. Men then accused the women who were demanding an equal share in society's resources and power of weakening the common struggle against the strangers who controlled the world. Men claimed that women were diverting energy from the task of national development.

The women only smiled, for they had broken the spell of God's condemnation. It was a beginning. Their immediate concern was to lessen the private pains inflicted upon them. And some even dared to hope for a movement whose primary task would be to lessen the institutional pain inflicted upon women by dismantling the structures of male dominance.

This book is a picture of how East African women — ordinary people in the urban and rural areas of Uganda and Western Kenya — are struggling day by day to lessen that 'pain'.

Christine Obbo

References

1. Garri tale recounted by Gudrun Dahl in *Report from SIDA*, Special Issue on 'The Woman in the World', 1975, p. 5.
2. The hardest of penalties (penas encimadas), original text by Carmen Soler Canale, quoted in *ibid.*, p. 12.
3. F. Engels, 'The Origin of the Family: Private Property and the State' (1884) in Karl Marx and Frederick Engels, *Selected Works*, (Lawrence and Wishart, London, 1968).

1. 'Women Hold Up Half the Sky'

Anthropology and the Question of Women

It has been claimed that the main problem for women has been their 'invisibility' in any serious study of history and society.[1] This has meant that nearly half the people of most societies have not been allowed the chance or space to articulate their thoughts, fears, and hopes on the subjects of labour, reproduction, child-rearing and sexuality. It has also been argued that by trivializing the roles of women and the questions feminists are asking, mainstream anthropology has not provided answers to questions such as the origin and development of sexism.[2] These are difficult questions to answer but social scientists have, until recently, tended to avoid issues concerning women. Even though ethnographies contain information on women as mothers, daughters, sisters and wives of male informants or power holders, the voices of the women themselves are mute.[3] Kinship studies by and large give more weight to men who are portrayed as building up power bases by using women to weave kinship, friendship and marriage networks. Women are seen as merely assisting their men in the quest for power by building strong networks based on visiting and gossiping with relatives and neighbours.[4] Rarely do these studies say what the women themselves have to say about all this.

The absence of studies of women or feminist issues in anthropology[5] generally is quite surprising in view of the comparatively large number of female anthropologists.[6] But the vast majority of women who survive training, fieldwork, degree-getting and publishing to give us information are themselves trained by men.[7] Some women scholars claim that, if they deal with questions concerning women, their data would be regarded as 'soft' and their work not academically serious. Even those who manage to do studies on women avoid quoting feminist authors, whose writing is seen as biased and creating new myths.[8] Apparently some scholars still believe in a value-free social science. Yet consider, for example, the fact that colonialism was a male-dominated system. In its early stages it consisted of an all-male corps (apart from local recruits) and was apparently 'disinterested' and free of racial feelings. The appearance of colonial women, as wives, coincided with a hardening of racist attitudes, due to the family and racial considerations that men could no longer ignore. Anthropologists and other scholars inevitably shared the superior status that all whites had in colonial society. Whether they wanted it or not, it was impossible for them to escape it. In addition, most anthropologists were studying small male-dominated societies in the Third World. In order to obtain adequate data they had to come to terms with the male leaders of the societies they studied, and women anthropologists were regarded as 'honourary males'. The resulting work correctly conveyed the message that it was men who mattered in the societies studied. Although some anthropologists were attracted to the study of matrilineal societies[9], the result was, again, the correct conclusion that, while women may have some advantages in certain types of matrilineal systems, there is still no doubt about the political dominance of men. Indeed, some societies which have yielded interesting examples of women in powerful positions, or at least exercising significant power on certain occasions, were not matrilineal.[10] As for male anthropologists, they, for complementary reasons, were usually excluded from effective access to female informants.

Taking all these factors into account, it can hardly be denied that anthopology as a whole has provided an essentially male view of Third World societies. While this *is* a correct reflection of male dominance in the societies studied, it not only threatens to give an account of only one half of the world, it also transgresses the anthropological ideal of letting the people speak for themselves, especially in situations where the establishment denies them the right. Yet some male authors, while not personally hostile to women, developed theories that were clearly 'mankind minus women'[11] or reduced women to mere cogs in societal machinery, even though the very same authors had data suggesting otherwise.[12]

Often anthropologists have not dealt adequately with the question of the different 'realities' for the segments of a cultural group. Male reality tends to be presented as equivalent to the whole group's reality,[13] a view which often reduces women to inarticulate young gigglers or old snorters. (Yet no scholar could claim to have talked mainly to women about men without provoking professional comment.[14]) It is not widely admitted that male informants may claim to know more about women than they actually do.

Their defence is that women as a unit of analysis are ideologically rather than scientifically generated.[15] Or at least that only anthropologists who have already studied communities as wholes and produced monographs on them should, as already established scholars, turn to women's problems.[16] (Audrey Richards did just this in producing one of the most detailed studies of women's rituals[17] twenty years after her fieldwork, having already published two monumental volumes and many articles on the Bemba.[18]) While it may be that women are not a 'scientifically' generated unit of analysis (whatever that may mean), in many societies women are economically, socially, and symbolically defined as a distinct category.[19] If it can be argued that there is a need for some rewriting of many ethnographic accounts produced by anthropologists under colonial conditions,[20] a similar case can be made about the neglect bordering on suppression of half the world's population by these same anthropologists — an argument only strengthened by Ardener's point that women are less accessible than the men.[21]

Ardener's point is best illustrated by the classic and stimulating works of Evans-Pritchard on the Nuer of Southern Sudan. Scattered throughout his detailed accounts are indications of a much more complex situation with regard to residential patterns and the marriage options available to women.[22] He stated that payment of bridewealth required that the woman had to live with the husband's people (virilocally) after marriage,[23] that 'there were no unmarried women in primitive societies,'[24] and that the agnatic (patrilineal) principle was supreme.[25] First of all, his data shows that poor men who could not afford cattle for bridewealth did not bring their wives to live with them on marrying. Instead they resided with the wife's people who, in return for his services, would forego some of the marriage payment and even give him cattle.[26] Secondly, it appears that in every Nuer village there were one or two unmarried women who had refused marriage to particular men. Some living independently[27], as well as widows, could refuse to be inherited by their deceased husband's brothers or sons by other women, and either take lovers[28] or return with their children to their fathers' houses.[29] Lastly, the Nuer lineage structure seems to have been flexible enough for families and individuals to move about whenever they chose and attach themselves to a community of their choice. The result was that it was convenience which dictated whether or not afffinal ties were emphasized, as in the case of poor men,[30] or cognatic ties as when affines and descendants of aristocratic women claimed affiliation to the dominant lineage of residence.[31] In other cases, descent was even traced through women.[32] These examples betray the fact that Evans-Pritchard had no access to the Nuer women's perspective which appears muted although women were social actors who even turned the dominant male ideology upside down at times.

Inaccessibility of women is partly due to traditions that protect women against strangers and partly due to researchers' assumptions that men are better informants because they seem involved in the crucial cultural activities.[33] Many researchers have had to solve the problem of information that seemed crucial but which later turned out to be something men assert and women deny.[34] Material deriving from male-centred perspectives should be neither taken for granted nor regarded as an insoluble problem. As long as anthropologists consider their strength to lie in humility in the face of empirical evidence, women's perspectives must be sought out and presented. This should go some way towards solving the 'problem of women' created by their position in anthropological models and will result in more balanced monographs.

Social Change

Some social scientists working in the south of Uganda and based at the Makerere East African Institute of Social Research did write about women.[35] This can be attributed in part to the fact that the area exhibited all the symptoms of capitalist penetration — cashcrop farming, migrant labour and rural-urban migration. The present study belongs to that tradition but goes further to describe not only the social environment, but the goals, choices and strategies of women within certain social, political and economic constraints. Originally I set out to study the single unattached migrant woman and the ubiquitous stereotype by which such women were held responsible for most perceived social evils such as marital instability and its train of consequences: illegitimate children who, for example, grew up to be violent robbers (*kondos*) if they were boys or prostitutes if girls. But after a preliminary survey, the study became focused on finding out how and why women migrate from rural to urban areas in the first place; what they do when they arrive and how this affects relationships between men and women. As the study progressed, I realized that these questions could best be answered by looking at women's strategies and the options their circumstances allowed them.

The women in this study had never heard, and probably will never hear, of the Women's Movement in the West, but they have created their own patterns for emancipation and, in the process, are spearheading social change for better or for worse. For example, some of the women questioned male supremacy in all aspects of life as well as the associated myths of the inevitability of marriage, the undesirability of illegitimate children and the general problem of the way women's place is assumed to be subordinate and dependent upon men as fathers, brothers and husbands.

These ideas will in time influence women from all social strata. In fact the idea of women having independent bank accounts instead of joint ones with their husbands began with the uneducated women, who asserted that 'economic autonomy begins with separate savings'. One Ganda woman told me, 'Money enables one to implement decisions instead of sitting around wishing for luck!' This was repeatedly confirmed in conversations with women from all walks of life in different African countries, who modestly acknowledged that the source of their inspiration for separate incomes or savings was the conventional wisdom articulated by their unschooled relatives.

Thus it was economic autonomy which seemed to be the prevailing concern of women everywhere. My talks with women traders in cities as far apart as Dakar, Lagos, Nsukka and Nairobi all revealed life histories, ambitions and problems similar to those I had recorded in Namuwongo and Wabigalo in Uganda. For example, in 1977 I found that the unskilled women traders of Lagos had taken a public stand on the issue of men withholding money from their wives, a problem they knew about either at firsthand or from conversations with the victims. It was common knowledge that if a man showed up at the market he would be overcharged on the assumption that he was either withholding money from his wife or stinting on her housekeeping expenditure or suspecting her of putting money away to spend on her relatives or for a rainy day.

By contrast to these market traders, the majority of elite women I talked to merely muttered about sexism in job promotions and the unpleasant consequences that followed if they stood up to men either individually or as a group, but it will be a while before any organized confrontation between men and women takes place on these issues. The aggressive style of the market women who can dictate prices to the consumers is thought to be inappropriate for a professional woman trying to gain promotion. However, such caution in avoiding confrontation and embarrassment can lead to women being completely ignored.

The women in the present study claimed that they too wanted power, wealth and status and that this created tension and conflict between the sexes. Women found that, because men depended on them for achieving these goals themselves, they regarded any direct attempt by women to seek the same goals as women becoming uncontrollable! The need to control women has always been an important part of male success in most African societies. The women, however, whether married or single, had definite strategies for achieving economic autonomy and hence improved social conditions — strategies such as migration, hard work and manipulation. *Migration* involved mobility and hence escape from obstacles to individual progress in favour of creating or taking up more options. *Hard work* brought direct rewards for their labour and enabled them to feed, support and rear their children. Through *manipulation* the woman engaged in 'strategic planning' and thus mobilized needed resources and engaged in certain actions that led to institutional change.[36] The women put pressure on traditional ideologies to create options that enabled them to share in the resources and alternative life-styles available in their societies. Children were one of the counters used in the game of manipulation as played by both men and women.

The strategies were known to all but were disseminated discreetly in private conversation or as knowledge stored up from childhood observations of female relatives. Although most village women took care not to let the children know their strategies by speaking in riddles, such caution would be forgotten in moments of stress. The men also knew them from hearing stories about or talking to those who had been 'victims' of their wives' scheming; some men were even instrumental in the success of such schemes by helping their sisters escape from unsatisfactory marriages through providing village women with income or by buying small quantities of coffee from them knowing very well that they had taken it from their husbands. This study takes the view that although these strategies had their roots in the rural areas where the majority of women lived, it was the urban areas which offered more scope for realizing them. Individuals applied the strategies to suit their particular circumstances and to achieve definite goals, but the cumulative effect was a general pattern of social change. Individual women were thus unwitting agents of change.

It is unfortunate that social scientists often describe and analyse past social change, rather than the on-going purposive social change in the lives of individuals. When changes are actually in process, they are defined as social *problems*, rather than as social *opportunities*. Yet, if the people being studied are treated as actors playing a game[37] manipulating other players and circumstances,[38] then an attempt can be made at describing and analysing on-going social change. This solves the 'problem' of female invisibility by treating women as social actors with definite views about strategies applicable to certain problems in their situations and the ends they hope to achieve. In order to meet present-day circumstances, the women in this study were perhaps unknowingly trans-forming their cultures in important ways that men regarded as a threat. The implicit assumption in the East African folk view was that change, when it concerns women's roles, is risky.

Papanek[39] has pointed out that women are often presented with ambiguous signals from men in order to curb rapid social change. There are fears and doubts about women changing their roles, in particular, women's increasing participation in political and economic life. The result is often that women become defensive and even begin to doubt the desirability of change, prefer-ring the security of tradition which at least does not cause increased anxiety. While men often urge women to march forward with them, women's interests are often perceived as in conflict with their own. Elite women frequently actually support the men when patriarchal opinions preventing women from speaking out on issues of social and economic change are spiced with national-istic sentiments.

Contemporary Stereotypes

The stereotyped views of women expressed in speeches by Ugandan public figures and letters and articles in the press are very revealing. Trends of social change can also be gauged from public utterances, often in praise of the *status quo* against some impending or threatening change. Since in Africa there is little investigative reporting on political matters which does not simply repro-duce the official line, articles on social issues tend to be what journalists know will reflect the prejudices and beliefs of the (male) people.

While using the press as a source of information may be objectionable to some anthropologists for whom authentic data is obtained only from actual utterances of informants supplemented by participant observation, use of news-paper sources can be defended since the problems of partial information and personal bias are bound to come up whether informants talk or write. While elsewhere in the world, electronics have turned the mass media into an inde-pendent myth-making organization, in Africa, the media are still an important source of social and historical information that can enable us to see 'the city and its behavioural links to the larger society.'[40]

Accordingly, we will examine public views reported in the urban press, using quotations mainly from the four English language newspapers, two published in the capital city of Kampala (Uganda) and two published in Nairobi (Kenya). (The latter were widely read in Uganda before 1974.[41]) These views represent a small randomly selected fraction — both in quantity and timespan — of the familiar opinions and themes that recur in public dis-cussions. However the complex and diverse views do converge on one prob-lematic point — woman's place. This includes such issues as whether or not women should engage in wage labour at all, let alone be in towns; the fact that earning power enables women to resist pressure from men; and the impact of official legislation and statements on women's participation in public discussions or politics. So, although the migrant women studied here were illiterate, what was written in the urban press directly affected them by perpetuating certain stereotypes of the 'urban woman' in the popular mind. I was intrigued by the way contradictory views about women could be held simultaneously by the public: women were seen as both unwelcome competitors in the job market and as a wasted resource, as the upholders of traditional ways of life and those most vulnerable to Western influence.

Job Poachers or Wasted Resource?

The question of urban migration and its perception came into existence as soon as the first towns were established in East Africa. During the 1950s a commission of inquiry was appointed to study the problems of urban migration in Tanzania (then Tanganyika). Molohan, the Commissioner, travelled all over East Africa and many of the things he reported applied to Uganda and Kenya as well. He claimed that women in towns were a liability rather than an asset because they had nothing to do.[42] He recommended that women should be trained to obtain paid employment, and he further declared that although opportunities in industry were not yet very great, 'it is ludicrous that domestic service in Tanganyika should be a perquisite of the male. The territory cannot afford for much longer the luxury of locking up so many able-bodied men in this unproductive sphere of employment for which women are far more suited.'[43] No doubt meaning well, this kind of recommendation has led to women's participation in urban labour being regarded as a threat to economic development, with women seen as adding to the overwhelming unemployment problem by competing for jobs with men whose labour was assumed to be more valuable.[44] Consequently, women are often overlooked when technical ideas are being introduced, although they do not let this hinder their contribution which therefore relies heavily on personal initiative.[45] Women migrating to urban areas usually continued their traditional, rural-based, 'female' tasks within the expanded occupational structure of the city;[46] lack of education, skills and experience and negative attitudes made them ill-prepared for full involvement in the modern sector.[47]

The other view maintained that women in the urban areas were a wasted resource because they did not work hard like rural women who worked even on Sundays and public holidays,[48] but spent their time gossiping, dancing and drinking[49] and often using their bodies immorally to support themselves.[50] Both points of view are concerned with what happens to women in towns and cast doubt on the desirability of female migration. Both are reflected in journalistic treatment of the question of women.

It is appropriate to open this review of opinions expressed in the press with one of the rare quotations from a male correspondent in defence of women. It also illustrates the issues around which the debate rotates.

Men call illiterate women fools and uncivilized. Then when the women

7

become educated and are able to avoid running after men for money, the men complain that women are not caring for them . . . When men are criticized by women for their mistakes, they say they are beginning to rule over them. A woman is not a man's slave. Give love to your woman and she will give you the same. We are all equals as long as we walk on two legs.[51]

Some men feel strongly that women abuse the privilege of working by becoming too 'big headed' to accept the superior position accorded to men by the Bible and the Koran, supporting this view with the fact that young girls are reluctant to return to the villages while married women desert or divorce their husbands.

In any event, many women wind up as prostitutes.[52] It is not clear why the ambition to be economically self-supporting is so often fulfilled by prostitution. However, women, caught between the past and the present, are not fulfilling their culturally expected role when they do not cultivate the land and feed their families as their mothers did. It is not surprising that urban women are stereotyped as wasting money on expensive clothes and beauty products while their children suffer from kwashiokor — a protein deficiency caused by ignorance of the principles of nutrition and which occurs in both the rural and urban areas.[53] A well-known Ugandan joke depicts a large house with a car, usually a Mercedes Benz, parked in front while at the back the children suffer from kwashiokor. It in fact illustrates the misplaced priorities that lead men to engage in conspicuous consumption at the expense of their family's health. However, the men prefer to blame the women for failing in their role as food providers, especially if the women live in the towns.

It is argued that women cannot do justice to domestic work and child-rearing while simultaneously engaged in wage labour.[54] This provides additional support for the argument that the solution to male unemployment is the sacking of all employed women who are 'selfish' enough to hold other jobs in addition to marriage.[55] This view ignores the fact that women without a separate income are subject to the whims of men who may withhold support from their families while spending their money on drinking or other women. Women who work not only ward off starvation but they reduce that kind of unhealthy dependence.[56]

Women are constantly reminded, 'The pride of a proper woman is a husband'[57] with the warning that they may miss out on this blessing or fulfilment through insufficient submissiveness.[58] Spinsters and divorcées are said to owe their status to challenging male supremacy,[59] particularly so if the women are educated.[60] In all this there seems to be a refusal on the part of men to accept the changes taking place in society as a whole, and a misinterpretation of the real purpose of education. For example, in a debate concerning the effects of female education upon marital stability, a senior lecturer in history at Makerere University expressed great indignation against women who believed that education meant emancipation and equality with men.[61] Some men attempt to solve this problem by marrying women with little or no education whom they hope to impress and control by virtue of their superior station in society. However, this rarely works as the education gap proves either unbridgeable or a problem in itself. Three things happen: the women are neglected when either men turn to the town women whom in other contexts they categorize as prostitutes,[62] or to the more educated women from whom they attempted to escape originally;[63] or else husbands attempt to educate the women under their guidance and 'supervision'. However, as soon as women acquire some occupational skills, they want to work. The right to work can result in full or partial economic independence which enables women to make their own decisions. But however minimal women's successes may be, men resent them, despite the desirability of a second income to maintain the high living standards of the elites which have made women's employment acceptable even to men who previously would have prevented the employment of their wives in the public sector. In addition, the expansion of the informal sector which depends primarily upon individual initiative has lessened the male monopoly in decisions about whether women should work. 'Women these days are not controllable,' was the constant complaint of Namuwongo and Wabigalo men with regards to women's employment.

Fear and frustration in personal or professional relationships with individual women lead men to lash out at all women, particularly those in wage employment. Any attempt at self-reliance and economic independence is interpreted as a challenge to male juridical supremacy and, therefore, bad for African society.[64] Most men expect the impossible – an educated woman who will blindly obey their wishes and who will stay in the rural areas cultivating food.[65] The good woman stays at home in the village because, if she is in town, she is a source of worry for her husband. In East Africa there is a tendency to regard all urban women as sexually loose, especially any who work or appear well dressed. Thus, prejudice is extended by the general populace even to highly educated women attempting to enter professions.[66]

The Debate on Public Morality
In the first two years of the military government in Uganda, President Amin held many meetings with community elders, farmers, doctors, leaders of ethnic groups, university professors and women. During a meeting with representatives of women's groups, he said that women were no longer trusted by their husbands because they were too easygoing. In fact, men were even unwilling to give lifts to women as this could be misrepresented as 'befriending' them. 'As a father of the Nation' he strongly advised the women to be honest with their husbands and to avoid all temptation liable to cause instability in the home.[67] The women who participated in the meetings to some extent acquiesced in this divisive opposition between country and town; for instance, they were quick to condemn women who wore short dresses and tight or 'hot pants', insisting that 'women should not be judged on the standards of "town girls" who led easy lives, while the vast majority were perpetually slaving in kitchens and coping with frustrating conditions.'[68] Amin responded by reassuring women that they played an important role in Africa, but their

weaknesses had been pointed out so that they could change. He regretted that there were many women 'poisoning the image of Uganda: prostitutes in Mombasa [Kenya] who were doing "terrible things" with Europeans'. The women informed him that some of the Ugandan women were married to Europeans, so it was not a case of prostitution.[69] Elizabeth Bagaya, the chair-person of the meeting, called upon the goverment to eradicate male domina-tion as well as other evils that hindered women's progress.[70]

During the 1950s when women were first employed in the Ugandan indus-trial city of Jinja, the local African District Council representing the rural population spent four days debating the issue of female urban employment.[71] The issue in fact lay outside their jurisdiction, but even so appeals were sent for three years running to the District Commissioner and the Governor. They argued that urban life meant immorality and hence barrenness or the birth of half-caste children. The colonial government rejected the accusation that the employment of women encouraged prostitution, stating that it had the opposite effect.[72]

The point at issue was complex. Wage employment was seen as a direct result of urbanization, but the towns were suspect because they were the points of dissemination of Western and other foreign influences. As well as arguing that women's place had to be in the home in order to reduce female competition for taxpayers' jobs, lovers and husbands positively resented the employment of women because it brought them in contact with other men and afforded them some degree of economic independence.[73] The men wanted to have the best of both worlds – the urban and the traditional, and produced elaborate rationalizations to justify themselves. For instance, men regarded it as their duty to tackle the hostile Westernized urban environment and to protect their women from it. In other words, men can work for wages in towns, but women can only do so at the cost of moral corruption.

Such thinking resulted in capricious public policies. One day in June, 1973, some military officers alleged that all unmarried women were prostitutes and ordered them to vacate their homes in the towns (and return to their villages, perhaps!). Seeing that this was going too far, Amin was able to earn himself some credit by cancelling the 'shocking' order when he returned from a visit abroad.[74] But the public attitude towards the morals of urban women persisted, culminating in the humiliation of a female cabinet minister for alleged prosti-tution with a European. In 1975, it was widely publicized in the local and international press that the Ugandan Foreign Minister had been accused by Amin of having sex with an unknown European at Orly Airport in France. Airport officials claimed that she had only stopped for a few minutes; and she maintained that, besides being surrounded by bodyguards all the time, she never went to the toilets at the airport. She was also accused of using govern-ment money to purchase gold jewellery and other valuables, and the govern-ment newspaper printed so-called nude pictures of her taken some years back when she had worked as a model for international fashion magazines. She later escaped to Britain where she sued two British newspapers and was awarded damages by the courts.[75] However, the incident had further reduced women's prestige in Uganda. Even unemployed male vagrants in the capital would hurl insults at any woman with impunity, for they were blessed by the law and public sentiment.

The stage had been set for the suppression of immorality by a Presidential decree, a year after the 1971 coup d'état. In the name of ensuring that Ugandan women got the respect they deserved, female clothing 'injurious to public morale' was banned. This applied to all females above 14 years of age.[76] This was declared to be courageous by an editorial in the Kenyan *Sunday Nation* condemning the exhibition of the female body, and maintaining that it should be a private thing, especially if a woman was attached to a particular man. The editorial called upon Kenya to follow the example of Malawi, Tanzania and Uganda in controlling immorality by regulating female attire.[77]

The women who ignored the warnings were so zealously rounded up, that some magistrates had to acquit them on the grounds of wrongful arrest,[78] but in most cases, the women were fined by the courts.[79] Women also suffered verbal and physical abuse at the hands of ordinary men, police and soldiers.

Ironically, the male power holders who believed in being 'independent economically, politically and in every aspect of life'[80] condemned women's dress for aping the West while they themselves wore finely tailored three-piece suits of imported wool and polyester cloth 'just to look civilized'.[81] Some writers found this deplorable,[82] while others satirized it as 'going to any length for the sake of decency'.[83]

Women therefore find themselves scapegoats not only for male confusion and conflict over what the contemporary roles of women should be, but for the dilemmas produced by adjusting to rapid social change. Where man have given up traditional customs and restraints on dress, but feel traitors to their own culture, they yearn for the security and compensation of at least knowing that women are loyal to it.

Take for instance an article on 'Marriages Across Colour Line' that appeared in the *Times of Zambia*.[84] The journalist took up the fact that a Ugandan woman had married an older white man at the University of Wisconsin, and then went on to allege that the woman was in her 20s and that it was a 'marriage of survival' to enable her to become an American citizen. He told his readers that according to rumours she was destitute because her husband, on whom she was so dependent, not only mistreated her but was always ill. These were lies but he had written a fine sounding story. Exaggeration and imaginative concoction seem more important to African male journalists than objectivity and fair-mindedness when writing about African women. This article is interesting not only for its notions of what 'lets down Africa' but also because of the author's assertion that Africans in mixed marriages are more susceptible to influence by foreign powers. Yet recent world events concerning the workings of foreign powers show how simplistic are such views of who their agents are or will be. Do some people point fingers to divert attention? A look around Africa will show that quite a sizeable number of the power elites either entrust sensitive state matters to foreign secretaries or are married to foreign women. Perhaps we are expected

to believe that it is only African women, not men, who engage in the evils of
spying, prostitution, etc. African women are constantly obliged to demon-
strate that they are not brainwashed by foreign ideas, keeping out of the
political limelight and avoiding controversial issues like women's rights.

Political Equality and Disillusionment

Just before Uganda gained political independence there was a great wave of
enthusiasm as elite women prepared for full political participation alongside
the men. This was a genuine response to calls by politicians that every man,
woman and child was needed in the great task of nation building, and that
human and other resources were needed to fight the war against ignorance,
poverty and disease. The women assumed that the right to vote would be the
weapon for fighting traditional restrictions. For example, the letter below
urged women to move with the times and participate in the elections for the
Buganda Parliament (Lukiiko).

> Our votes will mean a lot in installing the government we like. The
> government which will look after the interests of women and raise our
> status and standards . . . It is futile to help a person who does not help
> herself. It is high time women woke up and helped to choose a government
> of their country . . . It has been a custom among people to think that
> women cannot think, men think for them [and, therefore] they have to
> accept what they tell them to do and follow their husband's likings. In the
> past men monopolised higher education giving an excuse that women do
> not become chiefs, therefore why educate them for long? Let them learn
> enough for them to get married and bear children, do not let them waste
> time.[85]

This female correspondent concluded by calling upon the women to forget
their personal grudges and choose a government that would ensure freedom,
equal rights and justice for women.

Male response can be summed up by the following typical letter. The
correspondent felt that women were going to confuse issues if they felt and
saw:

> nothing wrong in their being leaders in the party. Insane talk! . . .
> A woman — every blessed normal one of them — is created to be a
> mother. A mother's place is in and about the house. Where there is a man
> there is a house, where there is a woman there is a home . . .
> The 20th Century is morally corrupt mainly due to children delinquen-
> tly brought about by the silly notions that a married woman has to work
> for livelihood. The children find an empty house after school. They go off
> to seek company. The corruption starts there.[86]

This represented a very widespread view, so women soon found their hopes
of equality and participation rudely dashed by men who categorically stressed

that the value of women lay in their avoiding British or American influence.[87] This affected the stance of women in public. For example, in 1966 on returning from New York where she attended a United Nations committee discussion on the status of women, Mrs. Enid Mboijana, a radio personality and wife of a prominent lawyer, told the press several contradictory things. On the one hand, she was of the opinion that women's education would 'prove an indirect means of solving many problems' because it would equip women to understand their roles more clearly as mothers and as citizens as well as make them aware of their economic, legal and other rights. But at the same time she insisted that this was not 'a matter of enticing women to compete with men, but urging women to make their full contribution with the men for the sake of national development.' After all, she claimed, women had enjoyed the same rights as men for at least two generations![88]

This defensive attitude which has plagued Ugandan women since the mid-1960s contrasts sharply with the early enthusiasm. For example, the first two women Members of Parliament, Mrs. Sugra Visram and Mrs. Florence Lubega, who were both mature, economically secure and politically sophisticated, at first participated actively in parliamentary debates but gradually turned apologetic and defensive.[89] Mrs. Lubega seems to have reached her defensive stage when she became Parliamentary Secretary to the Ministry of Community Development and President of the Uganda Council of Women. For example, in a welcoming speech to Prime Minister Obote at one of the Council's meetings, Mrs. Lubega urged women to use the vote as a tool for active participation in politics, but insisted that the Council was mainly concerned with 'the challenge of nation building and not to organize a rebellion against men'.[90]

A minority of elite or Christian women who engaged in public discussion about the rights of women with regard to pre-marital chastity and permanent monogamy were often ridiculed by both men and the majority of women.[91] It was, therefore, expedient to be cautious. This point can be illustrated by a letter of the Uganda Council of Women issued to the press.

> There have been in recent months many letters published in your column about the status of women. We note with interest that the majority of your correspondents are men and we wish here, on behalf of the Uganda Council of Women to thank those men who undoubtedly have advocated for a woman equal status to that of a man. We would like to point out, however, that the majority of women in Uganda are not primarily interested in theories of equality, superiority or even inferiority. They are interested in being treated with justice and with respect due to human beings.
>   In many parts of Uganda it still happens that when a man dies his widow is left destitute. His heir and relatives come and take all the property even the widow's cooking pots, chickens, tables and chairs.[92]

The Council attacked bridewealth which made inheritance of a widow legally recognized by the courts,[93] and the letter concluded by stressing once again that women were motivated to write by the desire for stability in the

home and nation.[94] In fact, it became fashionable for women to put in paren-
thesis the main issues they wanted to raise and instead devote much space to
stressing the responsibilities of women as wives and mothers for maintaining
sound homes.[95] Furthermore, conferences and meetings convened to discuss
women's issues were often addressed by male politicians or their wives. Thus,
men could appear progressive by urging women to 'move away from the
"tentacles of tradition" that imprisoned them' and to modernize and to stop
being docile and uncritical; and by calling upon women to help in the task of
'nation building' as their position was in no way inferior to men.[96] I feel that
these lectures were being delivered to the wrong audiences. It certainly does
not take much courage to speak up against injustices against women to a
predominantly female audience. It made men sound and feel good telling
women in vague terms to do just those things which, if they claimed seriously
to do themselves, would lead to attack and ridicule. Some even confessed that
because they were men some of the things they said had to be 'taken with a
grain of salt'.[97]

Professional women became further trapped in the double standards that
distinguished 'good' and 'bad' women.[98] Here the issue concerned unwanted
sexual advances from male employers as well as the familiar bias against 'urban
women'. Elite women continued to be troubled by the total lack of distinction
in the public's mind between the 'lady of the twilight' and a 'genuinely decent
married woman'. The difficulty was partly due to the fact that both categories
of women were smartly dressed and wore rings. This made some 'decent wives'
vulnerable to abuse from men who might mistake them for prostitutes.[99] One
woman told me that it was particularly difficult for married, as well as unmarried, women to go out to bars or restaurants and enjoy themselves alone
or with friends, male or female, without being suspected of being prostitutes.
Some women resorted to advertising their motherhood by packing their
children into the Mercedes Benz or Peugeot or Citröen and driving around
town. But this is neither fun nor a solution. The 'other woman' is often
blamed for the husband's infidelity and poor economic support. Wives often
assume that women who work in offices and public places are bad women. A
distinction is not made between the higher civil servants and professionals
whose earnings and access to subsidized housing and car loans are the same as
those of men, thus making them genuinely independent; and the more lowly
working women, secretaries in particular, who may have cars and live in
houses lavished upon them by their 'boyfriends' (probably out of public
money). Some women urge that such women be sacked from their jobs and
refused contraceptives.[100] This is a rationalization that might show up the
'rotten potatoes' among women but neither solves the problem of the stereotype nor deals with the real culprits.

Some women find themselves in situations where they either have to
submit to their bosses' propositions or lose their jobs, particularly if they are
not highly educated and would find it difficult to get alternative employment.
Being highly skilled and strong in character are the only means with which to
ward off unwanted sexual advances, yet this is not always enough. A university

graduate told me of an occasion in 1973 when she was due for a job promotion in the foreign company she worked for. The African head of her department propositioned her, and when she turned him down he told her that she had lost her promotion. When she threatened to take the matter to the directors, he laughed at her, 'Do you think that those men will believe you?' The directors did not believe her and she lost her job. In farewell her boss told her, 'You are such a fool'. She claimed that in both private companies and the Civil Service men usually got promoted before women, and even when women deserved promotion, they sometimes had to pay for it with their bodies.

Unwanted 'sex on the job' is by no means unique to Uganda.[101] However, as long as the problem remains in the private sphere, women who have been victimized for refusing sexual advances cannot appeal to the law or public opinion to support their demands for compensation or reinstatement.

Summary

In Africa both ordinary men and the male power elite agree that women's morality must be controlled. It is only when restrictive measures have already been passed that elite women realize that they too are threatened. Should they wish to improve their legal and economic status, they must expect to lose honour and respect.[102] However, the way men in power positions claim the right to guard womens' morals while themselves perpetuating immorality is an issue that needs to be faced and examined. Speaking of Tanzania, Professor Mbilinyi has pointed out the double standards of men who, despite their own practice, do not want their wives to work because they will sleep with other men and do not want their wives to use contraceptives because that would remove the wages of sin.[103]

The arguments become more complex when colonialism and African 'authenticity' are invoked. It is said that women, as bearers of African culture, should be protected, with or without their consent from the corrupting influences of Western culture such as cosmetics, wigs or short dresses. The real issue of course is that, if the primary colonial and neo-colonial forces that keep Africa in subjection cannot be adequately dealt with, at least women should be kept pure for the sake of African authenticity. In many ways this is an attempt to reconcile the dilemmas posed by conflicting ideals of individual advancement based on self-interest and choice, on the one hand, and the development of the community at large, on the other.

The weight of moral pressure, often backed by law, is exerted on women in order to reverse or hinder possible changes in the power and authority relationships between men and women. For example, male concern over women's dress and morality directly hinders women's effective entrance into and performance in the political arena. It is doubtful whether anyone will pay heed to individuals or to a group who are being constantly corrected. The few women who brave it to engage in politics are reminded by hecklers and friends that their rightful place is 'beside the three cooking stones with the children'.

If they persist and are single, rumours soon bring their sexual morality into question in order to discredit them. It is not unusual to hear women being criticized for not being reticent or avoiding political involvement.[104] However, the political dominance by men weakens the impact of female criticism of male behaviour,[105] and the majority of women assume a 'silence is golden' stance because they lack the confidence or education to deal with male dominance. However, other women assert their social and economic independence, in defiance of the orthodox male view on the role and status of women.

This is not a propagandistic study on behalf of women. Rather it attempts to explore fairly the strengths and idiosyncrasies in the lives of women in the low-income Namuwongo and Wabigalo suburbs of Kampala. The women were articulate, yet they were reduced to speechlessness when dealing with the wide arena of the city. The scenario set by the public views outlined above contributed to this. Also, during the time of research, the military government had declared all political activities illegal. This meant that most women did not view themselves as potential political actors. If politics is defined as behaviour and action which secure the desired public goals of a group or community, they were right.[106] However, if individual private goals are considered to be important, then the women's behaviour and attitudes had quite a few political implications. It is therefore imperative to take seriously what women do and say for, if ignored, they can bring about an unwitting revenge upon society when it comes to solving the problems of poverty, ignorance, disease and overpopulation. The successful implementation of political decisions aimed at solving societal problems depends upon the co-operation of women.[107]

References

1. Ryna R. Reiter (ed.), *Towards an Anthropology of Women*, Monthly Review Press, (New York, 1975) and M.Z. Rosaldo and L. Lamphere (eds.), *Women Culture and Society*, (Stanford University Press, Stanford, 1974).
2. Reiter, *ibid.* p.12.
3. *Ibid.*
4. Cynthia Nelson, 'Private and Public Power: Women in the Middle Eastern World', *American Ethnologist,* Vol. 1, No. 3, 1974; Barbara C. Aswad, 'Visiting Patterns Among Women of Elite In A Small Turkish City' and Peter Benedict, 'The Kabul Gunu: Structured Visiting in An Anatolian Provincial Town' both in *Anthropological Quarterly*, Vol. 47, No. 1, 1974, issue on 'Visiting Patterns and Social Dynamics in Eastern Mediterranean Communities'.
5. The exceptions were: Sylvia Leith-Ross, *African Women: A Study of the Ibo of Nigeria*, (Faber and Faber, London, 1939); Denise Paulme (ed.) *Femmes d'Afrique Noir*, (Mouton, The Hague, 1962); Maria Leblanc, *Personalité de la Femme Katangaise: Contribution a l'étude de son*

acculturation (1960); Phyllis Kaberry, *Women of the Grassfields: A Study of the Economic Position of Women in Bamenda, British Cameroons,* (HMSO, London, 1952).

6. To name only a few in addition to those in notes 5 and 9: Margaret Mead, Ruth Benedict, Ruth Bunzel, H. Powdermaker, J. La Fontaine, Laura Bohannan, L. Spindler, Elinor Leacock, Monica Wilson, Lucy Mair, Dora Earthy, J. Goodale.

7. Reiter, *op.cit.,* p.13.

8. Hanna Papanek, 'Purdah: Separate Worlds and Symbolic Shelter', *Comparative Studies in Society and History,* Vol. 15, 1973.

9. For example, K. Gough, E. Colson, A.I. Richards, M. Douglas.

10. Among others: on the Turu, see Harold Schneider, *The Wahi Wanyaturu: Economics in an African Society,* (Aldine, Chicago, 1970); on the Fipa, see Roy Willis, 'Sex, Power, and Symbolism in a Pre-Colonial African State: The Case of the Fipa's Female Magistrates', paper read at 77th Annual Meeting of the American Anthropological Association, Los Angeles, California, Nov. 14-18, 1978); on the Barabaig, see George Klima, 'Jural Relations Between the Sexes Among the Barabaig', *Africa,* Vol. 34, No. 1, 1964; on the Igbo, see Victor Uchendu, *The Igbo of Southeast Nigeria,* Holt, Rinehart and Winston, (New York, 1965); H. Harris, 'The Position of Women in a Nigerian Society', *Transactions of the New York Academy of Sciences,* Series 2, Vol. 2, No. 5, 1940; J. Van Allen, 'Sitting on a Man: Colonialism and the Lost Political Institution of Igbo Women', *Canadian Journal of African Studies,* Vol. 6, No. 2, 1972; on the Mende and the Sherbro, see C.P. Hoffer, 'Mende and Sherbro Women in High Office', *Canadian Journal of African Studies,* Vol. 6, No. 2, 1972; on the Lovedu, see Eileen Krige and J.D. Krige, *The Realm of the Rain Queen,* (Oxford University Press, London, 1943; on the Hausa, see Mary Smith, *Baba of Kano: A Woman of the Muslim Hausa,* (Philosophical Library, New York, 1955).

11. Lionel Tiger, *Men in Groups,* (Vintage, New York 1970).

12. Evans-Pritchard, see note 22.

13. *Reiter, op.cit.,* p.12.

14. Edwin Ardener, 'Belief and the Problem of Women', p.138 in Jean S. La Fontaine (ed.), *The Interpretation of Ritual: Essays in Honor of A.L. Richards,* (Tavistock Publications, London 1972).

15. Anthony Leeds, 'Women in the Migratory Process: A Reductionist Outlook', *Anthropological Quarterly,* Vol. 49, January 1976.

16. A.I. Richards, *Africa,* Vol. 22, No. 1, 1962, p.8.

17. Audrey I. Richards, *Chisungu: A Girls' Initiation Ceremony Among the Bemba of Northern Rhodesia,* (Faber and Faber, London, 1956).

18. A.I. Richards, *Land, Labour, and Diet in Northern Rhodesia,* (International African Institute, Oxford, 1939).

19. Ardener, *op.cit.,* p.139; T.O. Beidelman, *The Kaguru: A Matrilineal People of East Africa,* (Holt, Reinhart and Winston, New York,1971); Marilyn Strathern, *Women in Between: Female Roles in a Male World: Mount Hagen, New Guinea,* (Seminar Press, New York, 1972).

20. Dell Hymes, *Reinventing Anthropology,* (Random House, New York, 1972); Archie Mafeje, 'The Ideology of Tribalism', *Journal of Modern*

African Studies, Vol. 9, 1971; Diane Lewis, 'Anthropology and Colonialism' *Current Anthropology*, Vol. 14, 1973.

21. Ardener, *op.cit.*, p.137.
22. E.E. Evans-Pritchard, *The Nuer*, (Clarendon Press, Oxford, 1940); *Some Aspects of Marriage and Family Among the Nuer*, The Rhodes-Livingstone Institute Paper 11, 1945; 'Nuer Bridewealth', *Africa*, Vol. 16, 1945; 'Kinship and the Local Community Among the Nuer' in Radcliffe-Brown and Forde, (eds.) *African Systems of Marriage*, (Oxford University Press, London, 1950) and *Kinship and Marriage Among the Nuer*, (Clarendon Press, Oxford, 1951).
23. *Ibid.*, 1951, p.98.
24. Evans-Pritchard, *The Position of Women in Primitive Societies and Our Own*, 1965, p.45.
25. Evans-Pritchard, *op.cit.*, 1951, p.125.
26. Evans-Pritchard, *op.cit.*, 1950, p.389; *ibid.*, 1951, pp.26-7.
27. Evans-Pritchard, *op.cit.*, 1945, p.20.
28. *Ibid.*, p.16.
29. *Ibid.*, p.17.
30. Evans-Pritchard, *op.cit.*, 1940, pp.226-8; *ibid.*, 1951, p.57.
31. *Ibid.*
32. Evans-Pritchard, *op.cit.*, 1940, pp.243-4, 247; *ibid.*, 1951, p.122; *ibid.*, 1950, p.384.
33. Reiter, *op.cit.*, p.14.
34. Phyllis Kaberry, *op.cit.*
35. Walter Elkan, 'The Employment of Women in Uganda' (mimeo, 1956), pp. 1-6; also published in *Bulletin de l'Institut Inter Africain du Travail*, Brazzaville, Vol. 4, No. 4, 1957, pp. 8-23; Josef Gugler, 'The Second Sex in Town', *Canadian Journal of African Studies*, Vol. 6, No. 2, 1972; A.W. Southall, 'On Chastity in Africa', *The Uganda Journal*, Vol. 24, No. 2, 1960; Melvin Perlman, 'The Changing Status and Role of Women in Toro (W. Uganda)', *Cahiers d'Etudes Africaines*, Vol. 6, No. 4, 1966.
36. Charles Lindblom, *Politics and Markets*, (Basic Books, New York, 1977); John Friedmann, *Retracking America*, (Doubleday/Anchor, New York, 1973).
37. Frederik Barth, 'Models of Social Organization' (1966), *Royal Anthropological Institute Occasional Paper No. 23*, 1966.
38. F.G. Bailey, *Stratagems and Spoils*, (Blackwell, Oxford, 1968); Marc J. Swartz, Victor Turner and Arthru Tuden (eds.), *Political Anthropology*, (Aldine, Chicago, 1966); John W. Bennet, *Northern Plainsmen*, (Aldine, Chicago, 1969).
39. Hanna Papanek, 'Development Planning for Women', *Signs: Journal of Women in Culture and Society*, Special Issue on Women and National Development, 1977.
40. Richard G. Fox, 'Rationale and Romance in Urban Anthropology', *Urban Anthropology*, Vol. 1, 1972.
41. After 1974 the Kenyan and other foreign newspapers were banned in Uganda.
42. Molohan, *Detribalization*, (Dar es Salaam Government Printers, 1957), p.41.
43. *Ibid.*, p.42.

44. Ester Boserup, *Woman's Role in Economic Development*, (Allen & Unwin, London, 1970), p.19.

45. Kathleen Staudt, 'Agricultural Productivity Gaps: A Case Study of Male Preference in Government Policy Implementation', *Development and Change*, Vol. 9, 1978.

46. Margaret Byangwa, 'A Mug and a Woman's Attitude towards Work Outside the Home: A Study of the Economic Status of the Married Woman' (Makerere University, Kampala, Sociology Working Paper No. 53, n.d.), p.38; Christine Obbo, *Women in a Low Income Situation: Namuwongo-Wabigalo, Kampala* (Makerere University, Kampala, Dept. of Sociology, M.A. dissertation, 1973).

47. Marjorie Mbilinyi, 'The New Women of Tanzania', in *Journal of Modern African Studies*, Vol. 10, No. 1, 1972, p.28.

48. J.K. Nyerere, 'The Arusha Declaration: Socialism and Self-Reliance', *Freedom and Socialism/Uhuru no Ujamaa: A Selection of Writings and Speeches 1965-67*, (Oxford University Press, Dar es Salaam, 1968) p.2.

49. *Ibid.*, p.244.

50. Elkan, see note 35.

51. *Daily Nation* (Nairobi) 1 July 1973.

52. *Sunday Nation* (Nairobi) 8 July 1973, also 24 July 1973.

53. *Sunday Nation*, 8 July 1973.

54. *Sunday Nation*, 17 June 1973.

55. *Ibid.*, 24 June 1973.

56. *Ibid.*, 8 July 1973.

57. *Daily Nation*, 1 July, 1973.

58. *Uganda Argus* (Kampala) 8 July 1972.

59. *Ibid.*

60. *Ibid.*

61. *Ibid.*

62. A.W. Southall, (ed.), *Social Change in Modern Africa*, (Oxford University Press, London, 1961), p.57; p'Bitek, Okot, *Song of Lawino*, (East African Publishing House, Nairobi, 1966).

63. p'Bitek, *op. cit.*

64. *Daily Nation*, 5 May 1973.

65. A.W. Southall and P.C.W. Gutkind, *Townsmen in the Making: Kampala and Its Suburbs* (East African Institute of Social Research/East African Studies Series No. 9, 1957).

66. Southall, *op.cit.*, p.53.

67. *Voice of Uganda* (Kampala) 8 December 1972.

68. *Uganda Argus*, 30 November 1972.

69. *Ibid.*

70. *Ibid.*

71-73. Elkan, *op.cit.*

74. *Daily Nation*, 5 July, 1973.

75. The award was merely reported as substantial.

76. *Uganda Argus*, 7 June 1972.

77. *Sunday Nation*, 11 June 1972.

78. *Uganda Argus*, 14 June 1972.

79. *Ibid.*, 27 July 1972.

80. *Sunday Nation*, 11 June 1972.

81. *Ibid.*
82. Okot p'Bitek, *Africa's Cultural Revolution,* (Nairobi, 1973), p. 3.
83. *Daily Nation,* 13 June 1973.
84. *The Times of Zambia* (Lusaka), 11 July 1977. I want to thank Dr. Ilsa Schuster for sending me this article.
85. *Uganda Argus,* 10 January 1962.
86. *Ibid.,* 14 February 1962.
87. *Ibid.,* 29 November 1965.
88. *Ibid.,* 2 February 1966.
89. *Ibid.,* 13 December 1962.
90. *Ibid.,* 23 November 1965.
91. Southall, *op.cit.,* p.53.
92. *Uganda Argus,* 17 October, 1962.
93. *Ibid.*
94. *Ibid.*
95. *Ibid.,* 5 December 1962.
96. *Ibid.,* 23 November 1965.
97. *Ibid.*
98. *Ibid.*
99. *Ibid.*
100. *Sunday Nation,* 15 August 1971.
101. *Capital Times,* (Madison, Wisconsin), 20 April 1977, p.8.
102. Southall, *op.cit.,* p.58.
103. Marjorie Mbilinyi, 'Barriers to the Full Participation of Women in the Socialist Transformation of Tanzania', paper read at Conference on the Role of Rural Women in Development, New Jersey, 2-4 December, 1974, p.9.
104. *Voice of Uganda* 8 December 1972; *Africa,* 1972, p.20.
105. Southall, *op.cit.,* p.53.
106. Swartz, Turner and Tuden (eds.), *Local Level Politics,* (Aldine Publishing Co., Chicago).
107. Sullerot, Evelyne, *Women, Society and Change,* (World University Library, London, 1971), p.248.

2. The Background of Change

Urbanization and Colonial Policy

Negative attitudes towards the social change resulting from urbanization have characterized both colonial and independence governments. Ambivalence and opposition to rural-urban migration became strongest when women started migrating to the towns. Historically, the problem of rural-urban migration in East Africa was created when administrative and trading centres were set up in the 1920s. Throughout the 1950s, a paternalistic anti-urban mentality found expression in the concern over 'detribalization'. It was felt by the colonial authorities that urbanization would affect Africans by separating them 'from family, clan and tribal authority as well as social codes of behaviour, discipline, custom and perhaps religion which originally guided their thought and actions with the object of making them useful members of the tribe or community to which they belong.'[1]

This is how the problem was described by Molohan, chairman of a committee set up in 1956 to study the problems arising from African 'detribalization' with its concomitant problems of 'separation' and 'stabilization' as they relate to urbanization and migration in general. The purpose of the report was 'to find the most effective means whereby these new communities could be assisted to settle down peacefully and contentedly in their new environment and become good citizens.'[2] Although the committee was specifically set up for Tanzania, he travelled to Uganda and Kenya as well for purposes of comparison. He found that, in Uganda, Kampala and Jinja had a serious problem of urban sprawl, due to the fact that until 1956 both towns were, in effect, non-African enclaves situated within the local government areas. Town workers lived in thickly populated villages surrounding the towns.[3] For example, in 1957 one researcher estimated that about 100,000 people lived within a five mile radius of Kampala.[4]

In some cases the peri-urban areas lay within the boundaries of towns but taxes were paid to the administrative local authorities even though they did not provide services in the towns. The mushrooming of densely populated, unplanned settlements on the edges of towns may have been disturbing to the planners but the administrators and employers found them convenient. They could under-pay their workers because after all they were 'target' labourers, performing unskilled jobs with specific short-term goals in mind, and were thus merely 'temporary inhabitants of the towns'.[5]

In the Report of the East African Royal Commission of 1953-55, a section dealing with urban development pointed out that, although the opportunity for wage-earning had increased the African element in the urban areas, when urban authorities found it necessary to provide them with accommodation (for example, domestic servants, railway workers, security guards), it was on the assumption that they would work for only short periods of time in the towns, unaccompanied by their families, and would then return to their areas of origin.[6] The assumption that the town was not a suitable habitat for a permanent African society resulted in a tendency to look on the Westernized African with suspicion.[7]

The towns were regarded as centres of administrative and commercial activities as opposed to the (rural) 'tribal' areas which were fostered by the theory of 'Indirect Rule'. Town-dwelling Africans were regarded as the wards of the urban authorities rather than as citizens because, being neither tax-payers nor property owners, they had no stake in the conduct of urban affairs.[8] This was so despite the observations of a United Nations report that already in 1951 there was a perceptible drift of Africans from the country districts to the towns, and in many cases the numbers involved bore no relation to the industrial or commercial opportunities offered by the town.[9] In other words, the influx to the towns was directly related neither to the amount of paid employment available, nor to the higher wages offered there, nor to the number of houses available.[10]

Thus, while some migrants were becoming permanent 'townsmen', colonial researchers were mostly preoccupied with the 'target' migrant who engaged in urban wage labour to earn enough money for a specific object like a bicycle or house, and returned to the rural areas until another 'target' necessitated migrating again.[11]

The same researchers soon discovered that in fact what many migrants were engaged in was 'circulatory migration' that necessitated periodic movements between town and country.[12] For example, migrants worked for about two years in town and then took leave to visit their families and reaffirm their position within their original social networks and improve their property there.[13] The migrants contributed to the 'development' of the local rural communities by building houses and eventually returning home permanently.[14] All these activities necessitated the spending of hard-earned money. The migrant who did not generously provide the expected gifts or money was regarded as stingy. This attitude was reinforced by the fact that, by and large, wage employment was only to be found in towns and on plantations. It was useless to try to impress upon the often moneyless or impoverished villagers that one could actually work in town and still not have enough money or even none at all. Consequently, many migrants ate poorly while in town in order to save money. Men were therefore lethargic in their work, performed poorly and on occasion became involved in accidents. Some men eventually grew tired of it all and returned to the rural areas.[15]

But the burden of rural taxes usually forced them back to the towns. In Uganda, the system of taxation was structured so that the urban dwellers benefited from government expenditure, much of it paid for by the rural poor.[16] Throughout Uganda's modern history the agricultural sector has contributed the largest portion of government revenue because it was taxed at a higher rate than the non-agricultural sector.[17] The inequality in taxation between rural and urban areas was rationalized on the ground that without poll tax farmers would have no incentive to cultivate export crops, and without periodic increases in tax they would lack the impetus to expand the crop average.[18] The argument ran something like this: higher taxes would motivate Africans to work harder and low taxes would attract businesses and expatriates who would otherwise leave through lack of incentive. After political independence in 1962, the Ugandan elites inherited the colonial cities, and proceeded to spend money on social amenities for the better off urban residents.[19] Rural people were still being taxed at a higher rate but the tools and fertilizers intended for them usually ended up in the hands of those urban residents investing in the rural areas.

Urban Policy After Independence

In the euphoria of Independence, as the elites moved into the large colonial houses with their rose gardens etc., ministers revealed that the government wanted to see more Africans living in the towns.[20] Most of the ministers moved their families to the capital city, Kampala, and found them accommodation in houses that had been ostensibly built for low or middle income families. It was easy talking about encouraging people to migrate.

With the rapid increase in the number of unskilled migrants in the city of Kampala and other towns, the problems of unemployment, lack of housing and schools and hospitals were exposed. Migrants flocked to Kampala and other towns looking for work that did not exist. The government, the largest employer, could not absorb everyone into the formal economic structure. Rural-urban migration had become a political problem. The unemployed could be accommodated by either taking account of their needs in urban planning or simply ignoring them.

The misapprehension about the factors underlying urbanization in Uganda was reflected in demands by elites that the migrants should be returned to the rural areas where they belonged and where they would be gainfully employed. However, the elites themselves had unskilled relatives and friends who were following them to the urban areas and for whom they were obliged to obtain employment. Thus, although the urban elites could successfully discriminate against unskilled rural-urban migrants as a whole, they made exceptions for those individuals whom they knew. The practice was known as 'back-door introductory note recruitment'. At a meeting of the ruling party, the Uganda People's Congress, concern was voiced over the fact that the task of nation building was being frustrated by the nepotistic recruitment practices of those in business or in government.[21]

It was becoming obvious to observers and policy-makers that the future depended upon rural development. But this was contingent upon speedy reduction of the disparity in the relative levels of economic and social welfare between the rural and urban areas. There was still hope among planners that the process of rural-urban migration could be reversed. Politicians were telling the people that Uganda depended upon 'the masses' who produced the cash crops which earned most of the revenue; that Uganda's greatest assets were men, women and children who had to help the government in the task of 'nation building' by playing their part. Accordingly, the government waged a war against ignorance, poverty and disease. Schools, hospitals and roads were built in some rural areas. Uganda joined other African countries in adopting planned development. The declared goals of all the successive five-year development plans (1962-76) were to control urban development by providing urban services and fruitful employment to populations already in the towns and discouraging rural-urban migration. Economic opportunities in the rural areas were to be expanded and rural life made socially and culturally attractive as a long-term strategy for solving the problems of urban unemployment.[22]

In all the Ugandan development plans is the implicit assumption that unemployment is due to the basic imbalance between the rapidly growing urban labour force swollen by rural-urban migrants, and the slower growth of job opportunities. Many migrants were leaving the villages to escape rural poverty which they characterized as 'too much work for little economic return'. In fact, many learned to rely on their own initiative for employment once they arrived in the towns.[23] They thus became part of the 'informal sector' of the urban economy not usually enumerated in the government employment statistics which narrowly define the 'labour force' in terms of wage labour.

The outcome of the U.N. Development Decade (the 1960s) showed the crystallization of a pattern of asymmetrical 'development'. The elite had access to loans from overseas aid agencies and credits from banks, as well as kickbacks from foreign firms operating in the country. They had priority when it came to schools or overseas scholarships for their children, and their wives shopped in Paris or London. But while the elite minority enjoyed all these benefits, the so-called 'masses' were called upon each year to make more and more sacrifices for the sake of 'nation building'.[24]

This unhappy trend was attacked and deplored by social scientists and some politicians who believed, for instance, that most of the social ills affecting Africa in general and Uganda in particular were indigenous. The dominant minority who formed the ruling group had failed to reorganize resources to solve the problems of the village-dwelling majority of the population that was ill-fed, ill-clad and illiterate.[25]

However, although the elite could sympathize with the problems of the masses (which, after all, included their own relatives and friends), they seemed incapable of formulating any practical solutions. Throughout the 1960s the elite, particularly the politicians, constantly called upon the government to return all unskilled migrants to the rural areas, where 'unskilled' often meant all people in self-employment – i.e. the informal sector.

International factors also contributed to the reaction of the elite, as reflected in various government policies. For example, because of the increase in foreign tourists visiting Uganda, the elite wanted to eliminate or hide the 'ugly' aspects of the city – the hawkers and the unauthorized housing. It is not surprising that illegal activity in the city provided employment and housing for the unskilled rural-urban migrants. The elites regarded as slums the suburbs where the migrants lived and designated their style of making a living as unemployment; hence they resented the migrants as spoiling their vision of what an ideal city should be. This problem has plagued not only Kampala, but other cities in Africa such as Nairobi and Lagos[26] where low-income housing was bulldozed and replaced by skyscrapers for the sake of national prestige. Commenting on the underdeveloped countries generally, Marris has charged that the allocation of important national resources is made in the name of progress for the benefit of those who are already rich, at the cost of growing injustice.[27]

When the military leaders came to power in 1971, this emerged as their strongest argument: '. . . the principle of a wealthy class of leaders who are always talking of socialism while they grow richer and the common man poorer.'[28] Alleged evidence of this elitism was shown in the falling price of cash crops such as cotton and coffee, and the soaring taxes, cost of food, and cost of education.[29] However, after the distribution of the formerly Asian-owned businesses, the new merchants, some of them members, relatives, or of the same ethnic group as members of the military, started to complain about dwindling businesses, claiming that hawkers were hoarding essential goods. The main cause was, in fact, their inexperience and ignorance about the international network for importing commodities. However, in 1974 the government did take action against town dwellers who operated in the informal sector. On April 27, early in the morning, the police assisted by the military police and prison warders, invaded all trading settlements in and around Kampala to arrest hawkers who did not have valid operating licences. Over 1,000 people were rounded up, including tailors, dressmakers, sellers of cloth, food and soft drinks. A woman who sold soft drinks typified their protests at being taken to the police station: 'I am not a criminal. Why should I be taken there?'[30] One hawker was accused of having a bag of sugar concealed under his stall. Fines of up to 200 Uganda shillings or twelve month gaol sentences were imposed on those found with goods.[31] The anti-hawkers operation went on for some time, making no discrimination between the licensed and unlicensed.

Five hawkers and traders of the Kampala Car Park complained about the operation in a letter to the Minister of Commerce and Industry. They blamed slow procedures at the City Hall for their lack of licences, claiming that in June 1973 they had met the Minister and filled in the relevant forms. Since then they had been waiting to pay for the licences. They begged him to issue them so that they could resume earning their living and so afford to pay taxes, support their families and send their children to school.[32] At about this time two Kenyan women were acquitted on the grounds of insufficient evidence when the police accused them of illegally importing large amounts of beer into Uganda.[33] Obviously it was not only the unskilled, unschooled town dwellers who were being squeezed out of the informal sector by means of long delays in the issue of licences, but even those with licences had difficulty while their activities were located in the informal sector of the economy. These are the sorts of official tactics that can be used to make it difficult for people to migrate from the rural areas to towns, or to stay there once they come. Some poor people did not understand why fellow Africans would not want them in towns. This they regarded as worse than the policies of the colonial government. A man once asked me agitatedly, 'What was the point of independence?'

The policy makers refused to accept that urbanization led to asymmetrical parasitic development. Rural-urban migration was in fact part of the general movement of labour between alternative economic opportunities. For example Hutton found that people were willing to stay in the rural areas if opportunities existed. The unemployment of landless people who came to the towns determined to find work was not in this case caused by unwillingness to work on the land.[34] This observation was the result of her study of two small-scale rural development schemes in Uganda. The first one was a Tobacco Growers Scheme situated in West Nile District which began in 1965-66. The group she specifically focused upon were the Lugbara who had a long history of migrating to the south of Uganda in search of better cash crop opportunities. She found that, although the Tobacco Scheme had brought identifiable increases in cash earning opportunities for a privileged minority, the Scheme had no impact among the 'have nots' who continued to migrate.[35] The second scheme involved resettling school leavers in Ankole District. The government obtained a grant from Inter-Church Aid to build and run a farm school. It was hoped that by educating boys who would otherwise be unemployed in modern agricultural methods it would be possible to produce farmers with high potential earning ability. There was a lot of enthusiasm for the scheme. Yet it remained true that the cultivators in both schemes were still worse off than the educated in wage employment, for whom most good jobs were reserved anyway. And in both districts Hutton was told, 'It is not the farmers who are driving cars.'[36]

Women and Rural-Urban Migration

The subject of female migration is controversial throughout Africa generally and in East Africa in particular. Females migrating alone have always been seen as a problem by both urban authorities and migrant men. In Kampala during the 1950s there were laws requiring the repatriation of all single women found 'loitering' in town.[37] All single female migrants were branded as 'prostitutes' or 'loose' women who were intent on satisfying the sexual needs of the male migrants and consuming some of their money, but who were not

destined for marriage.[38] Some ethnic groups such as the Luo and Ruandans
punished and repatriated all women deemed 'loose' and therefore a blot on
their ethnic reputation.[39]

East African towns have always been full of men because wage employment
had begun on the basis of male labour.[40] But, as Table 1 shows, even as late
as 1969, the ratio of men to women was still high among foreign migrants.
However, the local ethnic group in Kampala, the Ganda, already showed a
balanced ratio by 1959 compared to other closely related groups, as is shown
in Table 2.

Table 1
Male Migrants in Kampala, 1969

Nationality	Total Numbers (Male + Female)	Proportion of males (%)	Proportion of Total Kampala Population (%)
Kenyans	35,409	61.5	30.1
Tanzanians	4,657	67.1	13.9
Ruandans	4,235	71.3	2.6
Congolese	3,053	72.0	4.8
Sudanese	2,588	65.7	1.1
Rundi	659	82.0	1.7

Source: *Atlas of 1969 Population Census in Uganda*, Vol. 3, Table 1
(Langland, 1974).

Table 2
Kampala: Migrants by Ethnic Grouping, 1959

Ethnic Group	Women	Men
Ganda	102	100
Soga	76	100
Kiga	20	100
Nkole	24	100

Source: A.W. Southall, 'The Growth of Urban Society', pp. 479ff.[41]

The tendency after the early 1960s has been for the numbers of male and
female migrants to even up. A far more settled population is emerging
partially as a result of the educational facilities offered for African children
in the towns,[42] and partially due to the stabilization of the urban labour
force and rising wages.[43]

However, the general attitude that still prevails in East Africa is that urban
migration is bad for women because it corrupts their virtue, leads to marital

instability and erodes traditional norms. This leads to the weakening of the family structure, an increase in juvenile delinquency and violent crimes. But the worst perceived influence of the towns is the idea that prostitution is encouraged among women. This seems to be the rationale for the pre-occupation of the public and the law and policy makers with the problem of female migration. Branding female rural-urban migrants as prostitutes has been a strong weapon repeatedly used to discourage female migration. But its deterrent powers are failing since the rural areas still do not offer the same facilities and opportunities to women who, for one reason or another, may be dissatisfied with the kind of life they are leading.

For a long time the towns were regarded as a necessary evil for, while they provided wage employment, they were also morally corrupting. Therefore, women as bearers of culture should be discouraged from migrating, and thus protected against the evil influences of the city. Women were better off in the villages where they would be gainfully employed growing food and cash crops for feeding and educating their families. The assumption here is that, if women migrated, they would inevitably neglect their families and spend their energy on other 'useless things'.

This book will show that, even for women in town, nourishing their families physically, emotionally, and socially is still a major concern. Over 70 per cent of the women in the sample, for example, spent some of their savings on sending their children to school. Most respondents felt that education held the key to improved social and economic status and that anyone without it was greatly handicapped. The respondents were speaking from experience. They knew what it was like to be unskilled and wanting to improve one's economic status.

As we have seen, the reasons why people in general migrate from the rural areas are little understood or appreciated by politicians, bureaucrats and planners. This is even more true when women are involved. The 1954-55 East African Royal Commission reported, 'A desire for economic and social freedom which they may be unwilling to sacrifice by establishing new marital ties, may bring both men and women to towns.'[44] The Report further observed that there was a large number of Africans who lived in towns with no recognizable means of support.[45] There was as yet little opportunity for women to find employment outside domestic service, although a few firms had started to employ women despite opposition from the 'traditional elements in tribal society'.[46]

Women's roles and contributions in the rural areas as farmers, wives, mothers, and homemakers often prove a hindrance to female emancipation. In order to keep women in the villages, the majority of men have developed arguments justifying women's role as part of African tradition. However, even rural women insisted: 'Traditions that break women's backs, that take women's work for granted without any reward, that keep women at home, that insist on morality for women only, must be forgotten.'[47] This informant of mine who argued so lucidly was saving money to buy a water cart and a plough, and she was planning to use the cattle purchased by her sister who had migrated to town.

Her statement is significant in view of the fact that all the women I spoke with or interviewed at Namuwongo-Wabigalo stated that town life was easy because they were less controlled by men, and they did not have to dig. Digging, they pointed out, makes one grow old quickly because it is monotonous, strenuous, and 'breaks the back'. For these women one indicator that a person was an urbanite was that they were not obliged to dig, either through freedom of choice or lack of garden space in town.

While many women migrated to the towns in search of less 'back-breaking' jobs, in the villages I also found women who normally refused to touch a hoe, unless it was for a monetary reward. Thus, the policy of returning women to the villages would not solve the problem of why they migrated originally: the nature of cultivation work, labouring without pay or rewards, and in some cases wasting their energies on underproductive land. The latter point is illustrated by the case study below which involves a woman who tried to save her children from starving to death in the village.

Case Study

In 1972 a Nkole woman brought a complaint before the parish chief that her husband was pestering her to return to the village. She had come to town because her husband had been away for six years. He worked as a house servant but had never sent any money home. They had three children. She had sent messages, but there had been no response. She suspected there may have been another woman in town. She and the children traced him by visiting various Nkole 'colonies' in Kampala. He was not happy to see them. She claimed that, in the six months they had been with him, they had eaten only beans and cassava, when everyone else was eating fish and meat. Even so, it was better than in the village where food was so meagre that their children were on the verge of starvation.

The husband begged the chief to convince his wife to return home, i.e. to the village, because his salary of 146 Uganda shillings could not support the five of them. He was already four months in debt with the shopkeepers. He promised he would economize and send money to his family. The wife said that those were only promises but, when the chief promised that every month he would remind the husband, she agreed to return to the village.

By 1974 she had returned to town once more, divorced her husband, and with the help of a friend had found a job as a City Council road sweeper. She made little money, only 80 shillings a month. She rented a 15 shillings mud-wattle room which she shared with rats and cockroaches that shuttled between her room and a nearby rubbish dump. But she insisted, 'it was better than starving in the village.'

No one can seriously blame men in the lowest income brackets, who were often prevented by their situation from bringing their wives and children to stay with them. By the time they had paid rent, bought food and occasional second-hand clothing, and paid taxes, the money was gone. A lot of migrants saved on clothing by buying second-hand clothes. An advisory board appointed in 1964 to inquire into the wages of unskilled workers in Uganda found the cost of minimum requirements for a family of four in Kampala to be 267 shillings per month.[48] The minimum wage in Kampala was consequently raised, but still only from 120 shillings to 150 shillings. Not only is this well below the minimum level needed to support a family in town, but since then there has been 300% inflation, according to unofficial reports.

In the case above, the women sought legal aid from the chief but the matter was really beyond his control. Apart from collecting taxes, there was little he could do in that type of family dispute. The man himself was barely subsisting, and he felt that his wife and children were better off in the village where they could grow food and support themselves in that way. He had forgotten that he had originally come to town because 'there was not enough to eat' as the soil was too exhausted to produce sufficient food and it was difficult to find employment in the village. These were the same reasons the wife had set out, but the man would not hear of them, putting forward the usual argument that women and children can subsist in rural areas, even on unproductive land. This is understandable wishful thinking on the part of less successful men for whom rural land represents the ultimate security against the vicissitudes of urban life.[49] They visited the village only for a few days, for example if a death or illness occurred in the family. Otherwise they preferred to keep away from their rural relatives' pestering demands for money. They lived, died, and were often buried in the urban area, but until their last breath they would maintain that the town was an evil (albeit a necessary one) and that they hoped to retire in their home areas, the villages.[50] Men, who like the one in this case study, 'disappeared' in the towns, had poorly paid jobs, or had failed to find employment, and were living meagrely alone or with friends. They were too ashamed to keep in touch with their relatives or wives in the rural areas.

Six women in the present study were in town ostensibly to try and locate their husbands who never sent money or visited. However, the migrants who succeeded in securing jobs or creating employment for themselves either regularly visited their wives and children in the rural areas, or brought their families to live with them in the towns.

References

1. M.J.B. Molohan, *Detribalization*, (Government Printer, Dar es Salaam, 1957) pp. 1, 11-12.
2. *Ibid.*
3. *Ibid.*, p. 15.
4. Personal communication with A.W. Southall.
5. East Africa Royal Commission, *1953-1955 Report*, (HMSO, London, 1955), p. 200.
6. *Ibid.*

7. *Ibid.*, p.201.
8. *Ibid.*, p.247.
9. *Ibid.*, p.205.
10. *Ibid.*
11. Walter Elkan, *An African Labour Force*, (East African Institute of Social Research/East African Studies Series No. 7, 1956); Walter Elkan, *Migrants and Proletarians: Urban Labour in the Economic Development of Uganda*, (Oxford University Press for Makerere Institute of Social Research, London, 1960).
12. J.C. Mitchell, 'Structural Plurality, Urbanisation and Labour Circulation in Southern Rhodesia,' in J.A. Jackson (ed.), *Migration*, (Cambridge University Press, Cambridge,1969) pp. 156-80; T.S. Weisner, *One Family, Two Households: Rural Urban Ties in Kenya*, Ph.D. thesis, Harvard University.
13. William Watson, *Tribal Cohesion in a Money Economy*, (Manchester University Press for the Rhodes-Livingstone Institute, 1958).
14. J.L. Watson, 'Restaurants and Remittances: Chinese Emigrant Workers in London', in G.M. Foster and R.V. Kemper (eds.), *Anthropologists in Cities*, (Little Brown, Boston, 1974).
15. Walter Elkan, *The Employment of Women in Uganda*, (mimeo, 1956, pp.1-6); also published in *Bulletin d' Institut Inter Africain de Travail*, (Brazzaville), Vol. 4, No. 4, 1957, pp. 8-23.
16. V. Jamal, 'Taxation and Inequality in Uganda, 1900-1964', *The Journal of Economic History*, Vol. 48, No. 2, 1978.
17. *Ibid*
18. *Ibid.*
19. *Ibid.*
20. *Uganda Argus* (Kampala) 13 December 1962.
21. Milton A. Obote, *The Common Man's Charter*, (Consolidated Press, Kampala, 1968),p.13.
22. *Third Five Year Development Plan*, (Government Printer, Kampala, 1971-76), pp. 110-11.
23. Christine Obbo, *Women in a Low Income Situation, Namuwongo-Wabigalo, Kampala*, Makerere University, Kampala, M.A. Dissertation, 1973.
24. Although nearly all African countries had development plans, and many attempted to implement them, to date only Tanzania has seriously stuck to the strategy of rural development as a basis for systematic social, economic and political change as spelled out in the 1967 Arusha Declaration. It is a difficult road to travel but they are trying hard.
25. Okot p'Bitek, *Africa's Cultural Revolution*, (Macmillan Books for Africa, Nairobi, 1973) pp.6-7; Milton A. Obote, *The Common Man's Charter, op.cit.*, p.12.
26. *East African Standard* (Nairobi); 20, 21, 23 January 1970. Peter Marris, *Family and Social Change in an African City: A Study of Rehousing in Lagos*, (Northwestern University Press, Evanston, Ill., 1962), p.viii.
27. Peter Marris, *ibid.*, p.ix. The urban elites usually consider anyone who is less fortunate to be a blight. This was true of Ancient Athens (see Alfred French, *The Growth of the Athenian Economy*, Routledge and Kegan Paul, London, 1964, p.40) and is true today of small cities in America

where street hawkers meet opposition and harassment from established merchants. (National Broadcasting Corporation, Madison, Wisconsin, 23 June 1978).

28. *Voice of Uganda* (Kampala) 28 April 1974.
29. *Ibid.*
30. *Munno and Voice of Uganda* (Kampala) 25 April 1974.
31. *Ibid.*
32. *Munno,* 4 May, 1974.
33. *Ibid.,* 10 May 1974.
34. Caroline Hutton, *Reluctant Farmers?,* (East African Publishing House for Makerere Institute of Social Research, 1973) p.155.
35. *Ibid.*
36. *Ibid.*
37. Buganda Laws, *The 1918 Adultery and Fornication Law and the 1914 Law to Prevent Prostitution,* (Uganda Bookshop, Kampala, 1957) p.2-6.
38. A.W. Southall and P.C.W. Gutkind, *Townsmen in the Making: Kampala and Its Suburbs,* (East African Institute of Social Research/East African Studies Series No. 9, 1957) p.90.
39. David J. Parkin, *Neighbours and Nationals in an African City Ward,* (Routledge and Kegan Paul, London, 1969) p.95.
40. A.W. Southall (ed.), *Social Change in Modern Africa,* (Oxford University Press for the International African Institute, London 1961) p.51. See also note 38.
41. A.W. Southall, 'The Growth of Urban Society' in Stanley Diamond and Fred Burke (eds.), *The Transformation of East Africa: Studies in Political Anthropology,* (Basic Books, New York/London; 1966).
42. Adrian Hastings, *Christian Marriages in Africa,* (SPCK, London, 1973), p.132.
43. Josef Gugler, 'Urbanisation in East Africa', in John Hutton (ed.) *Urban Challenge in East Africa,* (East African Publishing House, Nairobi, 1970), p.14.
44. *The East African Royal Commission 1953-1955 Report,* (HMSO, London, 1955), p.205.
45. *Ibid.*
46. *Ibid.,* p.208.
47. Christine Obbo, unpublished field notes.
48. Uganda Government, *Report of the Minimum Wages Advisory Board,* (Kampala, 1964) p.12.
49. Josef Gugler, *op.cit.,* p.14.
50. For a similar utterance in Nigeria, see Leonard Plotnicov, 'Nigerians: The Dream is Unfulfilled' in William Mangin (ed.), *Peasants in Cities,* (Houghton-Mifflin, Boston, 1970), pp.70-74.

3. Marriage and the Family

Focusing research on female rural-urban migration threw light on the overall problem of different reactions by men and women in different social systems to the challenges of differing contemporary situations. The introduction of cash as a dominant means of exchange was responsible for changes in marriage arrangements as well as personal relationships.

This book deals with low income women in Kampala and with rural women. It was not possible to obtain rural and urban data on all the ethnic groups encountered in Kampala. Consequently, three groups will be used for purposes of comparison whenever necessary. The groupings are: (1) the Ganda who were the dominant group in Kampala and Buganda together with the neighbouring peoples of similar culture, the Toro, Rwanda and Nyoro, some of whom lived in Kampala and rural Buganda as well; (2) the Luo, studied in Kampala and rural Western Kenya; and (3) the Muslim Nubi.

This chapter will examine the common male complaint that 'women are not controllable these days,' which usually referred to marital conflicts, female rural-urban migration and women trying to earn their own living. The analysis has a three-fold goal: to show how descent systems and types of marriages influence residential arrangements; to show how the marriage regulations that were introduced during the colonial period affected the ways in which people viewed marriages as institutions and relationships; and lastly, to show how relationships within marriage were influenced by the penetration of capitalism, heralded by the introduction of cash economies based on cash crop farming and rural-urban migration.

Descent systems and residential rules governing married people greatly affect the strategies and options available to women. As actors in the economic sphere, women are determined by the position they occupy within a family structure which shapes their relations to resources, competitors, patrons and clients.[1]

Customary and Christian Marriage

The societies in this study traced descent through the male line. They had three marital residential patterns which involved either the wife living with the husband and his people, or the couple establishing themselves away from relatives, or the husband joining the wife with her mother and other relatives. Anthropologists refer to these types of residence as virilocal, neolocal and uxorilocal respectively. The two dominant marriage systems encountered in this study have been described and characterized elsewhere as Nilotic and Interlacustrine.[2]

The Nilotic system is found among the Western Nilotes such as Alur, Acholi, and the Luo; the Sudanic Lugbara and Madi; as well as the Eastern Nilotic Teso and Karamojong, and characterizes the second group mentioned on p. 33. The Interlacustrine system is characteristic of the Bantu peoples of Southern Uganda such as the Ganda, Soga, Nyoro and Toro,[3] and is found in the first group mentioned on p. 33.

Bridewealth and polygyny (multiple wives) are the key factors for understanding the dynamics of the Nilotic system. High bridewealth in the form of money and cattle was given to the bride's people; in exchange the woman's sexual and reproductive powers were surrendered to the man and his lineage. Under this system, the children belonged to the husband irrespective of who had begotten them. The social father (*pater*) in his role as husband counted for much more than the adulterous genitor. In the case of illegitimate children, the woman's male relatives claimed custody of the woman's children and the biological father's rights to custody and filiation were only transferred upon the payment of compensation.

Divorce was rare but separations were common. However, the latter did not bother men because women were not allowed to take their children and this always forced them back.[4] The elders usually worked hard to reconcile the separated couple and to discourage divorce,[5] which was very complicated. Some of the cattle transferred upon marriage (and to offspring) were non-returnable to the husband because they were regarded as compensation for services already rendered by the woman to her husband during the period of marriage.[6] These services included labour used in the growing and preparing of food, reproduction of children and their rearing and socializing, and sexual partnership. In theory, when everything the woman had rendered to her husband had been calculated in terms of cattle, the rest were returned to the husband. But there was usually nothing left.[7] This would tend to weaken the argument usually put forward by anthropologists that high bridewealth necessarily deters divorce.

Upon marriage, the wife lived and became identified closely with her husband's lineage group and her links with the group into which she was born correspondingly weakened. Widows were inherited by a brother or son of another wife of the deceased husband. A woman owned virtually no property, having only right of usufruct over land for purposes of providing food for the family. She was even unable to sue anybody who tried to take part of the land that had been left by her husband, and instead had to ask one of the men to sue on her behalf.[8] Since women were outsiders to the descent system, they were excluded from ownership because land had to circulate within the family. Thus, although quarrels sometimes caused families to separate, men of the same descent lived together as neighbours in corporate territorial lineages.[9]

Polygyny was common but not universal. However, the practice afforded some women leverage within a male-dominated descent system. Women, as mothers, were necessary for the formation of the lineage descent lines since there could be no recruitment of men by descent without the nuclear families headed by wives as mothers, who were themselves recruited by marriage. Luo theory assumes that jealousy *(nyieko)* exists between co-wives who form the segments of a polygynous family,[10] and institutionalizes it. Each woman with her children forms a matrifocal residential unit that competes with the other residential units within the family for resources, the husband's patronage etc. This is articulated in Luo theory as the principle of *libamba*, i.e. complementary opposition between segments of the lineage (headed by the wives) that are co-ordinated to form a minor lineage headed by the father/husband. However, in cases of irreconcilable disagreement, sons of one wife can transform their segment of the family into a lineage that is separate from the other segments. When this occurs, Luo ideology explains it in terms of jealousy between wives who foster it in their sons.[11]

The Interlacustrine marriage and family system, on the other hand, was characterized by low bridewealth consisting of either a cash payment of not more than 400 shillings ('to buy a blanket for the father, a long gown *(kanzu)* for the brother and salt for the mother' as one informant put it), or several calabashes of banana beer, clothes for the wedding including those of the bride, bridesmaids, matron of honour or father's sister, a tin of kerosene paraffin and matches for the mother, and miscellaneous gifts for other in-laws. Although the husband and his close agnatic kinsmen claimed exclusive sexual rights over the wife, they did not completely own her reproductive powers. Children born to unmarried women or in adultery belonged by descent to the genitor regardless of whether compensation had been paid for the offence or not. Bridewealth was not refundable.

A Ganda woman never joined her husband's clan and the strong links with the group into which she was born were exemplified by the strong tie between brother and sister. The brother usually arranged or at least consented to his sister's marriage and later gave her protection and a home if her marriage broke down.[12] Divorce was frequent, and women often sent their children to live with their brothers. Richards, in a study of a Ganda village, has observed that uterine nephews and nieces were sometimes more numerous in a Ganda village than the men and women of agnatic descent.[13] Although clans and lineages were dispersed, brothers and parallel cousins as well as sisters and their children still depended on the household heads in a quasi-client relationship. In any home, the number of dependents varied with the social status or economic means of the particular relative.[14]

The Nilotic and Interlacustrine marriage and family types reacted differently towards British colonial rule. Previously, both systems had been flexible. In the Nilotic marriage, chiefs did not intervene in marital disputes unless they were personally involved or if a dispute led to serious breaches of peace. Bridewealth varied with economic circumstances, rising in times of prosperity and falling in times of drought, famine and cattle epidemics.

Bridewealth also depended upon the economic status of the groom and his people, as did the transfer period. However, the early colonial administrators brought marriage within the ambit of the new courts and tried to standardize the transfer time and amount of bridewealth in cash. All this led to abuses. For example, a bridewealth debtor was likely to be taken to court and committed to prison by default. People sought cash payments for bridewealth at the time of marriage or after divorce when the bridewealth had to be returned to the groom's people. Compensation for adultery and seduction was also often demanded in cash. All this greed led to a calculating approach towards a girl's beauty and education standards in terms of possible value or incurred expenses. This was often upset when a girl became prematurely pregnant. Not only did this reduce her chances of being married to a bachelor, but her male relatives received little 'compensation' in bridewealth for her virginity. Such girls found themselves wives of old polygynous men who had the means or social standing to rescue the honour of the girl's patrilineage. The crucial point was that the girls should give birth at their husband's and not at their parents' homes.[15] In effect, women had become pawns in the hands of men, as fathers and brothers demanded exorbitant bridewealth, and husbands sometimes tricked them in order to extort compensation.

According to one Luo woman I talked to, the Church did not offer women any better leverage with the men either. Many of my informants said that a large number of Luo marry under customary law because the hypocrisy of the Church people drove them away. They cited examples of missionaries who preached against drunkenness, illegitimacy and adultery while practising these things themselves. According to one woman in her 50s who was a prominent member of a breakaway church in Namuwongo, 'Our traditional customs were simpler and clearer.' Thus, it would seem that the double standards of some preachers and missionaries forced the Luo to ignore the marriage laws introduced by the colonial administration. As one man put it, 'We Luo live according to tradition and that means staying married.' Certainly, in the study I undertook, Luo marriages were outstanding by their apparent stability (see Table 3).

Other Luo men and women in Namuwongo and Wabigalo agreed with this assessment. They also claimed that the custom of giving bridewealth was the cornerstone of marriage which, if tampered with, would weaken the whole institution. For example, even in cases where a town man eloped with a village girl, the bridewealth was eventually paid through the insistence of the woman. As both men and women agreed, 'A woman should not appear as if she is desperate to be married by offering herself without bridewealth as an assurance of good intentions. That is only done by *Jomwa* [Bantu-speaking people], but unfortunately some of our women in the towns are doing the same.' Indeed, the most memorable part of interviewing Luo women was the emphasis they put on the amount of bridewealth involved in their marriages. They usually claimed the maximum of ten head of cattle. However, I later found that usually only four to five cattle had been given.

The Luo women displayed traditionalist tendencies only in insisting that their married status depended upon bridewealth being given to their guardians, fathers and brothers. Forty of the 47 women in the sample had married under customary law. There were four childless monogamous marriages. Two women married in church had divorced. However, if the majority of marriages survived, it was not because women accepted male authority unquestioningly. According to Namuwongo residents, Luo women were 'notorious' for constant arguments with their men in the home and in public places such as the bars or water taps. Issues were thrashed out either in private or in front of an audience. The men always threatened to beat their wives or to return them home. But perhaps 'getting things off their chest' also helped Luo marriages by bringing the problems out in the open. This seems to have eased some of the strains.

In other ethnic groups women acted in a subservient manner, but harboured resentment against men; hence the frequent separations. However, as will be shown shortly, the changes brought about by the money economy in the rural areas and the changed circumstances of the urban areas, had not left the Luo women untouched.

Interlacustrine marriage was also greatly influenced by the colonial institution of Christianity. Ganda chiefs insisted upon monogamous and indissoluble marriages. For example, in 1919 the Chief Justice of Buganda, Stanislas Mugwanya, issued a circular officially refusing to recognize customary marriages as they were potentially polygynous. This put pressure on Muslims and Christians to have their marriages registered or else be considered pagans. Because chiefs publicly discouraged the hearing of marital cases in their courts, bridewealth, adultery and divorce became private family matters. This occurred despite the 1917 Adultery and Fornication Laws which in principle recognized these matters.

The attitude of the Christian chiefs led to many changes in marriage. First, being married in a church or mosque and wearing a ring accorded elite status and, in the case of women, great respectability. Marriage with a Christian rite was regarded by most people as the ideal for social rather than religious reasons.[16] The conspicuous consumption displayed at Church weddings also contributed to the further reduction and even elimination of bridewealth. As one informant explained,

> The prestige of a person depended on how much to eat and drink there had been at their wedding. How many people had been transported by lorries to the wedding. Whether or not photographs had been taken. Sometimes families would decide that there was no need for bridewealth if the wedding was going to be spectacular. The parents of the bride would, however, request garments to wear on the occasion.

Another informant asserted that weddings were expensive because people had to stage two receptions. Between 4 and 6 o'clock at the church grounds tea, bread and cakes (bought at an Arab Bakery) were served. By the 1950s some people were serving soft drinks, but the reception was still known as the 'wedding tea party'. On returning to the village, the second reception followed. Banana beer was served and musicians and dancers entertained people from sunset until late into the night. The practice was frowned upon by the churches and it was not unusual to hear sermons by African clergymen condemning 'drunkeness' and 'seductive' dances. The 1917 Adultery and Fornication Laws also prohibited 'native' dances of an indecent or immoral nature. Any person guilty of the offence was liable to a fine of 10 to 100 shillings or imprisonment of two to four weeks, or both.[17]

By the late 1950s the rank and file of the Anglican Church in Buganda was concerned about the instability of marriages throughout the country. But this was not a new phenomenon.[18] Taylor also reports that 75 per cent of Anglicans who had been married by 1958 had not been married in church.[19] This was partly due to financial considerations. Not only was it expensive to stage a wedding and reception, but there were so many little fees to pay at the church that most people felt that the church was simply exploiting them. Also, clergymen and priests discouraged mixed marriages between Anglicans and Roman Catholics, although most villages had a population of mixed religion. The Anglican Church shared the official view that African customary marriages were 'potentially polygamous'. All people not married in church were regarded as 'living in sin' even where the marriage was monogamous and stable, and were automatically excommunicated. The women so married were referred to as *malaya* (prostitutes).

Genuine converts or those who received baptism in order to get married, found that they had to be married for life, however unsatisfactory their marriages might turn out to be. The Marriage and Divorce Laws did not cover the customary laws so that professing Christians were unable to contract valid marriages by African custom.[20] The Catholic Church did not allow divorce, and the Anglican Church did not allow remarriage after divorce. The law required that marriages registered under the Marriage Ordinance could only be dissolved, while the parties were alive, under the Divorce Ordinance and only on the grounds of adultery. Furthermore, the divorce law as transplanted from Britain to Uganda was 'medieval'[21] in that it allowed more rights to men than women. For example, a man could ask for dissolution of his marriage on the grounds that his wife had been guilty of adultery. But the wife could not get a divorce on grounds of adultery alone, but had to prove that her husband had *forsaken Christianity* and taken other wives, or that he had committed adultery coupled with some other wrongdoing such as desertion or cruelty.

In addition, the common people could see that the chiefs were secretly 'living in sin' by keeping one woman at the official residence and placing several others on their various landholdings. The rich peasants followed suit by buying land plots in different counties and placing as many as three different wives on them. In the final analysis, it was the wives of poor polygynous

men who suffered. The Church specified that any man who wished to be
baptized or married had to abandon all his wives but one. While this was
supposed to work in favour of women, not all women agreed that polygyny
was so bad after all. One woman who was married to one of the important
men at the turn of the century and who had been married under customary
law said, 'It is better to be married to a man with many wives because it
gives each woman more control and autonomy since the man cannot control
them all. In a monogamous marriage the man claims all your labour. Sometimes he may even bring home illegitimate children!'

Most women were attracted to the customary law because of its flexibility.
If a marriage was unsatisfactory for reasons such as incompatibility or impotence, the woman could separate (*kunoba*), from her husband. The woman
did not have to furnish proof that her husband had committed adultery. Thus
one obstacle at least to female emancipation and advancement had been
removed: customary law marriages, living together by consent, or cohabitation
and concubinage all became conventional. Mair found that it was common
for Ganda couples to live together without being married.[22] In 1952
Richards found that 13 per cent of the marriages in a village she studied were
cohabitations.[23] There also appeared to be an increase in the number of self-
supporting women living alone.

The changed perceptions of marriage were reflected in the frequency and
styles of Interlacustrine marriages. For example, as Table 3 shows, only three
Ganda women married whereas 27 had acquired the status of single woman
through a series of marriages or cohabitations.

The case histories also revealed that most of these cohabitations occurred
and originated in the rural areas. This is important because the public view
held by policy makers, reformers and writers is that it is the breakdown in
social controls in the urban areas that has weakened the marriage institution.
While it is not unreasonable to suppose that urban influences could account
for the frequent separations and remarriages, there are other causes also
responsible for social change.

While some rural women may have been resigned to their station in life as
producers of food and children, dependent on men for land, status in the
community and economic distribution of the fruits of their labour, others
were doing something about it. These women either migrated or tried to make
rural life viable by exploiting every available opportunity to make themselves economically independent of men. Accordingly, women were constantly
devising strategies for achieving some degree of economic autonomy. This led
them to clash with the men.

Personal and Financial Relationships

The women I was investigating were always complaining that their husbands
never gave them any money. In both the rural and urban areas women accused
their husbands of either misusing money or denying it to them. Rural Luo

Table 3
Types and Frequency of Marriages

	Kakwa	Lango	Acholi	Nubi	Teso	Nyole	Gisu	Ziba	Nyamwezi	Chagga	Kikuyu	Kamba	Luyia	Nkole	Ruanda	Rundi	Kiga	Luo	Ganda	Soga	Toro	Total
Traditional (Mosque or Church)	2		2	1	1					1	2	1	7[a]		9			40	6			72
Traditional + Single Church							2	1										2	2			7
+ Single																			6			6
Traditional + Traditional																1	3		1			5
Traditional + Traditional + Single						1								2					1			4
Traditional + Cohabitation		2	1										1	1	1				1			7
Traditional + Cohabitation + Single															5[c]				8		1	14
Traditional + Traditional + Cohabitation				1	1[b]														7			9
Church + Traditional + Cohabitation				1										1	1				6			9
Single				1									1						5[d]		1	8
Single Cohabitation							1		1				1						3	1		7
Multiple Cohabitation															2[e]		3[b]	5[b]	6[b]			16
TOTAL	2	2	3	4	2	1	3	1	1	1	2	1	10	4	18	1	6	47	52	1	2	164

Key: a = widowed after interview
b = one had cohabited 3 times
c = four had cohabited 3 times
d = one had cohabited twice; one had cohabited 3 times
e = one had cohabited 5 times

women claimed that month after month they waited for money that was not forthcoming from their urban employed husbands; some men even went so far as to demand that their wives hand over the whole of whatever income they had managed to earn.

Rural Ganda women whose salaried husbands were commuters or self-employed farmers claimed to be in the same position because they never saw their husbands' pay from one month to the next. In the urban area studied by me, Ganda women and women from other ethnic groups hinted that men's stinginess with money was largely responsible for the break-up of their marriages, whether in the rural or urban areas. Married women in both areas modelled themselves on the women who were self-supporting and single.

In the urban survey questionnaire an open-ended question was included to solicit information about the savings patterns of married women. Single women were asked what they had done during their previous marriages, or what they would do. The answers, shown in Table 4 below, plus the observations recorded, revealed women's endeavours and strategies to achieve economic autonomy.

Table 4
Savings Patterns of Couples

	Separately	*Together*	*No Answer*	*No money to save*	*Single*	*Total*
Rundi	1					*1*
Ruanda	3	4	2	9		*18*
Nyamwezi					1	*1*
Ziba					1	*1*
Acholi	2			1		*3*
Lango	2					*2*
Kakwa		2				*2*
Nubi	4	1				*5*
Teso		1			1	*2*
Nyole	1					*1*
Kiga	2	3			1	*6*
Luyia	6	4				*10*
Toro	1				1	*2*
Kamba		1				*1*
Kikuyu		1	1			*2*
Chaga		1		1		*2*
Gisu	1			11	2	*4*
Luo	15	12	6	5	3	*41*
Ganda	23	5			19	*47*
Soga					1	*1*
Total	*61*	*35*	*9*	*27*	*30*	*162*

Table 4 shows that only a minority of married women saved jointly with their husbands, and, except for 19 single women, the rest had residential relationships with men. Six claimed that they had no money to keep. Those who saved separately often added, 'We leave the schooled to save with their husbands . . .' followed by a sarcastic laugh. One woman elaborated:

> Educated women marry in church and save with their husband. What a waste of time! Until death parts them then they stop living in the same house? And if the women did not save money, there would probably be none to save as the men spent most of their earnings elsewhere. We, here, lead a completely different life and don't care what anyone thinks.

These remarks disturbed me because I knew that something important was being said to me, but I did not know what. An examination of the case histories of the more cynical respondents revealed that they had been through a series of marriages. The first one was usually a church, mosque or traditional marriage and the remainder were cohabitations or affairs varying in duration. The respondents who dared to say this to me were also Ganda. So I concluded that women made scathing remarks about 'ring or church' marriage because they had been involved in unsuccessful marriages or had never found anyone with whom to have the experience. Yet my conclusions bothered me because they did not really answer the claim that elite women saved money with the husbands out of some acquired habit, and stuck to their marriages because they were more concerned about social status than the less schooled women.

I would guess that the crucial issue was whether the wives of elite men knew what my informants and I knew, that some elite men had women friends in Namuwongo and Wabigalo whom they visited regularly, in some cases with money for child support and to see their children. It appeared that some of the elite men were spending a lot of money in the area. In fact, the desire of most women seemed to be getting a share in this wealth. But, along with this desire was the strengthened belief among women in Namuwongo and Wabigalo that men could not be trusted with money for, if they did 'not drink it all, they spent it on women'. But if men and women claimed they did not trust each other particularly over money matters, what were they doing about it?

> If it doesn't itch, don't scratch it.
> If it does itch, scratch a little but not to
>   irritate.
> If it is over irritated, try to cool it down.
> If it is cooled down it will not itch.
> Ha-ha-ha, everyone knows an itch.

> *Song of Namuwongo Drunkard, 1972*

These words of wisdom from a resident poet dressed in rags, covered with jiggers and smelling like a gin distillery, always brought tears to people's eyes. Namuwongo and Wabigalo residents interpreted the words to fit their particular circumstances or to illustrate any argument they wished to advance. Those selling stolen goods or illegal brews and gin saw 'the itch' as the law enforced by the chiefs and the City Council officials. 'In order to keep the "itch" down, greasing the elbows a little is necessary to enable the law to turn a blind eye.'

The unemployed saw 'the itch' as the authorities and employers who never had enough jobs or, if they had them, either refused to hire them or fired them after hiring them. However, almost everyone knew that any negative decision on the part of an employer could be turned into a favourable one if 'ghee to cool his tongue' was produced. All in all, Namuwongo and Wabigalo people regarded bribing public officials as their most constant and irritating 'itch' that had to be handled carefully. Anyone who has ever suffered from a mosquito bite or been 'burnt' by a poisonous plant can appreciate what is involved in dealing with an itch. To let it calm down is the ideal solution but most people give in to the impulse to scratch, thus creating an even worse situation.

For Namuwongo and Wabigalo women, the 'itch' was any obstacle that came their way. Most of the things catalogued as itches were drawn from male/female relationships. For example,

I hate having to beg for money on my knees like a child. I work too, I don't make him kneel before he wears the clothes I have washed or eat the food I have cooked.

Or

Since I started this business, my husband is always short of money to buy beer or cigarettes. He does not want me to have any money, so he helps me spend it.

Or

He denied responsibilities for my pregnancy but now that my daughter has turned out beautiful and I have worked hard to send her to a good school, he is very interested in her.

And

I have told my clients to pay me when my husband is not at home because seeing me get over one hundred shillings or so throws him in a temper. He starts threatening me 'if I had not brought you here, you would not be selling those mats. The money you make belongs to me'.

The relationships between men and women were greatly influenced by the introduction of cash as the dominant means of exchange. Economic matters concerned all women — those who enjoyed their marriages, those who grumbled about them and women who were unmarried. Regardless of whether they were vocal, manipulative, active or passive, the women in this study had played an active role in the changes that had taken and were still taking place in the institution of marriage for better or for worse.

Traditionally, Ganda women had limited property rights. However, the *mailo* land system introduced by the 1900 Agreement with the British enabled women to inherit freehold land, and to rent or purchase land under customary tenure, thereby offering them the possibility of independence. Some women, particularly the wealthy, could no longer tolerate their traditionally authoritarian husbands and preferred lovers whom they visited or who visited them in their homes. In other words, they had a choice: they could do what was 'proper' and get married, or they could remain single and do what they wanted to do. In fact, women in the rural area studied commonly cited 'buying a piece of land' as the major reason for saving money. This can be traced to the turn of the century when cash crop production and imported consumer goods were introduced. Most women I knew owned a plot (or were saving for one) in their villages or elsewhere, sometimes as far as 80 miles away.

The discovery of such activity usually resulted in quarrels or separation. As one woman put it,

> Men fear that once you have bought a piece of land it is a sign that the wife is planning to leave them. This is not necessarily the case. I have some old friends who have owned land ever since I can remember, but who have never left their husbands. It makes life easy for the woman to know that in the event of a separation or divorce they can at least be assured of somewhere to go and where they could be self-supporting. In the past a woman would go and stay with her brother, but nowadays it is not easy to stay in people's homes.

This woman told me later that she personally would never dream of migrating to the city or any urban area, but she considered rural-rural migration as a legitimate form of activity. However, what she had to say about a 'rainy day' was shared and expressed by both rural and urban women.

In the case of Buganda, the potential for rural-rural migration was there. Women constantly visited their relatives, guardians or brothers. Women went home one or two weeks after the wedding to fetch chickens and bananas for the first meals they cooked at their husband's home. They also went home during pregnancy to talk to their mothers.

During my fieldwork in a Ganda village, it was taken for granted that once in a while, every few months or once a year, a woman would want to make such a visit. Except in the case of a death or illness, the woman gave her husband notice four weeks or so in advance, partly seeking permission and partly informing him of the impending visit. If the man was employed in wage labour he might give her money to take with her or to buy clothes, shoes, bangles, or scarves for individual members of the family if the family was small. Otherwise, money would be given to the wife to buy milk, bread, and so on for all the visited family members to share. The very young children would go with the mother, but the older children would remain at home. In cases where a relative or in-law resided with the family, the children were left under their care. In such cases where there was 'someone at home', the wife's visit might extend up to a month.

There were several instances where the women who visited more frequently in the end deserted their husbands and migrated. For some it was rural migration, for others it was urban migration. The women on their regular visits would stay in a friend's or brother's home selling pancakes, brewing beer, or distilling gin, or labouring as coffee pickers. The money earned would, after a few years, be invested in buying land and building a house on it. The most desirable land was a plot near or within an urban or rural centre. Other women used the money to start businesses such as hairdressing, market trading or selling items to snack like groundnuts and oranges at bus stations. This was the category of women who migrated to the larger towns by staying first at small urban centres. Each stage in the migration process represented an expansion of business and an increase in opportunities to do other things. Thus, meaningful change for the Ganda women has been brought about by their manipulating social customs to their own ends.

The Ganda were very polite and, unless drunk, rarely quarrelled in public with their partners. But this gentility covered up the unspoken antagonism between the sexes. Men and women suspected each other of cheating, scheming and keeping secrets. These issues were never discussed, but instead were smothered by courtesy, the women kneeling while greeting or serving men and addressing them as 'sir' (*sebo*), the man addressing the woman as 'madam' (*nyabo*).

During my research, I heard of several, and witnessed four, cases in which men would not let their wives take their clothes with them on separation. The men would tear or burn the clothing. The argument was that every man should provide for his wife, so if a wife was leaving him for another man, the latter assumed the responsibility to buy clothes for her. However, I only once witnessed clothing of any value destroyed. In the other three cases the women had stored their clothes with friends. I was told that the common practice in the village was for women to keep clothing with their friends, neighbours or relatives — husbands being kept ignorant of this. A woman storing clothing for a friend made sure that her husband was aware of this. Either the friend was to come at a time that the husband would be home, or the clothing was left lying where the husband was bound to spot it and make inquiries. Since the men only wanted to destroy clothes that they or their own money had bought, the stored clothing usually remained intact.

The most common talk by Ganda men in the villages and in the Namuwongo-Wabigalo area was that women these days are 'too much' (*bayi-tiridde*), 'difficult to deal with' (*tebasoboka*), or 'wild' (*balalu*). These remarks were often followed by some story about a recent incident to illustrate the point. One day at a beer party in the village a story proved to be too exaggerated in the eyes of the women present. One woman reported, 'If we are wild, surely Nambi [the daughter of Heaven Gggulu and wife of Kintu, the man who allegedly unified the Ganda clans into a political state] was also wild. (*Oba Tuli balalu Nambi naye yali mulalu*.)' The men responded in unison,

45

'Yes, but see what her stubbornness brought us — Death *(Walumbe)*.' The women then reminded them that, while it is true that Nambi's insistence upon returning to pick up the things she had forgotten enabled her brother Death to follow her to earth, without her there would be no bananas or chicken which Ganda men liked so much. At this point, everyone laughed and the conversation was changed.

On another occasion five women from the same village were sitting by the road side waiting for a bus, and as usual discussing who had given birth to a child and who had divorced or separated. One of the three men also waiting for the bus commented, 'Was it not a pity that women were separating from their husbands too much!' Another man expressed disgust that the women were constantly deserting their husbands *(kunobanoba)* and roaming from one liaison after another *(kufumbirwafumbirwa)*. One woman disdainfully told him, '*Irene nga teyakwatibwa nsonyi*. (But anyhow Irene did not feel ashamed)'. This was a reference to Irene Namaganda, the Queen Mother and widow of the 34th Kabaka of Bugunda, Daudi Chwa II, who had caused a scandal by remarrying, and a commoner at that. This remark silenced the men because, in the words of one informant, it was obvious that 'If the King's wife can break the custom, then there was no reason for ordinary men to swell up like frogs that have been beaten or frightened.'

A woman who had lived in a chief's court in the 1920s, and who had frequently been sent to wait on one of the princesses, remarked on their sexual freedom. 'This one was rich, unmarried, and did what she wanted.' This story seems to have been divulged to support the argument that women should be left to do as they please for, after all, they were just copying those at the top of society whence power and authority emanated.

It is a well-documented fact that princesses usually enjoyed more privileges than ordinary women. The denial of normal marriage to daughters of the royal clan occurred in the Interlacustrine region — Buganda, Bunyoro and Buhaya. In Buganda, it has probably had important results, and may explain the reputation of Ganda princesses for sexual freedom. But the enthusiastic reception of Christian teaching by the Ganda ruling class gave a real incentive for the transformation of traditional roles, while the *mailo* land system and the right of women to own and inherit property had usually made Ganda princesses wealthy as well as independent in outlook. They had no good economic reason for taking to prostitution, as their Haya counterparts may have had.[24]

Although kingship and all that went with it had been abolished in 1966 by Uganda's republican government, it is interesting to note that women were rationalizing their actions by reference to a high society that was now past.

Luo women were also facing a conflict over being good wives and mothers while at the same time making an independent living. While all the Ganda women I studied were cynical about trusting men with money, some Luo husbands and wives did trust one another. In cases where couples jointly owned businesses, for example, shopkeeping and trading or carpentry, they seemed to have joint responsibilities with regard to the disposal of the money, for example, whether or not they should build a house in Kampala or in the rural areas, or reinvest in the business. I knew many Luo couples that had extensive discussions over how to use their money. Some working men often gave their entire salary to their unemployed wives for safe-keeping. Others deposited large percentages of their income in a Post Office Savings account and gave their wives the savings account book to keep. One Luo man informed me that, since his wife could count but not read figures, she was safe. This man made his wife feel trusted and yet what he seemed to trust was her illiteracy!

If the wives were working, the couples agreed on who would be doing what for example, in one case the wife paid the school fees while the man provided the uniforms for their six children. The woman also sent 20 shillings regularly to the people who looked after their home in the rural areas. While the man paid the rent and provided money for buying their staple food, the woman took care of purchasing other things like vegetables and meat.

However, over one half (27) of the Luo women in the sample had to rely upon their husbands' income. Except for three single women, 15 women said they saved separately, 12 said they saved jointly, 6 gave no answer (4 of whom were unemployed), and 11 said they had no money to save (see Table 3).

Almost two-thirds of the Luo women spent most of their time shuttling between the rural and urban areas. They never stayed in town long enough to settle, a fact that their men were proud of: their women were not staying in town and being corrupted. And it is from this group of women that my informants came. Those who did not have to shuttle between the urban and rural areas were said to have learned the ways of Ganda women. What this meant was that they were seeking ways and means to have independent sources of income. So, in fact, they were not learning Ganda behaviour but the facts of urban life, i.e. the lesson that everyone needs to have some economic support.

The Ganda women had been exemplars of this, but generally I found that women felt the need for money after living for as little as a week in Namuwongo and Wabigalo. I prefer to interpret this desire to have an independent source of income as a strategy to loosen the total dependence on men faced by urban women with no occupations. Men used various ways to curb women's appetites for money. They either meticulously counted every penny spent to ensure that their wives were not misappropriating housekeeping money (or wasting it), or they actually forbade their wives to engage in marketing activities. The case study below illustrates the conflicting interests of the good wife who at the same time wishes to have an independent source of income.

For some time Wilfreda had been selling sweet bananas on the verandah while her husband was at work as foreman for a shirt factory. She had also discovered that she could buy fish cheaply if she went to the market after six o'clock, even though it was a rush to prepare supper because her husband always returned home between 7.30 and 8.00. But she managed to save some money. Then one day some 'Bangladesh' arrived, i.e. a second-hand clothing seller working for Indian second-hand stores. She bought three nice chiffon dresses and some head scarves. When she showed the clothes to her husband he was very upset and demanded to know where she got the money. She told him. His reply was, 'I wonder if you would be doing these things if I had not brought you to town. You wear nice clothes and sit here waiting for men to come buying bananas. You are returning to the village at once.'

The woman packed her things and left by train for Kisumu three days later. In 1974, when I met her again, she was involved in a very complex trading arrangement. She had a trade licence to sell fish from Uganda to Zaire and Kenya. From Kenya (Kisumu and Nairobi) she sometimes bought sugar or beer or cooking oil or cement to sell at Namuwongo. From Zaire she bought some Dutch batik cloth which she sold to elite women in Kampala at 100 per cent profit. She occasionally stayed with a female friend whose room was next door to her ex-husband's. She had lost her husband but gained economic autonomy.

The case is interesting for several reasons, but particularly for the fact that women were expected to be content with the money their husbands earned, which in most cases was not very much. Men feared that financial independence might give their women ideas of independence in other areas, namely sexual independence. As one Luo man put it, 'Once women have their own money they will do anything. Look around Namuwongo, the women with money are not married because they can no longer listen to a man.' This was not an isolated view. However, in my view, the Luo men had least cause to worry about their wives.

The Nubi, an Urban Phenomenon

The Nubi, like the Luo, had a reputation for having their women under control. But they could not pretend that the good woman lived in the rural areas or that engaging in an economic activity necessarily made women 'big headed' and uncontrollable. Furthermore, while the other ethnic groups could mourn the decline of their cultures because their chief bearers, the women, were exposing themselves to corrupting urban influences, the Nubi men could not use such an argument because their culture was actually the result of transformations that had occurred in the urban areas. Thus, while some of my informants could vaguely refer to themselves as coming from some ethnic group in Southern Sudan, they mainly identified with the urban areas. At first it was the army posts in Sudan, then the barracks in Uganda and Kenya and finally as landowners, real estate managers and speculators, taxi-owners, shopkeepers and cobblers in the suburbs of Kampala and small urban centres.

Nubi women, when they married non-Nubi rural Muslims, conducted themselves in ways that most people agreed were urban. For example, they insisted on using charcoal stoves instead of firewood; they had a porter hired whenever possible to do most of the manual work of digging and fetching water; they made exquisite meat and rice dishes, as well as fried cookies from simsim, rice and flour.

The only bone of contention was the children. Nubi women insisted on bringing up their children as Nubi. They instructed them in Islam, taught them the Kinubi language, dressed them in long loose shirts and caps if they were boys, and insisted that they wear ankle length bloomers if they were girls. Also, they would usually travel long distances to join other Nubi in large urban centres to celebrate most Islamic holidays.

Correspondingly, when Nubi men married other women, the children were still automatically reared like Nubi and the wives had to assimilate Nubian culture. This involved conversion to Islam, learning to speak Kinubi, wearing knee length dresses and ankle length skirt wraps of special striped cloths (*bikoyi*), and covering their heads with bright coloured thin materials of cotton khanga (*lesu*) popularized in recent years in Tanzania, or, for special occasions, women who were well off used brocade silk or net shawls. The converts made doubly sure that they were indistinguishable from other Nubi women by adopting the special Nubi cornrow hairstyle, adorning themselves with real gold nose plugs and earrings, and wearing necklaces of either amber or strings of mixed black, white, yellow and red glass beads. This claim to ethnic identity was complemented by ethnic dress so that 'To a distant observer, such persons would appear as Nubi in all aspects of social life.'[25]

Nubi men had convinced everyone that they indeed controlled their women. In the two Kampala wards of Namuwongo and Wabigalo the residents seemed to believe the Nubi community to be morally uncorrupted. This was a myth but it was perpetuated by careful maintaining of certain images. For example, the Nubi claimed and seemed to observe all the laws or pillars of Islam, particularly the dogma on women's behaviour. They were disdainful of the non-Nubi Muslims, particularly the Ganda, whom they accused of being morally loose because they were not strict in observing the five pillars of Islam, namely: daily prayers, fasting, alms-giving and pilgrimage to Mecca.

Although some women were assimilated by marriage, the majority of the women who became Nubi were single and unattached. These were mainly Ganda, Soga, Lughara, Toro, Kakwa and Acholi women. The process of Nubinization is best understood if we regard it as a strategy used either to acquire respectability by counteracting negative stereotypes and images of urban women, or as a cushion against the rootlessness resulting from separation from the rural home.

The myth of male control went hand in hand with the myth of female submission. Informants revealed that the bridewealth given for Nubi girls had dropped from the two thousand and the one thousand shillings which supposedly their grandmothers and mothers respectively had fetched. As an elderly Nubi woman put it, 'This is an indication that Nubi girls have become morally loose too!' This contention was supported by my findings. I discovered that when mothers said that their daughters were very ill or bewitched and therefore could not see visitors, it usually meant that they were pregnant.

The houses of affluent Nubi had shrub or tree hedges around them. The houses of poor Nubi had huge verandahs at the rear where women did their work. Rich men installed water taps in the kitchens; poor Nubi either fetched the water and washed clothing for the family themselves or hired a water carrier. After observing five men washing clothes for a month, I was full of admiration for them for I assumed that they were men who had transcended sex role stereotypes and did not mind helping their wives. However, when I asked the women, they told me that the men were washing the clothes so that the women would not be seen hanging about at a public well for long periods of time. It was an open secret that most affairs in the area began and flowered through encounters at that well. Men usually washed the clothing in front of their houses. If a man was washing clothes, other Nubi men would come visiting or would chat to him as they passed by. He did not miss out on anything, and he had the support of the men who approved of his stand. However, the women had to wash clothes at the back of the house with co-wives or children for company, stopping once in a while to entertain visitors. It would seem, therefore, that there was little difference between Nubi women and those of other ethnic groups, but the men wanted to convince everyone that there was. The following incident illustrates the point.

When I was doing fieldwork, my landlord was a Nubi. The house I lived in had eight 'doors' (rented rooms), six of which were rented by single, unattached women. One day when one of the women was unable to pay the rent, the landlord came early in the morning and accused her of selling herself like other Ganda women to raise the money required for the rent, and even threatened to expel her from the premises because he 'did not want her filthy money'. No sooner had he uttered those words than two of the woman's friends started warning him. They reminded him that he had two illegitimate children at home (another neighbour corrected the number to three and several of those gathered around confirmed it). They requested him to stop moralizing because it was a shame that such a pious man had such a family including a daughter who would have children by a non-Muslim who was by definition uncircumcised and therefore unclean according to Islamic law. The audience laughed at this sarcastic reference to Nubi women. The women advised him to sweep his own house thoroughly before worrying about the morality of Ganda women. They insisted that, while the man's tenant had once supplemented her income through dubious ways at the bars, she had reformed and even acquired a steady boyfriend. The women told me later that they had supported their friend because they objected to the Nubi 'holier than thou' attitude that condemned people forever despite their reforming. They agreed that, while the Nubi did not wash their linen in public, 'it did not mean that their women were morally above other women'. In fact, Nubi women themselves generally expressed agreement with the Namuwongo drunkard's ballad, 'Women control themselves. Don't let anyone deceive you that a man can control a woman. It all depends on what she wants!'

Summary

Men of all ethnic groups expressed the view that urban employment made women too 'big headed' to accept male control. Even those whose wives were not working lamented that women did not need men; 'they only need our money' as one man put it. But it would seem that men were no less susceptible to the compelling attraction of money. Men in situations of financial insecurity also employed strategies to ensure that the situation did not get worse. About 20 young men admitted to me that before they became serious with a woman they often asked her if she was employed. Men of all ethnic groups wanted a woman who would be a financial asset rather than a liability.

Nevertheless some men, particularly the Luo, did want a woman who would be willing to live in the village and not have any fancy ideas 'about being employed in town'. At the beginning of a relationship, a working woman would be showered with presents in the hope that she would reciprocate. The relationship would become sour if the woman seemed reluctant to spend easily. The name of the game was making a living. Men as well as women were struggling to save money so as to have some economic security and this seemed more important than romantic notions about whom they wanted to sleep with. Novels and books have hitherto recorded this only of women in urban areas.

In this study it was found to be true of men as well. Since most young women were unwilling to support their boyfriends, some young men attached themselves to older women so as to save money. I knew students, clerks, and unemployed school drop-outs who had no worry over accommodation, food or clothing. They enjoyed the financial comforts provided by older women, but still liked to sleep with younger women whom they accused of being mean with money.

In one instance, I found a man who had bought land in the village, built a house on it and even married thanks to the generosity (or ignorance!) of his lover, who had secured him a job as a coffee maker at a government office through her contacts. Many Ganda informants insisted that there were such men in the rural areas too. In my research I found that successful independent female householders usually had younger resident lovers whom they fed, clothed and even gave money to for taxes.

The amount of bridewealth determined the extent of the vested interest male lineage members, particularly fathers and brothers, had in their women. In the Nilotic family, the high bridewealth made men jealously guard the chastity and fidelity of their sisters, daughters and wives. This meant that women under this system of marriage spent all their lives under the control of men, unless, of course, they could discover loopholes or options. The men exchanged high bridewealth at marriage or in the event of divorce.

Although the Luo women I interviewed took great pride in telling me, and sometimes exaggerating, how much bridewealth had been given for them, some were in fact saving up to pay back the bridewealth themselves because they had failed to convince their male relatives that they and their husbands were incompatible. In this virilocal residential pattern, women could not own land, but could use it only by virtue of their roles as wives and mothers. If they expanded the acreage under production, the husbands could always claim the entire output. Luo women, therefore, greatly depended upon the charity of their neighbours, husbands and brothers. In other words, they occupied a niche that offered limited scope. However, it will be shown later how some Luo women did attempt to deal with this handicap.

On the other hand, under the Interlacustrine marriage system, as bride-wealth among the Ganda became a symbolic token, male relatives were bereft of a vested interest in the chastity and fidelity of their sisters and daughters. The freehold system of land tenure had two effects upon marriage. First, there was increased mobility as men bought land in places far away from their patrilineal relatives, making the residential patterns for most people virilocal or neolocal. Even when the couple stayed in the same village as the husband's father, the avoidance taboo between daughter-in-law and father-in-law usually forced the couple to seek residence some distance away. Secondly, after the turn of the century, women could legally own land in their own right without depending on fathers, brothers or chiefs.

While men from other ethnic groups lamented the passing of 'the good woman' as urban influences corrupted women, Nubi men tried to convince everyone that they were in control, even if this was no longer because women needed men but loved their money. It was, however, found that Nubi men, too, attached themselves to successful women who took care of their economic needs.

References

1. F. Barth, 'Models of Social Organization', *Royal Anthropological Institute Occasional Paper* No. 23, 1966.
2. A.W. Southall, 'On Chastity in Africa', *The Uganda Journal*, Vol. 24, No. 2, 'Problems of the New Morality', *Journal of African Studies*, 1974, (Los Angeles: University of California at Los Angeles, African Studies Center, University of California Press), pp. 381-3.
3. *Ibid.*
4. John Ndisi, *A Study in the Economic and Social Life of the Luo of Kenya*, (Scandinavian Institute of African Studies, Uppsala, 1974), p. 72.
5. *Ibid.*, p. 73.
6. *Ibid.*
7. *Ibid.*
8. *Ibid.*, p. 15.
9. *Ibid.*
10. A.B.C. Ocholla-Ayayo, *Traditional Ideology and Ethics Among the Southern Luo*, (The Scandinavian Institute of African Studies, Uppsala, 1976), p. 40; A.W. Southall, *Lineage Formation Among the Luo*,

(Oxford University Press for International African Institute, London, 1952), p. 20.

11. *Ibid.*
12. A.I. Richards, *The Changing Structure of a Ganda Village,* (East African Institute of Social Research, Kampala, 1966), Study No. 24, p. 21.
13. *Ibid.,* p. 22.
14. *Ibid.*
15. Simon H. Ominde, *The Luo Girl From Infancy to Marriage,* (Macmillan, Nairobi, 1952), p. 177.
16. John V. Taylor, *The Growth of the Church in Uganda: An Attempt at Understanding,* (S.C.M. Press, London, 1958), p. 123.
17. *Buganda Laws,* (Uganda Bookshop, Kampala, 1957).
18. Taylor, *op. cit.,* p. 169.
19. *Ibid.*
20. H.F. Morris, 'Marriage and Divorce in Uganda', *The Uganda Journal,* Vol. 24, No. 2, 1960, p. 199.
21. *Ibid.,* p. 197.
22. L.P. Mair, *Native Marriage in Buganda,* (Oxford University Press, London, for International Institute of African Languages and Cultures, 1940), Memorandum No. 19, pp. 23-8.
23. A.I. Richards and Priscilla Reining, 'Report of Fertility Surveys in Buganda and Buhaya, 1952' in Frank Lorimer (ed.), *Culture and Human Fertility: A Study of the Relation of Cultural Conditions to Fertility, Non-Industrial and Transitional Societies,* UNESCO, Paris, 1954), p. 384.
24. A.W. Southall and P.C. Gutkind, *Townsmen in the Making: Kampala and Its Suburbs,* East African Studies No. 9, East African Institute of Social Research, 1957, p. 83.
25. Barri Wanji, 'A Preliminary Postgraduate Research Paper on the Nubi of East Africa', Makerere University Working Paper No. 115, 1971, p. 7.

4. The Research Sites

Namuwongo-Wabigalo

Something of the vivid and outwardly chaotic scene in the rapidly growing urban areas, known to the outside world only as slums, peri-urban areas, squatter settlements and shanty towns, may be conveyed by a few glimpses of Namuwongo-Wabigalo (Kampala) which was the urban area I focused on.

An attractive woman rushes to grab her child from the road where a fast moving lorry is approaching in a cloud of dust. A tall thin woman calls out to a small boy with a running nose to come and have his bath, while two freshly washed little girls stand nearby drying themselves in the sun. The woman and her neighbours talk about the day's happenings. They laugh, gesture and sigh, 'That's life!'

A little distance away laughter drifts from a room out of which a man staggers followed by a woman yelling, 'If you do not pay, I am going to call the chief. Why did you pretend you had money? No one drinks my gin for free.' She grabs his parcel of fish and returns to the room where a hubbub of animated conversation can be heard. Under a tree a woman sells roast chicken and pork to beer and gin drinkers. Another woman, returning from her distillery in the valley with a four gallon tin of gin balanced on her head, meets a sub-chief near her house. He falls in step with her and asks, 'Are you at it again?' The woman laughs and does not answer. They reach her house and he pours out some gin for himself. About an hour later he leaves and the woman tells her neighbours and customers, 'Those rascals took my income for three months. He is spying on me because he hoped that I would be totally broke. He directed the City Council rogues to my house because I had refused to give him some money last month. These chiefs are like jealous people who bring thieves to steal your things in the hope of retarding your progress. Not me, I am going to continue being successful.'

The same woman hails a woman carrying firewood and walking so fast that it looks like a trot. Several people help her to put down the heavy bundle while they talk, 'Is that good firewood for me?' asks the distiller. 'Yes, if you pay me more than you usually do. I had to walk a long distance to get it and it's a much bigger bundle.' 'Alright, put it at the usual place and I will pay you tomorrow.' 'I'm sorry. I can't wait. If you don't have the money today, I will sell it to someone else. You see, my daughter has a terrible fever and I want to take her to a private doctor for an injection. The tablets from Mulago (the main government hospital) have not helped at all.' The distiller buys the firewood and orders more.

A well dressed young man approaches a room, watched by about half a dozen people sitting on the verandah of the shop opposite. A wooden box, a blanket and some unfolded clothes lie outside a padlocked door. They are his belongings and his mistress seems to have thrown him out. He sits on his box, he swears, utters threats and eventually leaves as a crowd gathers.

Nearby, some schoolboys play football refereed by a teacher who is buying curried pancakes (*sumbusa*) from a veiled woman. They exchange meaningful glances. From the kindergarten room there comes the sound of slightly off tune singing and a din of tin musical instruments.

Two women enter and a man leaves the room of a diviner-curer who claims to be able to cure sterility and impotence and to help with court cases, job hunting and luck in love. At the taxi depot a man sits with his medicines spread out and chants all the problems he can cure. A woman buys a tooth-brush for her children to succeed in school. Another woman buys a piece of moulded clay for stomach pains. A man rolls up his shirt to have several incisions made and medicine rolled into his upper arm. This will induce the woman he has been chasing to love him, so the medicine man tells him, Medicines are rubbed into the incisions at the wrist of another man who has lost several jobs and wants to keep the next one. A tiny talisman consisting of a filthy piece of cloth stitched to look like a bean is given to a man engaged in a lawsuit over land.

A man and a woman stand at the doorstep of their room shouting instructions to a seven year old girl. 'I want you back here quickly. No playing along the way with the milk', says the mother. 'If you provoke those children on the way and they steal your money or throw it away, you will be in trouble,' adds the father. The girl skips on without looking back.

Two women returning from the market decide to buy a few things at a shop owned by a Ruandan. The one carrying three tomatoes buys a cup of cooking oil and the other carrying spinach buys maize flour. They leave complaining, 'I hate buying from these profiteers, it is a pity John (a Luo shopkeeper) was closed today,' says one woman. 'No wonder his shop is always robbed, must be people he overcharges,' declares her companion.

Four men returning from work stop at the cobbler's workbench situated on a shop verandah. They admire several new shoes and promise to have similar ones made at the end of the month when they get their pay. Mean-while, what they really need are a few stitches in their shoes. They wait while the shoes are being repaired. The cobbler continues to talk with his nephew who is visiting from the country. The home news is good and bad. Several people have died but the food harvest has been abundant. The nephew helps him to polish the shoes of the customers before they leave.

A church leader who has not visited his rural home in five years is brought up to date by neighbours who have recently been to the village. A woman and her friend talk and laugh loudly as they prepare to sell food. A shopkeeper sits on her verandah watching the passersby and offering a running commentary to her neighbours inside. People individually or in pairs drop into the various bars. A drunkard sings and recites commentaries on life to the applause or disgust of the hearers. Children play running around games and mothers tell them to be careful.

There is loud hammering of metal under a tree. A woman bargains unsuccessfully for a charcoal stove and oil lamp. She buys them anyway. Another woman comes to pick up the saucepan and pail she had brought to have the leaking bottom removed and a new one put in. She pays and praises the workmanship. From behind a house three women appear with long sticks chasing rats and mice which disappear in a mountain of garbage where dogs and cats are amusing themselves. A chorus of children cheer the women's efforts.

A Mercedes-Benz stands outside a carpenter's shop, where a man in a pinstripe suit is ordering some chairs, beds and tables. The carpenter looks pleased with acquiring so much business.

A few yards away, a man emerges out of a Fiat and ducks into a bottled beer bar. Rude remarks are hurled at a young woman wearing a miniskirt and high heeled shoes. 'It is disgraceful that women do not respect themselves anymore', men and women agree. 'I hope the soldiers spot her, they will teach her a lesson or two. The law banning these silly clothes is the best thing the military government has done,' declares one man to an amused audience that is still watching the disappearing figure of the woman.

Several women are returning from a nearby spring. Some are talking and others hurrying on. A Nubi man is hanging up the family's laundry. His wife and friends sit under a mango tree, braiding hair and plaiting mats. A Luyia neighbour has problems lighting his charcoal stove to cook beans. Nearby five Ruandan men sing as they construct a house from papyrus reeds.

There is an argument. A Luo man tells his wife, 'You should count yourself lucky to be in town. All your friends are in the village digging.' 'You call this a town? People back home think I'm living in a brick house with electricity and tap water. They think I walk on paved roads. But look at this leaking, grass roofed, mud wattle house we live in. Look at the dusty, corrugated roads. Look at the rubbish everywhere. One day when you have enough money to rent a decent house, I will consider myself lucky,' chided the wife. A laundryman (*dobi*) and a tailor look on sympathetically. However, their attention is attracted by City Council officials conducting a surprise weekend swoop on an illegal house being constructed. Several workmen are arrested but they plead that it is not their house and do not know to whom it belongs. The workmen are taken into custody. The tailor remarks, 'They will be back tomorrow and the house will be ready on Monday. Those city officials know that no magistrate will take action against these men. I worked once as a house builder and the wise builders used "to grease the elbows" of the chiefs for protection against this kind of raid. When the materials had been collected, workers were hired to put up the houses on weekends. If we were arrested, we pleaded ignorance! What a life it was!'

A customer laughingly says, 'Maybe that is what I will have to do. I have just paid 2,200 shillings for 50 square yards of land. That includes "greasing" the chief's palm, the surveyor's inflated fees, the tea that I gave the City Council official who approved my house plan and the architect who sold me the plan.' The listeners shake their heads in amazement.

Some women return from the market balancing containers on their heads. Two of them chat with a woman carrying her personal belongings on her head, a baby on her back and leading a four year old by the left hand while balancing the heavy basket with the other. Onlookers comment, 'Welcome to Namuwongo another villager. Why do you think she packed up and left the village?'

This is Namuwongo-Wabigalo, a ward of Kampala, where my main research was undertaken. It was only four miles as the crow flies from the city centre, but physically and psychologically isolated along a bumpy winding road full of pools in the wet season and clouds of dust in the dry (although the workmen responsible for providing the necessary services — road menders, garbage collectors, mosquito and vermin controllers — were reluctant to come and work here, the City Council law enforcement officers managed to get here frequently enough to arrest tax defaulters or illegal brewers and distillers who had failed to buy adequate protection).

So diverse is what is going on in the area that strangers to Namuwongo and Wabigalo find it difficult to distinguish between business and social activities. The place seems like one big party with some people very busy and others just sitting inside the houses or on the verandahs drinking or waiting for something to happen. But, as has been observed of two similar Kampala suburbs,[1] the people of Namuwongo and Wabigalo cannot be accused of lacking initiative in creating employment or trying to better their lives generally. The snippets of conversation and excerpts of action recorded here are representative of those urban areas inhabited by unskilled rural-urban migrants.[2] They also afford us glimpses of women who, because poor, are compelled to take a more realistic approach which may have some lessons for all.

Background and Present Situation of the Area

Kampala, the capital of Uganda, grew up adjacent to the capital of Buganda, Kibuga.[3] By 1969, it was a prosperous multi-ethnic city of 350,000 people.[4] All the country's major roads lead to Kampala where the ministries and parastatal bodies have their offices; the banks, the main hospitals, particularly Mulago, and Makerere University are all situated there. As a direct response to the commercial and administrative activities in Kampala its suburbs have, since the 1940s, been bursting with economic activity. As the number of migrants to these areas increased so did the opportunities for employment in service industries. Those not employed in the government or private companies could be self-employed.

Namuwongo and Wabigalo were such suburbs, situated east of the city and adjacent to the light industrial area — plants for car assembling, soft drink bottling, coffee and tobacco curing, and the manufacture of blankets, fishnets, shoes, batteries, clothing and so on. The urban ward in which Namuwongo and Wabigalo were situated consisted of the two parishes of Kisugu and Muyenga. Each parish *(muluka)* was under the rule of a chief assisted by four deputy chiefs *(batongole)*. They were responsible for collecting taxes, enforcing laws, and resolving minor conflicts. Although the parishes included areas of high income residence for elites such as diplomats and businessmen, the chiefs confessed that they spent most of their time in the low income localities where they had their offices and where they felt there was a great need to enforce law and order. The senior chief himself lived in the village of Bukasa outside the city boundaries, while his assistants who did most of the work had been in the area for over ten years and were property owners.

Settlement in the area was first stimulated by the development of rail and water transport. Goods from Britain and India were brought from the Indian Ocean port of Mombasa to Kisumu on Lake Victoria, where a steamboat then took the cargo to Port Bell which was linked by light railway to Kampala, the administrative centre. In 1931 the main railway line from Mombasa was extended from Eldoret to Kampala.[5]

All this created certain sorts of jobs, for instance labourers to shovel coal into the furnaces to run the steam engines of the boats and trains, and porters for loading and unloading goods from them. Porters became an essential part of the administrative and commercial centre, Kampala. By the 1940s, however, domestic service was the largest employment opportunity for migrants from Western Uganda — the Toro, Nyoro and Ankole — settling mainly in Wabigalo. At the same time, the Luo migrants from Kenya had settled on either side of the Port Bell railway.

Since the 1940s, the area has been a dormitory for unskilled and domestic labourers who migrated from the rural areas to seek wage employment in Kampala. However, until 1968 the area was part of the Buganda local administration. Landowners both rented out rooms and old houses and leased, sold or developed some of their land to meet the accommodation demands of migrants. The result was unplanned, and therefore, uncontrolled development. By 1954 the Medical Officer of Health for the Kampala Municipality reported 'The problem [of the unsanitary conditions] increases daily with rapid uncontrolled building which is taking place in the immediate environs of Kampala and this septic fringe constitutes a serious threat to the health of the citizens of Kampala.'[6]

The situation was still the same in 1968 when the government decreed amalgamation of the city of Kampala, the municipality of Mengo, and the townships of Natete, Kawempe and Nakawa, including the parishes of Kisugu and Muyenga in which Namuwongo and Wabigalo are situated.

In 1968 the City Engineer and Surveyor of Kampala City noted in his annual report that the Namuwongo and Wabigalo areas presented,

a scene of completely unregulated development without any semblance of visual order. A wide variety of types of buildings ranging from rows in mud and wattle and tin roofs to permanent structures. There is no drainage system. What serves as roads are only deeply eroded and winding tracks, impossible in wet weather, and water is obtained from natural springs. The conditions are to be found in other slum areas, such as Katwe-Kiziba, Kikubamutwe, Makerere, Kivulu and Mulago.[7]

The 1968 expansion of the city boundaries increased the size of Kampala from 8½ to 75 square miles. The city undertook not only jurisdiction for the area but responsibility for providing urban public services, which had hitherto been poor due to the local authorities' uneven revenue. The resident parish chiefs (*bamiluka*) and ward chiefs (*batongole*) were officially designated ward-based City Council officials. But since most of their duties such as arbitration in disputes continued to be the same, the people continued to refer to them as chiefs.

The chiefs, as City Council officials, did not waste any time, but immediately demanded public amenities — water, electricity, and garbage disposal. Through letters and weekly visits to the City Council headquarters, they engaged in discussions with the relevant officials, and persisted in their demands even when the authorities tried to drag their feet. When a pipe was eventually laid to a stream, it soon became obvious that it could not provide an adequate supply of water for the area. Ten water taps were then installed. Garbage was supposed to be cleared at least every two days, but no one was surprised when it took two months. By 1971, street lights were provided but few houses had electricity and even in those homes that did the people found it cheaper to use paraffin lamps and cook on charcoal or primus stoves.

One problem remained however — the imposition of city building standards in the area. Entrepreneurs would recruit casual labour to erect houses at night when no law enforcement officials were around. If the labourers were arrested, they could not legally be prosecuted because the law required that the actual owner be brought to court. Often the builders did not know their employer. The law weakened the effectiveness of City Council officials in their efforts to deal with the problem of unauthorized housing.[8]

Providing housing for the rural-urban migrants was one of the most profitable Kampala businesses by 1971. Closely related were landownership and land speculation. Between 1967 and 1970 a marked increase in the acquisition of land in the area took place. Land was divided into strips for sale to the highest bidder. Some long-time local residents bought land, but it was mainly the government ministers, top civil servants and rich merchants who scrambled to purchase it for residential building.

By 1972 the Luo were to be found in most residential areas around Kampala, but mainly at Makerere-Kivulu, Mulago, Kisenyi, Nakawa, Kibuli, Nsambya, Kololo, etc. But Namuwongo remained the 'original home' of Luo migrants. Everyone had 'something' in Namuwongo; a relative or friend whom they visited every Sunday. In fact, irrespective of where they eventually moved to, most Luo's first experiences of Kampala were at Namuwongo. The area came to be known as 'Kisumu Ndogo' (little Kisumu), referring to the main town of Kisumu in Luoland. Some Luo acquired land and built houses in tow In addition to individual entrepreneurial efforts, the Luo Union, through the investment of mutual aid funds, built houses that were rented out to members who could not afford the fees that were being charged by the local landlords. However, the efforts failed and the houses were sold off.

During the 1950s retiring King's African Rifles Nubi soldiers also used their generous gratuities to buy land in Namuwongo and Wabigalo where they settled. By the 1960s the demand for houses in the Kampala area became acute. The Nubi combined cobbling, running taxis and shopkeeping with house ownership, and prospered.

Not everyone in Namuwongo and Wabigalo was a migrant. There were ten indigenous *(banansangwawo)* Ganda families. Other Ganda had acquired plots of land in the 1960s and had moved in from elsewhere. But the majority of Ganda were also rural-urban migrants although, since the city was situated within their home area, they were regarded as 'hosts' to the migrant 'strangers from other ethnic groups.[9] The Ganda owned most of the land in the area, under the *mailo* system of tenure. *Mailo* is a corruption of the English term 'mile', and was used for the estates given under freehold tenure by the Uganda Agreement of 1900. Permanent freehold titles were granted to some 3,954 notable persons who had full powers of disposal over the land they received. In 1927 a legislative enactment gave peasants security in the occupation of plots of unspecified size *(bibanja)* which they held from the *mailo* owners under customary tenure.[10]

Plot sizes in Namuwongo and Wabigalo varied from 20 to 100 square yards. This is in contrast to the national average holding (including large and small holders in the rural areas) of 9.75 acres.[11] Although owners were not allowed to sell land to non-Africans without special permission, five landown had mortgaged some of their land to Asian owned firms and banks in order to obtain financial loans. It is not clear what happened to the mortgaged land when the Asians were expelled from Uganda in 1972. There were claims that the government had given it to people other than the original owners.

The situation of uncontrolled development in Namuwongo and Wabigalo thus contrasted sharply with the pre-1968 City of Kampala public land that was mainly under leasehold and subject to land use planning regulations.[12]

Population of Namuwongo-Wabigalo

According to the 1959 census figures 33,570 Tanzanians, mainly Ziba, and 43,255 Kenyans were living in Uganda. The decade, 1948-57, had seen a net increase of 130,000 Ruandan men, women and children staying in Uganda. The 1959 census also showed that, of all the Kenyans in Uganda, 5,544 Luo were living in Kampala-Mengo and Jinja. While in 1962, migrants comprised 28 per cent of the total *urban* labour force, in 1969 the immigrants were only 5.1 per cent of the population of Uganda as a whole.[13] But the Luo and Ruandans still constituted a large percentage of the immigrants.

The 1969 population census showed that about 7 per cent of the total population of Uganda lived in urban areas of over 2,000 persons. The capital city, Kampala, had a population of 330,700 which accounted for one-third of the total urban population.[14] This was double the 1959 figure of 157,828 persons.

Table 5
Population of Kampala City, Administrative Areas 25, 26, 27, 28 and 29

Age Groups	Male	Female	Total
0- 4 years	2,532	2,618	5,150
5- 9 years	1,468	1,693	3,161
10-14 years	934	893	1,827
15-19 years	1,854	1,805	3,659
20-34 years	7,435	3,758	11,195
35-49 years	2,510	839	3,349
50-65 years	551	239	790
65+ years	186	111	297
Not stated	71	48	119
Total	*17,541*	*12,004*	*29,547*

Source: *Report on the 1969 Population Census,* Vol. 1, pp. 101-3.

Because Table 5 lumps together adjacent administrative areas,[15] it is difficult to delineate the population of Namuwongo and Wabigalo precisely. The different areas had varying population densities: Bukasa was a rural area with a density of probably less than 25 persons per square mile; Kibuli and Nsambya had densities of 200-423 and 100-200 persons per square mile respectively;[16] Namuwongo and Wabigalo were estimated at 50-100 persons per square mile.[17] In this study the population of Namuwongo and Wabigalo was estimated to be just over 4,000 people on the basis of the number of the rooms in the area. (There were 1,000 rooms in the area, each accommodating an average of four persons.) The chiefs and City Council officials felt that their tax records did not account for all residents because of constant residential changes within the city. The officials themselves had long given up trying to estimate the number of residents because raids on tax dodgers usually caught twice as many as the number of recorded tax-payers. Thus, any method used for enumeration could only be an approximation.

Occupations of People Living in Namuwongo-Wabigalo
Among the categories of people attracted to the area by 1971 were students, school leavers, civil servants, clerks, medical assistants, secretaries, telephone operators, nurses, as well as the unskilled rural-urban migrants. Some Namuwongo and Wabigalo residents were employed in the industrial sector as nightwatchmen, sweepers or odd job men loading and unloading goods.

People stayed in the area because it was cheap and made saving possible. For example, one person could eat for as little as 40 shillings a month; rooms for 15 or 20 shillings were available for those prepared to endure leaking grass or flattened four-gallon tin (*malebe*) roofs and crumbling mud walls. Decent rooms were available from slightly more to double these prices. The city centre and industrial area were both within walking distance of Namuwongo and Wabigalo. I estimated that people who walked to and from work and did not use taxis or buses saved on average 35 shillings a month. This can be contrasted with workers from other residential areas such as Kamwokya or Mulago who had to travel relatively long distances and spent at least two shillings a day on transportation.

The majority of residents were self-employed. This kind of employment has been referred to as the 'informal sector'. Characteristically, informal sector activities are small scale, labour intensive and individually owned. The enterprises in Uganda suffered from a high casualty rate for many reasons including market competition and lack of business know-how. However, some activities in the informal sector were economically efficient and profitable although small in scale and limited by simple technologies and little capital.[18] The informal sector in Namuwongo-Wabigalo provided goods and services both to local residents and to other parts of the city as well.

There were approximately 160 carpenters, 87 tailors, 58 food vendors, 10 taxi owner/drivers, 100 gin brewers and distillers (20 of whom had licences to supply the government-owned Uganda Distilleries), 60 market sellers, 37 fish mongers, 58 charcoal sellers, 40 firewood sellers, 120 shop-keepers, 4 tin smiths (making pails, drinking water containers, and oil lamps), 6 blacksmiths producing charcoal stoves and coiled pipes for distilling gin, 3 bicycle repairers, 2 primus stove repairers, 10 cobblers, and 12 cement building block makers. Even these activities are not exhaustive of the Namuwongo and Wabigalo occupations but have been singled out because they generated regular incomes for the residents.

Table 6
Approximate Monthly Income Ranges for Individuals in Various Occupations*

Women	Shillings	Men
Shop owner; house owner;	1,000+	House owner; shop owner
banana beer brewer	1,000	Shop owner
	998	Garage mechanic
	902	Shop owner
Distiller	800	Quarry supervisor
	750	Shop owner
	700	Private firm mechanic
Distiller	680	Factory foreman
Malwa** brewer	548	
	500	Bus driver; bank messenger

Women	Shillings	Men
Prostitute and dressmaker; house owner; shop owner	400	Bus driver; bank messenger
Kwete*** brewer; shop owner	357	Shoe shop porter
Fish and vegetable seller	310	Meat seller; lorry driver
Prostitute; house owner; malwa brewer	259	House painter; post office clerk
Mat maker; cooked food seller; banana beer brewer; cassava, banana and sweet potato cultivator; verandah trader	200	Factory guard; blanket maker
Distiller; dressmaker; fish trader	190	
	183	Night watchman
	179	Bakery porter
	168	Fish seller
Distiller; vegetable seller; banana seller; factory seamstress	150	
Distiller	136	Fish seller
	100	Odd jobs
Malwa brewer; verandah trader; banana beer brewer	90	
Cooked food seller	80	Clothes hawker
Honey beer brewer	70	
Verandah trader	60	
Cooked food seller; munanansi brewer; barmaid, and kwete brewer	50	
Munanansi**** brewer; malwa brewer; banana cultivator; verandah trader	30	
Verandah trader	20	
	10	Odd jobs

* Incomes varied even for people in the same occupation, and some people had multiple occupations.
** Millet beer
*** Maize beer
**** Pineapple beer

Views About the Area
The low income area residents were popularly stereotyped as vulgar in their language and behaviour, the men perceived as either lazy or thieves and the women as single or prostitutes. Professional people, while sitting in their comfortable offices, would refer to the area as an 'eyesore', a 'den of

thieves and prostitutes' who should be 'returned to the land'. Such views were held despite the fact that some of the elite lived next door to Namuwongo and Wabigalo, in the high income areas of Tank Hill and Kisugu, and employed house servants and baby sitters from Namuwongo and Wabigalo. During shortages, they even bought sugar, rice, salt, milk, bread, flour, bananas, charcoal, fish and cooking oil there. Furniture could be bought almost half price at Namuwongo and Wabigalo. Some elite men also had girlfriends in the area, while others entertained their girlfriends there discreetly.

If the elites were ashamed of living next door to Namuwongo and Wabigalo, some of the residents themselves were ashamed of the area. For example, students and those employed in the formal sector always pretended to live in the higher income residential areas of Muyenga or Kisugu. The image of Namuwongo and Wabigalo as one of the grimmest parts of the city was held not only by outsiders but local residents as well. When I was going to reside in the area, I informed the chief as all new residents were supposed to do, also telling him that, although I wanted to look at some rooms before entering, this was not possible. (Because of the high turnover, rooms were usually occupied within 24 hours of being vacated.) He thought hard and then advised me not to stay in the area. Pointing to the open sewers, crawling cockroaches and a woman throwing out two dead rats, he told me that I would be constantly ill. Motioning with his eyes towards two men in torn shirts and bleeding from beatings, he warned me against attacks by thieves. A few days later, he told me that he had found several spacious rooms with running water and electricity in the neighbouring high class residential area. The chief, of course, was motivated by the best of intentions. He wanted to treat me like an elite woman whose insulated mentality should be saved from traumatic experiences. Also, I was unmarried and needed to be protected if my reputation was to remain intact for the duration of my research. Finally, the chief himself commuted to the area to work from his home in Bukasa, an adjacent rural area.

He was not particularly enthusiastic about the room I eventually rented which was, among other things, near a bar. Yet it suited my purpose admirably. It was at the cross-roads in the middle of Namuwongo and Wabigalo where I could watch people going to and from work and the markets as well as observe many other activities without much effort, and gossip too with neighbours and passers-by without seeming nosy. My room was attached to a house with two shops. The house stood opposite a building that served on different days as an Anglican Church, school and clinic. I was within one to five minutes walking distance of three other churches. I had access to three food markets within five to fifteen minutes walking distance. I had easy access to all the ten water taps in the area.

Another example of the disfavour in which the area was held occurred in the following way. Once when I dropped in to interview a Namuwongo resident who worked as a newspaper reporter in the City Centre, I learned from his colleagues that he was out for lunch at a restaurant where apparently he lunched every day, while they were eating food bought from a woman food seller for two shillings a plate. (The same quantity and quality of food (steamed rice and fish) would have cost five shillings in a downtown restaurant.) On my way back to Wabigalo, I spotted a familiar looking figure at an open air restaurant. I told him how his colleagues had said he was lunching down town. Embarrassed that I had discovered his image-building tactics, he said, 'For one shilling I get food here that would cost me six shillings. Look at the chunks of meat and the large helpings. I am not married and I am saving money to buy a plot of land, a car and to marry.' Namuwongo and Wabigalo provided cheap and substantial meals, but one did not admit this to fellow elites.

By contrast I was amazed at the openly close relationships and regular contacts between Namuwongo and Wabigalo and the university. Although the student newspaper often carried disparaging articles written by male students about low income areas, some students had girlfriends and even children there. And the women students had their hair braided and dresses made in low income places like Namuwongo. In one extreme case of elitism, Anna, a fellow school and university student, disparagingly teased me about conducting research in such an area, but then by coincidence, I came across a gin brewer and seller in Wabigalo who claimed to be her mother. She had raised and educated three children to secondary school level. I remembered how high boarding school fees were and what nice clothes Anna used to wear and I could not help but feel great admiration for Nambi. Anna admired her too, as long as she herself did not have to live in the area.

However, the officials in charge of providing services to the urban population had nothing but disdain for the Wabigalo-Namuwongo residents, who, in order to avoid lengthy questioning or being browbeaten usually claimed their place of domicile to be Kiwuliriza.[19] Even though in 1971 this was a non-existent place for administrative purposes, this did not seem to bother the public officials or medical staff.

My Research in Rural Areas

After three months of acclimatisation and nine months of actually living at Namuwongo-Wabigalo, I decided to spend the following three months gradually pulling out of my research area and checking some of my findings in the rural areas which had a number of female migrants represented in my Namuwongo-Wabigalo sample. The women of low income areas were the least known and understood of all, so the study of Namuwongo-Wabigalo area was fundamental, supplemented by research visits to Luo and Akamba villages in Kenya, some rural and urban areas in Tanzania, and further research to give confirmation and precision to my prior knowledge of the modern communities of rural Buganda where I had been brought up.

British colonial rule in East Africa ended in the early 1960s when Tanzania (1961), Uganda (1962), and Kenya (1963) all achieved political independence. After some experimentation early in the century, there had been little white settlement or land alienation in Uganda, unlike in neighbouring Kenya. Effective indirect rule by the British was set up in Uganda partly through the leaders of the powerful Kingdom of Buganda.

Uganda has experienced a relatively prosperous economic development through cash crop farming by small-holders. The south of Uganda — Buganda and Western Busoga — is favoured with adequate rainfall and fertile soils, which have stimulated immigration into the area. Already by the 1920s two types of economic opportunities existed: (1) wage earning in the urban areas of Kampala and Jinja, and the sugar plantations at Kakira and Lugazi; and (2) in the rural areas cash crop farming by the Ganda and Soga as well as by the migrants who rented land on an annual basis, and paid cattle herding by Hima pastoralists who migrated from Ankole to Northern Buganda and Teso.

At the same time, transportation (road, rail and steamer) facilities between the south of Uganda and other parts of East Africa were improving. Temporary or permanent migration remained one of the most effective means of solving the economic, political, social and racial problems of the rural areas. The Ruandans, Rundi, Lugbara and Luo were migrating to relieve critical land shortages; the Hima Ankole migrated in search of pastures; people from Bukedi district migrated because of famine. There were people migrating for non-economic reasons as well. In each group, family quarrels, witchcraft accusations, poisoning, barrenness etc. caused migration. In the late 1940s and early 1950s during the Mau Mau struggle in Kenya many Kikuyu migrated to Uganda. In the 1960s Congolese (Zaireans), Tutsi from Rwanda and Burundi, and Southern Sudanese took refuge in Uganda to escape internal wars and possible genocide. Finally, there had been a movement in the opposite direction when many Ganda migrated to other parts of Uganda to escape the religious wars of the late 1800s and later, at the turn of the century, to serve as agents (soldiers and chiefs) of the colonial government. The mission of men like Semei Kakunguru, indeed, was to civilize the rest of Uganda to accept Christianity and colonial rule.[20] According to a conservative estimate, the proportions of Ganda living outside Buganda were as follows: 4 per cent in 1911; 4.2 per cent in 1931; 5.2 per cent in 1948; 4 per cent in 1959.[21]

A Ganda Village
The village[22] I decided to study was situated in the Kyagwe county of Buganda province. It consisted of two divisions, each under a parish chief (*muluka*) and two assistant chiefs in charge of villages (*omwami wekyalo* or *mutongole*). The area was situated 15 miles from Kampala, and three miles from a small township with a population of 3,532.[23]

The area had an Anglican church with a primary school attached to it. Around the railway station, a rural centre consisting of four shops and six restaurants had developed. This was only a few miles away from a weekly market to which butchers came from all over the southern provinces to buy cows from northern traders and to which Arabs and Somalis brought imported cloth from the northeastern coast of Africa. The women sold bananas, chickens and eggs, using the proceeds to buy cloth, plates, cups, saucepans, toys, scarves and jewellery from the city hawkers who turned up there.

The local people remarked on how the area should have developed in the past twenty years into a township or urban centre, but had not. The Asians could not build permanent buildings for shops because the land did not belong to them, and even though some landlords had been willing to lease out land to them, this was illegal since non-Africans were not allowed to own land in Uganda.

During 1959 Augustine Kamya, founder of the National Movement, held several meetings in the area inciting people to boycott non-African shops. Several Asian families had their houses burnt down while the neighbours watched. Although no Asians were physically molested, their businesses suffered and they were frightened about their prospects and so moved out. During the 1960s government policy prevented non-African traders from operating in rural centres, causing emigration of more Asian shopkeepers and coffee traders.

Local development was further hindered by the fact that the area was essentially a dormitory for urban wage earners. It accommodated clerks who worked at the local administration headquarters of the township, medical technicians and midwives, teachers, taxi drivers (who made several trips daily between the City of Kampala and the various townships and rural centres in Kyagwe County), charcoal makers who peddled charcoal on their bicycles to Kampala, fishermen who cycled throughout the villages selling fresh fish, and tree cutters who sold wood to the local carpenters and gin distillers.

A Luo Neighbourhood

The other area that was studied was a locality in the East Kano district of Central Nyanza (Kenya). The district had a total population of 63,463 including 31,316 men and 32,147 women.[24] The locality I worked in had a population of about 200 adults. The village had a primary school, a bar, three shops, a grain mill owned by a politician, and a drug store operated by a retired nurse. The buildings surrounded a square consisting of grass and eucalyptus trees where the chief convened meetings, and also where a twice-weekly market took place. This market specialized in local produce such as fish from a nearby river, green vegetables, rice, maize, milk and flour. Those who wished to buy meat, chicken, large fish, baskets, etc. had to go to a bigger weekly market at the township five miles away or alternatively to the daily market at Kisumu, the largest town in Western Kenya and situated ten miles away.

In the previous ten years there had been many changes in the area that were reflected in the migration trend. Hardly any women had migrated from the village although three elderly women told me that they had once lived in Jinja and Kampala in Uganda. Primary school graduates rarely continued with schooling. Some worked at the nearby township, while others worked at a sugar factory four miles away (some still grew sugar cane to sell to the sugar factory). There was a community centre that had been built by local efforts and the projects conducted there stressed health and improved farming techniques. The result of this was evident in the general enthusiasm for a local rice irrigation project.

Summary

The data from the Luo and Ganda villages were intended to answer the question why some rural areas were prone to female rural-urban migration and others were not. I had also isolated certain issues from the Namuwongo-Wabigalo data, which I hoped would be clarified by rural data. For example, I was eager to ascertain whether single independent women and female householders were exclusively urban phenomena or were to be found in the rural areas as well, and why. Further, I was keen to ascertain whether the desire for economic autonomy through participating in modern urban trade activities was an entirely urban aspiration. In other words, I was curious about the East African folk view that certain social categories, customs and behaviours were exclusively either urban or rural. After talking to both men and women, it became clear that the data from the village added some new dimensions which are important in understanding the dynamics of migration. For example, town and village women viewed the rural and urban areas as warp and woof of the same cloth and not as an either-or situation. When the economic opportunities and personal options became restricted in the rural areas, the urban areas represented an *expanded* spectrum of opportunities, rather than a totally different set of circumstances.

References

1. The hustle and bustle of urban life have been described for Kisenyi and Mulago in A.W. Southall and P.C. Gutkind, *Townsmen in the Making: Kampala and its Suburbs,* (East African Institute of Social Research/ East African Studies Series No. 9) 1957.
2. Wandegeya, Makerere, Kivulu, Nakulabye and Mulago were the low income areas nearest to the university and therefore where the most frequent contacts took place.
3. Southall and Gutkind, *op. cit.*
4. The Statistics Division, Ministry of Planning and Economic Development, *Uganda 1971: Report on the 1969 Population Census,* Vol. 1: 'The Population of Administrative Areas', (Government Printers, Entebbe, 1971).
5. H.B. Thomas and R. Scott (eds.), *Uganda,* (Oxford University Press, London, 1935).

6. Municipal Council of Kampala, *Sixth Annual Report of the Medical Officer* (1954), p. 3; also quoted in Southall and Gutkind, *op. cit.*
7. City of Kampala, *Report of the City Engineer and Survey* (1968), p. 66.
8. Personal communication with J. Kinene, the City Council Law Enforcement Officer (November 1971).
9. David Parkin, *Neighbours and Nationals in an African City Ward,* (Routledge and Kegan Paul, London, 1969), pp. 92-5; *Report on the Population Census, op. cit.,* Vol. 1.
10. *Uganda Laws,* Vols. 1 and 6 (1935 edition); A.B. Mukwaya, *Land Tenure in Buganda: Present Day Tendencies,* (East African Institute of Social Research/East African Studies Series No. 1, 1953); A.I. Richards, 'Methods of Settlement in Buganda' in her *Economic Development and Tribal Change: A Study of Immigrant Labour in Buganda,* (Heffer for East African Institute of Social Research, Cambridge, 1954), pp. 126-8; A.I. Richards, *The Changing Structure of a Ganda Village,* (East African Institute of Social Research/East African Studies Series No. 24, 1966).
11. Beverley Brock, 'Land Tenure and Social Change in Bugisu' in Peter Rigby (ed.), *Society and Social Change in Eastern Africa,* Makerere Institute of Social Research/Nkanga Editions No. 4, n.d.), p. 17.
12. H. Kendall, *Town Planning in Uganda,* (HMSO, London, 1955).
13. O. Dak, *A Geographical Analysis of the Distribution of Migrants in Uganda,* (Department of Geography, Makerere University, Kampala, Occasional Paper No. 11, mimeo, 1968) p. 53-8.
14. *Ibid.*
15. In personal communication, Mr. K. Hill, a census official. These areas included Nsambya, Kibuli and Bukasa.
16. M.A. Hirst,'Essays on the Social Geography of Kampala', *Geowest 2,* (Working Papers of the Department of Geography, University of Western Australia, 1974), pp. 7-8.
17. *Ibid.*
18. International Labour Office, *Employment Incomes and Equality: A Strategy for Increasing Productive Employment in Kenya,* (1972), p. 6.
19. In pre-colonial times there were several provinces designated as *Kiwuliriza.* Each was under a chief who periodically briefed the Ganda King on local affairs. Changes brought about by the 1900 land consolidations and the 1966 abolition of kingship had made the name redundant.
20. H.B. Thomas, *op. cit.*
21. O. Dak, *op. cit.*
22. A village (*ekyalo*) designated an administrative area that traditionally consisted of a river and valley. The undulating hills that are typical of the area made the designation simple.
23. *Report on 1969 Population Census, op. cit.,* Vol. 1. According to the census, the total village population was 500 of whom 151 represented migrants from 12 ethnic groups and the remaining were Ganda.
24. *Kenya: Report on 1969 Population Census,* Vol. 1, (Government Printer, Nairobi).

5. Migration

Types of Migration

Although migration is a very widespread phenomenon, hardly any people migrate simply because they want to migrate. It is a symptom of many underlying causes that affect an individual and a community. The overall picture that emerges from this and other anthropological studies is that, while the causes of migration are complex, they can be summed up as limited resources and personal dissatisfaction. Individuals migrate to escape poor positions in the socio-economic stratification system which limit their full participation in the rural opportunity system. These are determined, for example, by lineage membership, age, sibling order,[1] and having few family or friendship ties with the rural community as in the case of the unmarried members of small families, and those whose parents had died and left them landless.[2]

There is a vast accumulation of migration studies mostly and necessarily statistical (as is essential for general planning). However, statistical studies carried out by formal questionnaires never reveal the actual personal causes of migration decisions, as is recognized in the distinction made between 'rate' and 'incidence'.[3] Thus, within the overall structure of capitalist modes of production and development, the factors determining the situations conducive to rural-urban migration may be beyond the control of the individuals concerned.[4] However, there is a need to understand why certain people migrate while others stay behind. In other words, while economic factors may be the primary cause for rural-urban migration, not all poor people migrate.

The case histories in this study showed that there was a difference between the reasons claimed for migration, the real reason, and what actually triggered off the move (which may be, but is not always, the same as the claimed reason). For example, one Ganda woman claimed that she had packed up her things and migrated because her husband had married another wife without telling her. However, on closer examination, it turned out that she had been planning to migrate for some time and had been saving money and keeping her valuable clothes and china stored with friends. She was just waiting for the last straw to push her to the city.

Table 7
Reasons for Migration to an Urban Area

Ethnic Group	Accompanying Husband	Going Alone	Travelling to Visit Relative	Coming to Follow Husband	Born in the Area (1950 Settlers)	Total
Kakwa				2		2
Lango		2				2
Acholi	1		1		1	3
Nubi	2				2	4
Teso		1		1		2
Nyole				1		1
Gisu		2			1	3
Ziba		1				1
Nyamwezi			1			1
Chagga	1					1
Kikuyu	2					2
Kamba	1					1
Luyia	6	1	1	2		10
Toro		2				2
Nkole		4				4
Ruandans	3	6	2	6	1	18
Rundi		1				1
Kiga	2	3		1		6
Luo	26	26	4	13	1	70
Ganda	6		6	1	12	25
Soga	1					1
Total	51	49	15	27	18	160

Non-Migrants

As mentioned previously, Namuwongo and Wabigalo were not officially incorporated into the boundaries of the City of Kampala until 1968. I talked to twelve women who had been born and reared in the peri-urban areas that were incorporated, some of whom were daughters of migrants. The women in the latter category regarded the area as a *village* because they had land and could earn money by cultivation, whereas the second-generation migrants referred to the areas as *urban*. In most cases they had been sent to stay with rural relatives for part of their lives or for holidays. Sooner or later in the interview they would assert that the villages had the advantage of 'free things such as water, fuel and housing, that did not cost money, but the people worked so hard.' They idealized most aspects of rural life except for the low wages prevalent there.

Four of the women had settled in Namuwongo and Wabigalo during the 1950s. They had bought one or two acres of land in Muyenga, and supported themselves by growing cassava and sweet potatoes, and cooking both sweet bananas and bananas to make beer. There were markets for all these products: school children ate sweet bananas for lunch snacks, and divination activities in the city created a demand for beer. In 1972, Kyaddondo, the county in which Namuwongo and Wabigalo are situated, was the largest producer of cassava and sweet potatoes, providing 50 per cent of the total food supply to Kampala.[5]

Women Who Migrated With Their Husbands

Fifty-two women in the sample had come with their husbands. In some cases migrating as a family had been a mutual decision between couples, in others the wife had insisted on coming also. For example, widows, wives and sisters of short-term, Ruandan migrants were insisting upon coming with the men to the urban areas. This trend, I was told in 1972, had only started in the previous ten years; previously only men had migrated, for short durations, while their wives took care of the rural homes. In 1972 the women were claiming that life in the village was difficult for them to cope with alone and the money the men were bringing back was not enough. Two incomes were needed to meet minimal home requirements.

Case Study: The following case study illustrates the joint decision of a couple to migrate due to a loss of desire for a rural base. They became landless through choice, and hence it is an important case in that their commitments were urban in orientation even before they migrated. Unlike other people, they did not — once in town — waste money on lawsuits against rural relatives or neighbours who were encroaching on their land, but saved to invest and expand their business in the urban areas. In fact, they ended up employing other migrants who had come to the towns hoping for employment with the government or large private companies.

Filo had just got married when she and her husband migrated in the late 1940s to a village 21 miles from Kampala where she had inherited two acres of land from a maternal grandmother. Apart from the few banana and coffee trees immediately around the house, they had to clear a large section of the land. Several teenage relatives came to stay with them: two of her sisters, a sister-in-law and two brothers-in-law. Work was much easier because there were so many helping hands. The 1950s turned out to be years of prosperity. From the coffee and cotton, they built the first brick houses in the village.

By the early 1960s the relatives had married and moved away. The couple's two children attended a nearby school. Filo started to braid and plait hair for money. 'A lot of women flocked to my home. Some shied away after a husband cut off his wife's hair with a kitchen knife because she had wasted his money on a silly hair style.'

Filo became interested in a Community Development programme designed to help women improve their housekeeping skills. She began going twice a week to a township three miles away to learn sewing from a Luo tailor who worked for an Indian. She invested her hairdressing money and bought a rusty second-hand sewing machine. Soon she was making dresses for women.

Filo said she had only had a basic education, but then a dress was not a complicated thing to put together! Moreover, she only charged five shillings while the tailors in town charged ten shillings or more.

Filo used the income from dressmaking to purchase second-hand white-laced wedding dresses which she hired out to local brides. Sometimes it was necessary to adjust the hem or the sleeves. One day her daughter was ill and a teacher (who was English) brought her home. Filo gave her several bunches of sweet bananas. The teacher was so overcome that she asked what she could do to reciprocate. Filo asked for flowers which were delivered to her home by her daughter a week later. Since becoming a bride-dresser, she was expected to do everything — arrange hair, powder faces and even provide the flowers for the bride to carry and wear on the head. Before long, villagers were travelling up to 20 miles to come to her.

A Community Development Club was started by the wife of the county chief, an educated woman who wanted other women to share her experience. Twice a week Filo and women from her village walked three miles to where the club meetings were held. Classes included nutrition and cookery, basket- and mat-making, dressmaking and embroidery, reading and writing. Filo was particularly interested in the last two:

After about six months the club's membership had decreased. The women were interested in learning but their other duties were much more pressing. Coffee had to be harvested and dried everyday. It also rained frequently and once coffee gets wet it is useless. The women no longer had time to visit each other as they used to. People only dropped in on each other either on the way to and from the hospital or on the way to and from funerals. Sometimes this 'social call' took place at the garden.

For the previous seven years her husband had been participating in annual bicycle races sponsored by the Raleigh Cycle Company, each year winning an even better bicycle. He began repairing people's bicycles under a tree outside the house. People would stop in to have the punctures repaired and brakes adjusted.

My husband and I decided to sell the land and buy a small plot near Kampala. In 1964 we bought an acre, had a small garden and built houses on the rest. He is now a car mechanic and he also repairs bicycles and motorcycles. I am still a hairdresser and a bride-dresser and a dressmaker. I like it here very much. We had to migrate from the village because the women were so jealous of my prosperity that some accused me of having bought witchcraft that enabled me to prosper at their expense.

Several times armed robbers (*kondo*) broke into our house, tied us on the bed or beat us and cleared off with everything that looked nice. My rusty sewing machine always survived! Not only were the women scornful of my badly kept garden, they were also resentful of the fact that when I went to supervise the workman or to get potatoes or bananas from the garden or to fetch firewood from the forest, I wore Wellington boots which I bought at the second-hand store. Because many men in the village wore them I was accused of trying to be a man.

I wanted much more out of life than digging. I wanted to learn how to read and write. The world was changing and leaving the women behind.

This is an interesting case study from the point of view of how changes in traditional roles, behaviour and expectations make individuals less acceptable to other villagers. Filo and her husband were adopting new skills at a pace too fast for other people's comfort. By the same token the skills made them independent enough to sell their land and migrate to the urban areas. This confidence was lacking in most migrants, who retained their rural land as an insurance for when they would retire.

Migrants Visiting Relatives
Urban-dwelling relatives were an important link for some migrants. The relatives visited in town included mothers, fathers, sisters, brothers and cousins. However, 'relatives' could also mean boyfriends and girlfriends.

Some women had come as young girls to be au pairs for their sisters or brothers; some girls had come to stay with relatives while attending the city secondary schools. After a while some were attracted by the choice of life styles and economic possibilities in town. If an urban relative insisted that they return to the village, they would go and stay with another relative or move in with a friend. After some time they would acquire their own accommodation, which required that the migrant find employment. This was called 'becoming wild' by the rural people but was regarded as self-reliant and pragmatic by urban people.

Other young women were persuaded to leave the rural areas by urban-dwelling boyfriends. A Luo woman who left the area three months after I had been there told me that after six months in town she was returning home to the village because her boyfriend had brought her to town under false pretences: 'He used to return to the village in borrowed clothes. He looked smart and all the girls admired him. He talked of the football matches, and cinema he went to; he talked of the beautiful things that happened in town and in the end I followed him. I found he was lodging with a friend and was unemployed.' The 'bright lights' had gone dull once the girl experienced the realities of urban life: everything cost money but job opportunities were limited even for those with skills usable in the modern sector. Still, most of those seeking husbands usually stayed around for they had decided that urban husbands had more to offer than rural husbands.

Followers, Shuttlers and Circulatory Migrants
Twenty-seven women in my sample had followed their husbands to the city. The wife usually followed after a few months or years when the husband acquired suitable accommodation. Sometimes the women found the village atmosphere so oppressive that they followed without encouragement from

their husbands. A woman whose husband was away was much more restricted because everyone tried to keep an eye on her, usually reporting on her faults to her husband. Luo women in particular complained about their mothers-in-law, brothers-in-law and other relatives watching and supervising them. Women, therefore, insisted on migrating with their husbands partly because they could not face life alone in the villages, and partly because they hoped to combine housekeeping duties with some means of acquiring their own money which would not be a housekeeping allowance from their husbands.

Among the women who followed their husbands were those I have categorized as 'shuttlers' because they constantly moved backwards and forwards between town and country. The Luo predominated in this category. Their commitments as agricultural producers and mothers were perceived as situated in the villages but their duties as wives required that they periodically visit their migrant husbands in the towns. Being in town also served as a break from the rural agricultural work and domestic chores. The majority of Luo women came to visit their husbands three times a year, each trip lasting about a month. The visits coincided with the times when planting, weeding and harvesting had been completed. On each visit women took back money to pay school fees for the children, to hire labour, and to buy food. The women also usually shopped for clothing and utensils before returning to the villages. Women who had been shuttling for some time usually brought food, such as flour, for the urban family as well as food to sell, such as groundnuts and black-eyed peas. The women never told their husbands about these food sales because they would have had 'to surrender the money whenever the husband wished to have a beer or smoke a cigarette', according to several women shuttlers who hoarded their private incomes for personal needs and emergencies.

In some cases women who got tired of shuttling just gave up visiting their husbands in town. The reasons they gave for stopping visiting varied from 'I have no money and he has sent no money', to 'the children are ill', and 'I am not feeling well'. In such cases, the men made periodic visits to the rural areas.

Women Who Migrated Alone

As Table 8 below shows, women in this category stated the most diverse reasons for migrating to the cities. Although they all were employed, only 10 out of 51 stated that they had migrated to seek employment. However, economic concerns were behind expressions like 'to seek my fortune', 'to improve my opportunities', and 'to try my luck'. The respondents in this group included some school leavers and women who had engaged in entrepreneurial activities in the rural areas. These women had an open mind about returning to the village some day. Others had irrevocably cut off their rural ties and claimed that 'starting a new life' was their primary motivation for migrating. In this category were women who were 'tired of village life', 'tired of digging', 'wanted to be in the centre of the city', 'seeking something', and some school drop-outs who felt that they did not fit in the village because they had had some education, or who were pregnant and felt ashamed of having to face village gossip.

Table 8
Reasons Why Women Migrate Alone

Ethnic Group	Barren/ Divorced	Seeking Job or 'Fortune'	Stigma of Divorce	Sorcery Accusation	Read & write	Unsatisfactory Marriages	Widow	Tired of Village Life	Total
Lango	1	1							2
Kakwa									
Acholi									
Nyole									
Chagga									
Kikuyu									
Kamba									
Teso					1				1
Gisu	1					1			2
Ziba							1		1
Nyamwezi									
Luyia		1							1
Toro		1						1	2
Nkole		1				1		1	3
Ruandan		2				1		3	6
Rundi		1							1
Kiga						1		2	3
Luo							2	1	3
Ganda	2	3	4	1		11	1	4	26
Soga									
Total	4[a]	10	4	1[b]	1	15[c]	4	12	51[d]

a) One Luo woman in the sample had migrated with her husband and was still happily married though barren.
b) Four women in the sample had persuaded their husbands to agree to escape sorcery accusations.
c) Fourteen other women in the sample had migrated to escape unsatisfactory marriages but had remarried before moving to Namuwongo and Wabigalo where they arrived with their husbands.
d) Above all, 20 women in the sample had migrated because they were pregnant, but this was explained away as seeking future or tiredness with village life. There were five adventurers looking for more than village life offered. As one Nkole said, 'People in the village work all the time. There is no time for enjoyment.'

One Teso woman had migrated to town as a teenager because she wanted to learn to read and write. She became involved with various religious organizations and partly achieved her ambition. She could read the Bible and write letters, but still couldn't cope with clerical jobs requiring minimum literacy skills. She worked as a seamstress in a shirt factory. Most people in the area thought she was a Luo because she spoke perfect Luo, not associating with other Teso in the area, but spending most of her time with her 'saved' or 'born again' Luo 'brothers and sisters'. She had achieved double protection against accusations of being 'loose': although single, she was religious and enjoyed the friendship of the Luo who supposedly were strict with their wives.

Some widows said they had migrated because they had no land or had never fitted in with their in-laws. Others did not care to elaborate, but merely stated there was no future for them in the villages.

Sorcery accusations between co-wives or husbands and wives still occasionally provided the immediate reason for leaving the village. I even met a woman who had migrated because her husband's mistress had 'ensorceled' her, as evidenced by periodic swelling of her sex organs. The diviner-doctor had advised her to leave the village if she ever hoped to recover. She was pleased with her progress after eight months. Other women migrated in order to escape the stigma attached to divorces triggered off by witchcraft accusations.

Barrenness, coupled with divorce, was another cause of migration. My interviewees and informants claimed that women who were barren but not divorced were never ridiculed because it was supposed that the man was sterile. 'But for people like us village life can be difficult unless one has land or supportive relatives,' a barren and divorced woman pointed out. Thus, people who migrated for this group of reasons were expressing a need to escape from rural discrimination and stigmatization. It was more possible for a barren woman to be happily married in the urban areas, although pressures and even discrimination by other women were there too.

Sixteen women claimed they had migrated to 'escape unsatisfactory marriages' and the closely related reason of 'escaping polygyny'. Polygyny has been illegal since the beginning of this century but it still persists.

Although only five Ganda women were recorded as having rejected polygyny, I came across 20 women from different ethnic groups who felt it was better to live singly than to be married to a man who divided his time between his several wives. Some women said that they could be reconciled to polygyny if their co-wives did not live in the same house or compound as they did. Others had migrated because they objected to the fact that when their husbands consulted them about the matter, it was really to announce that they were getting another wife. It seemed that few women actually divorced their husbands over polygyny, they just deserted. Unsatisfactory marriages further meant that the personal relationships between the couple left a lot to be desired, i.e. the man was a miser, quarrelsome, etc. In the case of the Ganda it often meant that sexual life was not satisfactory. One woman informed me, 'Ganda men can send away *(Kugoba)* wives who had not elongated their *labia minora (nfuli)*; and women who constantly do not get orgasms can desert *(kunoba)* their husbands . . . . If sexual encounters are not sweet, then marriage goes sour and no one will blame (a woman) for seeking satisfaction *(okumattizibwa)* elsewhere.[6]

This has led some people to suggest that, with the weakening of traditional collective ties, sexual satisfaction assumed an inordinate importance in the relationship of the spouses.[7] Southall and Gutkind found that in successful marriages, clothes, money and kindness were secondary factors compared to sexual satisfaction.[8] Certainly, some Namuwongo and Wabigalo men attributed their sexual lust to the fact that women were oversexed.[9] Orley reported that some men in Kampala suspected their wives of going out with 'many' (five or more) men.[10] This was allegedly reflected in the prevalence of the 'disease of adultery' *(obulwaddebwobwenzi)*, otherwise known as *makiro* or puerperal psychosis (madness after birth), which attacked some women and could result in death for the mother and the newborn baby.[11] But when Orley asked 29 men whether it would be right to excuse their wives if they slept with other men if the husband was, for instance, in prison for a year or two, only three said that it would not be right.[12] The men bragged not about the sizes of their sexual organs, but how long it took them to have an orgasm. A potent man would last 30 minutes and an extremely potent man would last forty.[13]

On the whole Bantu and Nilotic women were concerned about the quality of sexual satisfaction, but it was only the Ganda women I heard threatening to leave their husbands if sex life was not satisfactory. Two Ganda women and one Kiga woman had deserted their husbands because they did not find satisfaction in marriage.

Still another reason for migrating was desertion. This was usually the result of women being 'tired' of particular marriages, or marriage in general, as illustrated by the following case studies.

Case Study 1: After 20 years of marriage, Nalumansi, a Ganda, packed up her things while her husband was at work and left *(kunoba)*. She took her belongings to her brother's house and went to a town three miles away. Her close friends were not surprised at the move. They had always known that it was only a matter of time before she left her husband. The children were grown up and, therefore, she felt it was time to make the move. People from the village who went to town on weekends to dance and drink European beer said they saw her working as a waitress in a bar that sold food, beverages and liquor. It was not long before her husband began frequenting the place where she worked, seeking a reconciliation, but she was 'tired of being married'. When she could not take his pestering anymore, she migrated to Kampala. After only six months she had a prosperous hairdressing salon where on most Saturdays brides were costumed.

She claimed that she refused to remarry and preferred to be independent. She bought land, built herself a house, and established herself as an independent householder (*nakyeyombekedde*). She rented a house in the suburbs of Naguru and each day commuted to the centre of the town to carry on her business at the bus station.

The women who said they were tired of marriage asserted it so firmly that there was no doubt they meant it. Even the attitudes of women who at first did not think this way changed once they arrived in Namuwongo and realized the frustrations they had endured in order to achieve economic independence. *Case Study 2*: Amina, a Lango woman whose stated reason for migration was 'to seek her fortune' in town, had had four unsuccessful marriages. She had lived in three small urban centres in the north of Uganda. She said she would have been happy to stay in any one of them but each time her gin distilling business was prospering she managed to attract men who soon became jealous of her entrepreneurial ventures. Every time a relationship ended she had to move or else be financially ruined by acts of sabotage. On one such occasion she decided to pack up her belongings and come to Kampala. A Lango woman, who later became her business partner, offered her accommodation for the night when they met at the bus station. Her distilling business was one of the most successful in the area. At the time of research she had only lovers and claimed she did not want ever to remarry.

If women were deserting their husbands because they were 'tired of marriage', it is reasonable to assume that husbands too must have been doing so. The most common type of desertion I came across in Namuwongo and Wabigalo was men who 'disappeared' in the towns, clearly exemplified by the case study on page 29.

Styles of Migration: How Women Came to the City

The decision to migrate is only half the story, and so in this section we shall examine the other question of *how* to migrate.

The reasons given for migration were often reflected in the style of migration: women who visited their husbands in town regularly, but who lived in the rural areas most of the time; women who followed their husbands and settled with them in the city; and women who planned on their own or jointly with their husbands to migrate to the city, but in order to do so had first to test out urban life in smaller towns. I have characterized these styles of migration as shuttling, direct, and stage-by-stage migration.

Shuttling

In the last section women who came to the city to follow the husband were divided into two categories: those who came to stay and those who visited periodically. The latter were characterized as shuttling migrants, and the description of their movements given above will suffice as an account of this style of migration.

Direct Migration

Most migrants moved directly to the city to solve immediate problems or to escape certain conditions that weighed heavily on them. Some had never thought of migrating until they actually found themselves doing it. Others had thought about it but had not yet found a specific reason for migrating. In most cases the immediate reasons were mentioned, but there were other associated causes reflected in the case studies.

Case Study: Lita, one of the most successful Ganda shop owners, had been planning for ten years to move to town, and her stated reason, when asked, was 'to improve my business'.

She began by selling cigarettes and sweet bananas at home in Bulemezi county. Then she sold pens, books, and soda drinks. Finally she started selling sugar, salt and beer. Although her in-laws lived 23 miles away, they were angry at her business activity. Around that time her husband had a severe attack of malaria. His skin was pale and his urine black. After she nursed him back to health she was accused of having used sorcery on him because she was allegedly jealous of the other woman her husband was seeing. According to her, 'I knew of his relationship with another woman and all I wanted was to leave him in order to give him a chance to marry her. As it turned out, when I left she did not want to come and live with him, she was just a home spoiler, a *kirerese*. He begged me time and again to return to the village, but I had attained my own goal and I was not going to abandon it.'

Stage-by-Stage Migration

The women in this category had made migration to the town a long-term strategy. They did not move directly from the village to the city, but stopped in several intermediate towns before arriving at their eventual destination. In other words, they experienced urban life in small doses as they moved from the small rural centres to the city.

The stage-by-stage style of migration involved only 25 women out of the 164 in my total sample. They had a relatively greater commitment to the urban area than, say, the direct migrants. Having moved through different urban places of varying sizes, the city seemed the ultimate goal they consciously or unconsciously sought. As a woman figuratively put it, 'Migration is like a spirit spiral (*omuzimu*). Its size becomes bigger and bigger the higher and further it moves.' It is interesting that she gave this analogy of the whirl-wind. The Ganda and quite a number of other East African societies believe that whirlwinds are spirits that are moving around. While it is best to avoid them, once caught in them there is no telling what might happen to you.

The city represented a widening of employment opportunities and perhaps ultimate escape from whatever had caused them to migrate in the first place. It was like a kind of pipedream come true! The stage-by-stage migrants tended to stay longer in the urban areas and I would claim that they form the back-bone of the urban citizenry. The city represents the ultimate goal they had strived towards and for better or for worse some of them had to make a success of it. The case study below illustrates interesting aspects of the dynamics between town and country, and highlights different aspects of rural-urban interactions.

Case Study: In 1972 Eseza, a Ganda, was aged 45 and had been in Kampala for 20 years. In Namuwongo she owned three brick houses with three rooms each. She lived in one house and rented the other two to lodgers at 80 shillings a room. In 1972 her net income from the rooms and distilling was 2,000 shillings. She was thus one of the most successful distillers of the local gin, *waragi*. Eseza had a licence to supply 20 gallons a month to the Uganda Distilleries, but since she produced more than this she had local customers as well as a clientele in at least four low-income suburbs where the Namuwongo brand (made from maize flour) is famous. Since it is illegal to sell crude *waragi* which has not been redistilled at the government refinery, Eseza dis-guised her illicit activities by brewing *kwete, malwa* and *munanansi* beer made from maize, millet, and pineapples respectively. Because the work was becom-ing heavier and too difficult for one person, she employed five women (one Soga, two Nkole and two Toro) to work with her. She relied on male casual labourers for her water and firewood supplies, but was convinced that men were unreliable business partners.

Whereas most women in the area hoped to move eventually to one of the prestigious residential areas, Eseza seemed satisfied with things as they were. She had established herself in Namuwongo after an interesting career. After three years of marriage she had gone and stayed at her parents' home, a village 40 miles from Kampala. She sold tea and pancakes (*mandazi*) on the twice weekly market days. After six months, she decided to take her business to a tiny rural centre (consisting of four small shops, a butcher, bus stop, and village meeting green) one mile away from her parents' home. Finding commuting inconvenient, she rented the third room at the back of the shop which previously had been rented by a couple. Eseza learned to make *munanansi* which was the popular drink then. After she had been there for a year she heard of a job at a township five miles away. She went and became a cook and waitress for a *hoteli* (bar-cum-restaurant). She was happy because she was earning 150 shillings a month, enough to live on and save. Two years passed, then one day she met a childhood girlfriend who was working at a coffee curing plant in Kampala. During the conversation she learned that jobs with high wages were available in the city. She left for Kampala and found a job with the British American Tobacco Company which made cigarettes, but she lost it when she quarrelled with the foreman. He reported her to the bosses, accusing her of being constantly late. This hurt her because she had paid 200 shillings to secure the job. By this time she had moved from Makerere-Kivulu to Namuwongo and was living with a Tanzanian, a relationship which lasted eight months. She became the most well-known *kwete* (maize beer) brewer in the area and made friends with practically everyone — policemen, local chiefs, tax collectors, etc. After four years she was buying land, putting up houses, and expanding her brewery into a distillery. It should be added that owning houses and distilling *waragi* are the most profitable businesses in Namuwongo.

Eseza represents a success story. Most of the women who migrated in the stage-by-stage style were achievers and often succeeded in whatever they set their minds to do. Not all of them became as prosperous as Eseza, but all things considered, they definitely did well. One thing these women shared was the fact that they were independent householders; these are the women people referred to when they said that all town women were single. Their successes made them highly visible and the envy of their struggling counterparts as well as men in similar positions. Women like Eseza would probably have succeeded in the rural areas anyway, had not the town existed to offer them more opportunity.

Village Women

It is difficult to understand the position of migrant women in towns without a comparison with their village sisters, women who have remained in the village either alone or with their husbands or after their husbands have migrated to the town. While seeking one's fortune or escaping from unhappy marriages are two of the major reasons for migration, being tired of village life is equally important.

Even though urban women work hard — up to eight or ten hours a day — popular and scholarly views are agreed in seeing an escape from the life of drudgery to one of relative leisure as a prime reason for migration,[14] an impression as prevalent in the town as the village. When rural girls complained of digging or sweeping chicken and goat droppings, of eyes stung by smoke and soot-blackened hands, their mothers would scold: 'I pity you. If you live in the village you will have to get your hands dirty. You're behaving like a town person. God help you.' Urban women agreed that town life at least did not involve digging and fetching and carrying firewood and water, since town dwellers used charcoal or primus stoves, tapwater or purchased water, and did not have to hoe. Thus even long hours worked in town were regarded as light compared to rural work,[15] and backbreaking jobs done in an urban context, such as carrying produce from the market or even carrying firewood, were acceptable because they were directed towards earning an income.

Since most African countries are essentially agricultural and 80 per cent of agricultural labour is performed by women,[16] their life in the villages is hard, and especially so under changed circumstances such as cash cropping which are inappropriate to the traditional sexual division of labour. Apart from special occasions like market days, births and deaths and visiting sick relatives, there is such a thin line of differentiation between household tasks, farm work and leisure time that it is understandable what women meant by being tired of village life. Women clearly felt that their labours were not adequately rewarded and attempted to avail themselves of an independent income in a variety of ways, with or without the consent of men.

With Ganda women, in particular, there is a clear connection between their 'restiveness' and the introduction of cash cropping at the beginning of the century. When cotton growing began in 1904 with the encouragement of the government, the Church Missionary Society[17] and zealous chiefs,[18] it was regarded as merely an extension of women's traditional responsibility for providing sustenance for their families. Women did most of the cultivation[19] because men regarded it as a mark of degradation 'to stoop and dig the ground like a woman'.[20] Cotton paid for all the family expenditure on taxes, school fees, and imported consumer goods. The women of course resisted such increases in their work,[21] particularly as men saw their role as lording it over the women and children, watching, encouraging, and only occasionally lending a hand.[22] Clearly overworked already, the women were reluctant to expand the cotton acreage, this led to the drop in 1911 of cotton production in Buganda.[23]

What is more, women began to demand that their labour be rewarded in some form, insisting that 'if they were not supplied with European clothing . . . the banana supply for the family would stop; they would no longer cultivate, but go off and get work as labourers, and earn money with which to clothe themselves satisfactorily. In the face of this, a man wanting to live happily and with sufficient food has to supply the food and other luxuries demanded (such as better clothes and better houses).'[24]

It has been argued that the women's demand for clothes and better treatment can be attributed to the effect of missionary work with its Christian mores and the requirement of appearing suitably dressed for public worship reinforcing the traditional concern of Ganda women about their attire.[25] Certainly this study confirmed that there was such a concern, informants, for instance, quoting the following Ganda proverbs, apparently part of the advice to a bride and now popularized in the song: '*Awaba sali waliwo obufumbo; awaba jababa waliwo emirego* (Where there are beautiful clothes there is marriage; where there are poor clothes there is trouble).' However it was the men who apparently led the way to Western dress, to such an extent that the colonizers, while admiring the Ganda for their eagerness to absorb European culture, were disconcerted that they were 'greedy for cloth and every manufactured article'.

Apart from such concerns, however, there are strong reasons for taking the women's demand as specifically a demand for reward for labour. While by 1930 hired foreign labour (mainly Ruandan) had transferred the responsibility for tending cash crops to the men, wives of poor men and those in areas without such labour still continued to engage in cotton growing,[26] but were now asking not only for clothes but for small plots of land to provide a little extra personal income. If husbands refused, then women sought other ways, such as selling fruit and sugar cane.

The main source of income, however, was coffee, often the only means a family had for paying taxes, school fees and buying the basic manufactured commodities. The coffee was produced and dried by the women at home (itself a laborious job subject to the vagaries of the weather and the cares of supervising children). The husbands were in charge of its sale, but in their absence women would often sell small amounts to the men who came on bicycles from the township stores. Money earned in this way was either hoarded for a rainy day or invested in land. But such practices and the suspicion they induced could not help but exacerbate already strained family relations.

A typical situation for the Luo women, on the other hand, found them trying to cope with rearing a family while their husbands migrated to the city. Some Luo men had been in Kampala for 20 years or more and only visited the villages when there was a marriage, death or major illness in the family. The responsibility of maintaining the rural base fell heavily upon the shoulders of women. They shuttled between city and country at least two to four times a year, the number of visits depending on the range of their responsibilities in the village. Some women visited their husbands in between planting, weeding and harvesting food and cash crops, leaving their relatives to take care of the homes. Other women with no relatives visited their husbands in the city only twice a year, and spent the rest of the time farming and taking care of the younger children. Most Luo men I talked to insisted that the town was a bad influence for children who should receive their initial education in the village. So the women in this category visited their husbands for two major reasons: to obtain money for running the farm (eg. hiring labour) and to obtain school fees for the children.

More and more, however, Luo men could not take it for granted that their wives, even with the help of relatives, would assume responsibility for the agricultural work. In the East Kano district village studies, women were asserting that there was 'no free labour, even in the villages', indicating that they, like the Ganda women, were seeking rewards for their labour.

In general there was a strong belief among the women that their energies were best spent cultivating crops that could be sold. The acquisition of labour-saving technological devices such as grain grinding mills and ox ploughs greatly decreased the hours spent on digging, pounding and grinding, so women could devote their times to other things or even rest longer, and young girls stood a better chance of attending school instead of being kept at home looking after the babies. The presence of alternative economic opportunities encouraged people to stay in the rural areas, but also fed into the increasing resentment those who stayed in the village felt for those who were 'enjoying themselves in town'. The relatives and wives left behind did not see why they should labour to support the farms of unemployed migrants. So, only for extremely depressed rural areas, did the wages of migrants add anything significant to the family income.

Summary

Women in the study migrated for personal, matrimonial, social and economic reasons. They regarded the towns as areas of expanded opportunities and resources. Some had lived in the area before the city boundary enclosed it, others came with or followed their husbands, while still others migrated alone. In some cases migration was intermittent as in the case of the Luo women who shuttled between town and country. The reasons for migrating were often reflected in the styles of migration. An immediate reason such as witchcraft accusation, pregnancy or quarrels caused women to migrate directly from the country to the town. Long-term planning resulted in either direct migration or stage-by-stage migration through urban centres of varying size culminating in the city itself. Stage-by-stage migrants tended to be women who migrated alone and were highly motivated.

References

1. J.C. Mitchell, 'Structural Plurality, Urbanization and Labour Migration in Southern Rhodesia', in J.A. Jackson (ed.), *Migration*, (Sociological Studies Series No. 2, Cambridge University Press, 1969), p. 174.
2. D.D. Gregory, *Inter-European Migration and Socio-Cultural Change in an Andalucian Agro-town*, Ph.D. thesis, University of Pittsburgh, 1972; R.C. Taylor, 'Migration and Motivation: A Study of Determinants and Types' in J.A. Jackson (ed.), *Migration*, (Cambridge University Press, London, 1969) pp. 99-133.
3. Mitchell, *op. cit.*
4. S. Amin (ed.), *Modern Migrations in Western Africa*, (Oxford University Press for International African Institute, London, 1974) pp. 88-9.
5. J.J. Oloya and T.T. Poleman, *The Food Supply of Kampala*, (Makerere Institute of Social Research, Kampala, 1972) p. 24.
6. Women informants claimed that *nfuli* helped them experience both vaginal and clitoral orgasms and denied the suggestion often made by Westerners that *nfuli* are purely for male sexual pleasure.
7. This is an issue that is still not discussed in many societies. The *Hite Report* was such a sensational success in America and Europe because it revealed all the hidden desires and frustrations women have about their sexuality but had never dared articulate before. See Shere Hite, *The Hite Report: A Nationwide Study of Female Sexuality*, (Dell, New York, 1976).

8. A.W. Southall and P.C.W. Gutkind, *Townsmen in the Making: Kampala and its Suburbs*, (East African Institute of Social Research/ East African Studies Series No. 9, 1957).
9. *Ibid.*
10. John H. Orley, *Culture and Mental Illness*, (East African Publishing House for East African Institute of Social Research, No. 36, Nairobi, 1970) p. 5.
11. *Ibid.*
12. *Ibid.*, p. 60.
13. *Ibid.*, pp. 13-14.
14. Ester Boserup, *Woman's Role in Economic Development*, (Allen and Unwin, London, 1970) p. 191; M.J.B. Molohan, *Detribalization*, (Government Printer, Dar es Salaam, 1957) pp. 41-2.
15. A.W. Southall, and P.C.W. Gutkind, 'Townsmen in the Making: Kampala and its Suburbs', *East African Studies*, No. 9, East African Institute of Social Research, 1957.
16. H.B. Thomas and R. Scott (eds.). *Uganda*, (Oxford University Press, London, 1935) p. 127; P.G. Powesland, 'History of Migration in Uganda' in A.I. Richards (ed.), *Economic Development and Social Change*, (Heffer for East African Institute of Social Research, Cambridge, 1954) p. 22.
17. Powesland, *ibid.*, P.H. Lamb, 'Report on Cotton in Uganda' (Uganda Government Press, 1910) p. 7.
18. *Mengo Notes*, vol. 4, no. 4, April 1903, p. 21, Kampala (quoting the Pall Mall Gazette); Powesland, *op. cit.*, p. 18.
19. Powesland, *op. cit.*, p. 21.
20. C.W. Hattersley, *The Baganda at Home*, Religious Tract Society, London, 1908) p. 114.
21. Powesland, *op. cit.*, p. 23.
22. *Ibid.*, p. 109.
23. *Ibid.*, p. 21.
24. Sir Charles Eliot, *The East African Protectorate*, (Edward Arnold, London, 1905) p. 99.
25. Powesland, *op. cit.*, p. 22.
26. *Ibid.*

6. The Single Woman in Urban and Rural Uganda

The last chapter showed how the introduction of the cash economy, and new rules to regulate land and marriage brought about changes in people's attitudes towards labour and marriage. This was particularly clear in the attempts of women to achieve some kind of economic autonomy by keeping their savings separate from their husband's. This was just one of the things which led men to declare that modern women were uncontrollable. Yet the Ganda women could point to the first queen of Buganda and other powerful women who had all been 'wild'. As for Luo women, they were not making as much headway as the Ganda women but they were changing too.

The development of the towns, improved transportation, and the increase in communication, particularly the radio and other mass media, afforded women a wider field in which to seek marriage partners and to escape unsatisfactory marriages. While this can be seen in some respects as an increase in options, it also led to an upsurge of prejudice against traditional female options outside marriage. Independent single women who rented rooms in rural centres, townships and towns were indiscriminately referred to as prostitutes (*malaya*). It cannot be denied that there are prostitutes in the urban areas, but the labelling of all urban women as prostitutes reveals a double standard on the part of men who both want to control their women — wives, sisters and daughters — and still have relations with mistresses, concubines and prostitutes, thus contradicting as lovers what they strive to achieve as husbands and parents.[1] The diffusion of the urban notion of *malaya* into the rural areas further shows fixed male views which cannot cope with non-traditional roles for women.

Unattached single women are ubiquitous in East African cities and towns, in contrast to the rural areas.[2] Even the Secretary of the National Research Council which sponsored my research and the City Council officials in Kampala assumed that the low income women they usually saw or had to deal with were single, and that single women were on the whole disreputable. Yet in fact, in my sample of 164 Namuwongo and Wabigalo women, while 17 per cent were independent female householders, the remaining 83 per cent were married or at least cohabiting with a man. However, single women were in the forefront of social change, challenging the inevitability of marriage and children within wedlock, and this made them highly visible. For example, when, after the 1920s,

Ganda women began to own land legally in their own right, it gave them enough confidence to assert other rights controlling sexuality, reproductive and productive assets — in fact the three areas in which men were claiming loss of control.

Categories of Single Women

There were five categories of single women in Namuwongo and Wabigalo: (1) women who had never married; (2) women, including divorcees and widows, who were irrevocably tired of marriage as an institution and as a relationship between men and women and preferred having their own houses and being self-supporting; (3) women who belonged to the first two categories but lacked the resources to be self-supporting; (4) women who had migrated to have a change of life and hoped to marry urban men or rich rural men who frequented the city (they spent most of their time looking for 'Mr. Right', 'marrying' for periods varying from two weeks to a year); and (5) women who were caught up in the scramble for non-existent or underpaid jobs and often resorted to the 'skill that comes naturally' — sex.

We must briefly consider the question of prostitition, as it is always mentioned in the context of single urban women. For most women in Namuwongo and Wabigalo this skill was not be be relied upon for long; it was a temporary measure to tide over bad situations such as unemployment, low pay and difficult times. It is my belief that the strong religious feeling in this particular area made it impossible for a woman to sell sex blatantly like women in other low income suburbs.[3] The prostitutes entertained clients discreetly in their rooms and did not roam around the streets or bars like the sophisticated city operators (school-leavers and secretaries). Also, while not all single women are prostitutes or practise it continuously, it should be added that not all 'easy' sexual behaviour is urban.

In order to give a proper consideration of the prevalent view that the single woman is a purely urban phenomenon, it is necessary to consider rural areas as well, and we will find that at least some of the five categories listed above have definitely rural roots.

Independent Female Householders
In this section we shall look at several areas of Uganda in which this category of independent female householder has long existed. Even though the urban areas make such a lifestyle easier, they cannot be identified as its cause.

In the rural areas of Buganda women, known as *banakyeyombekedde*, had set themselves up independently either because they had never married, were widowed or divorced, or had simply deserted their husbands because they were 'tired of being married'. This was a well-known status, and men who courted such women hoped to stop them from 'shutting in', that is, having nothing whatever to do with men.

In the pre-colonial days when women could not own land in their own right and were reliant on male relatives, such a woman would have to move to another village and seek the protection of the chief in return for her allegiance (*kusenga*) if she had no male relatives or was on bad terms with them. According to one informant, she would have her house built next to the chief's compound, cultivate her own banana groves, make her own beer, and entertain her friends. Part of her duties included helping the chief's wife or wives entertain visitors.

The *nakyeyombekedde* often provoked envy in other women who noted the social and sexual freedom which such independent women seemed to enjoy. They were also suspicious of them because they were not sure what they were up to with their husbands, but the traditional *nakyeyombekedde* rarely had affairs with local married men, choosing mostly unmarried men from other villages. These relationships allowed both parties to keep their freedom but some informants remarked that the situation usually became uncomfortable if the man moved into her house permanently. Beattie found that among the patrilineal Nyoro certain women were known as *kyeyombekeire* because, when men married them, they deviated from the pattern of virilocal residence (in which the wife moves to the husband's people) and instead moved in with their wives. Such men were despised by the Nyoro,[4] and, similarly, for the neighbouring patrilineal Toro, free marriages (*nnabuisa*) with independent female householders were rare because they involved loss of prestige for the men.[5]

After the 1900 Agreement, when the land tenure system changed and women as well as men began to own land in their own right, a person did not have to depend on a patron-chief. Thus the independent female householder presumably living on rented, purchased, or inherited land from husbands, maternal or paternal relatives, came to be known as *nakyeyombekedde*. The Buganda word *nakyeyombekedde* does not include wives in polygamous marriages who may live in separate homes which their husbands visit regularly. The term also excludes wives who are left in the rural areas while their husbands migrate to the towns. *Banakyeyombekedde* were mature women aged 35 years or more. They were resented and referred to as 'husband snatchers' by Ganda women and as 'purse pinchers' by the men because they were expensive to maintain. Men went to great trouble to prevent their wives and daughters befriending the *nakyeyombekedde* for fear of their wives eventually leaving them for an independent life, and indeed many young women in their teens and twenties were renting rooms and setting themselves up as independent householders both in rural centres and big towns like Kampala.

These women had decided opinions about men. Some had tried marriage and had had their fingers burnt, but they all agreed that although men were necessary for a healthy sex life, they were a nuisance in general. Within this framework they usually enjoyed stable relationships with their lovers, but were very conscious of their rights. For instance, on six different occasions in 1972 women won child support claims against their lovers or boyfriends in a Kampala court.

In the Kampala suburb of Mulago, during the 1950s researchers reported a successful independent woman who obtained an income from selling beer and bananas, and renting out houses, and was said to be 'fastidious in her choice of lovers'. One day when a man called her a prostitute, she beat him severely and explained to the chief afterwards about the honesty of single women and the dishonesty of married women in sexual matters.[6] This pinpoints one important issue: if women enjoy a high degree of decision-making with regard to their sexuality, it becomes a threat to those men who observe or associate with them and have only limited categories in terms of which to think about female sexuality.

Elsewhere in Uganda, substantial numbers of rural independent women householders have been reported. In 1932-33, Mair found in Bowa that out of 58 people, seven (12 per cent) of the women were living alone: two having deserted their husbands, two had been deserted and three had been widowed.[7] Richards found that out of 299 householders, two per cent were women.[8] Taylor found that out of a sample of 76 households, 10 (23 per cent) were headed by women.[9] The percentages compare with Southwold's findings in four Ganda villages.[10]

Looking at Africa as a whole, researchers have found that women become *de facto* household heads with sole responsibility for production and family welfare when adult males migrate from the rural areas. For example, the incidence of female-headed households has been reported at about 42 per cent in some parts of Botswana,[11] 33 per cent in rural Kenya,[12] 17 per cent in Mali,[13] and 33 per cent in Ghana.[14] The point of all this is to show that the phenomenon of independent female householders is not peculiar to the urban areas, although that is where most studies have been done.

Turning to some of this research on urban areas, we find that in two other suburbs of Kampala, Kisenyi and Mulago, in the 1950s, 23 per cent and 34 per cent of the household heads were female respectively.[15] In Kisenyi the number of household heads in each group were as follows: 43 per cent Ganda, 35 per cent Haya, 13 per cent Toro, and 15 per cent Ruandans. The remainder were Soga, Swahili, half-caste, Teso and five other groups.

There is also comparative data collected during the 1950s from other cities in Africa such as Stanleyville: 33 per cent of the women over 16 years of age were living singly or as mistresses. Kahama had 22 per cent female household heads as compared to 2 per cent in the surrounding countryside. In Koforidua 70 per cent of the women were traders and 25 per cent lived singly.[16] The number of female household heads for Mathare, a low income suburb of Nairobi, has been put at between 60 and 80 per cent.[17] The majority of these women were Kikuyu, the dominant and host ethnic group.

Unattached Dependent Women
The women in this category did not have the resources or the fortitude to be even relatively independent of men. While both Ganda and Luo women suffered from these handicaps, lack of resources, particularly land, seems to make most Luo women dependent on men for most of their lives.

Unattached Luo Women: In the Namuwongo and Wabigalo sample, out of 47 Luo women only four were single. Two of them had lovers who lived with them and the other two claimed to be 'too busy to enjoy sex'. They had successful beer and distilling businesses, and in fact they were the backbone of the millet beer club that had been started by a businessman and to which most Luo brewers belonged and constantly contributed (see Chapter 8).

The Luo men and women I talked with at Namuwongo and Wabigalo flatly denied there were any single unattached women in their home area, and identified it as an exclusively urban phenomenon. Women whose marriages failed did not set up house independently. In fact, the socialization process more or less ensured that there would be no single women. While the men worried about the chastity and the economic value of their daughters, the mothers encouraged them to learn to read and write but not exceed their wifely duties. In the 1950s Ominde reported that while boys were encouraged to become clerks outside the home, the mothers opposed or ignored their daughters' education. Women needed the girls to help with the constant pressure of the household tasks.[18]

When I arrived at a village in East Kano, my host, who was a minimal lineage head (the smallest possible segment of a descent group), together with a circle of friends who referred to themselves as elders, asserted that Luo women never broke away from their families. They pointed out, however, that girls who had gone to school and married young were divorcing and migrating to Nairobi where they lived alone.

A few days later I went at dawn to watch the cows being milked and to have a chat with one woman who lived in the compound. I learned from her that she was the sister of the compound head. She had never married because she could never settle down. She had eloped twice, but her brothers fetched her back each time saying that the man had to pay bridewealth for her. In the first case the man refused to give even a calf, and the second one, who was willing to pay the required bridewealth, then died in a brawl during a dance. Several older men offered to marry her as a second wife. Her brother agreed, but the woman refused. Meanwhile she had two children, a daughter and a son, who also lived in the compound. She had her own three cows and some garden land she inherited from her mother. Although she lived in the same compound as her brothers and their wives and children, she supported herself by selling her agricultural produce or selling beer at the market. She obviously enjoyed greater latitude in decision-making, but sometimes when the work became too much and she had difficulties getting helpers, she would jokingly refer to it as her 'sentence for having let down the lineage'.

In the same compound the eldest wife's daughter also lived as an unmarried mother. At twelve she had been sent to school where, after five years, she became pregnant. She bore her baby in her brother's house. The child was referred to as *nyath simba* (child of the batchelor's hut). Her father then set out to find a husband for her. But since she had a child her fate was that of most girls in her position: marriage to a polygynous man, whose bridewealth payment made him the father of the child.

Even when married, she was constantly at her mother's house, and claimed that her co-wives gave her too much work and bossed her around. Her husband would not listen to her pleas. During one long visit to her mother the husband came and demanded to know what was going on. She informed him, in front of her mother and father, that she was not going back. The husband told her that her maize and millet were ready for harvest, but she told him to leave it to the birds. The husband then accused the mother of encouraging the daughter; the mother called him 'a stupid old man' and promised that the 'thin, bony cows' he had given as bridewealth would be returned at once. Next day the girl's father asked him to forget what had transpired, and the husband returned home, but when his wife did not follow him in five months he asked for the return of his bridewealth. When I visited, the girl lived on her father's compound with her child and there did not seem to be any pending marriage, although she had several boyfriends.

We can categorize single women among the Luo as follows: (1) widows who have refused to engage in leviritic marriages (in which widows are passed on to male relatives of the dead husband) and live in the same compound as their sons or live alone; (2) women who claim that they could never settle down; (3) women who force their husbands to divorce them; (4) young, unmarried mothers who refuse to live in polygynous marriages and women who have objected to a first marriage so strongly that they have taken the desperate step of running into a house or village where people were mourning or who have not finalised a wedding.[19] According to Luo belief this forbidden act might wipe out the lineage, village or clan.[20] Eventually the woman who had behaved in this way would have to elope along with her children or just remain single. However drastic a measure, I see such an act as an effective weapon for resisting being forced to marry against one's will.

Nearly everyone in the village had an unmarried female relative, however distant. It was all blamed on modern conditions. Girls were being taken away from their homes to the schools where they are getting all sorts of ideas. As one man lamented, 'Girls are marrying very young these days. In our days a girl had to be mature before she got married. The girls of today are so young they cannot grind a tin of millet and feed the family on the same day, a requirement for brides.' It is true teenage girls who left the local primary schools were already anxious to have a serious boyfriend, whereas older women claimed that they must have been at least 20 years old before they had married.

The serious question was not so much the age of marrying as whether restlessness and defiance among girls was a modern condition. Not so, according to older women, who would say when they were totally relaxed and swimming in the river that some of their friends or someone they knew had found ways to get out of marriages that they did not like. It seemed, then, that the ideology expounded was often contradicted by what actually happened. Wilson found a small class of women in the 1950s who had never married or had been married but had deserted or divorced. Such women who had turned their accumulated wealth into cattle, were in a position to marry wives to their own names or to their brothers' or fathers' names – a procedure which did not meet with the approval of the Luo elders.[21] They claimed it was modern, but some informants told him that traditionally a wealthy woman, 'might marry a wife to her own name or to a brother or to a member of her *libamba* in order to perpetuate her name in the lineage. Such women are said to be regarded as men and to establish a lineage as if they were men.'[22] These lineages descended from women must be distinguished from Southall's findings of uterine (*anyuola*) segmentation whereby the children of one mother break away from the compound family (*dhoot*) and claim to be descendants of their mother to separate themselves from the descendants of her co-wives within the patrilineage.[23] If it were a modern practice, relatives might be expected to violently oppose such practices and we would expect it to be common only among urban people or people who had been to school. Instead we find it not only happening in the rural areas today but, according to various old women, it also used to happen in the past. However, I found that as a general rule the Luo always tended to idealize their social structure and would not admit to any deviation from the ideological model.

This study suggests that in fact Luo women did have the option of staying single. Often this was achieved at the expense of lineage mystical pollution, as when they refused to marry, or at the expense of the 'brothers' or 'fathers' who had to pay back the bridewealth when the women provoked a divorce. So, in fact, even in the most completely patrilineal systems women have some leeway. The men cannot push their luck too far or else they lose. Evans-Pritchard found similar occurrences among the Nuer of Sudan whose patrilineal lineage principles are definitely somewhat similar to those of the Luo. He found that some stubborn girls could provoke divorce once or twice, until the parents, unable to 'crush her rebellious spirits' and to avoid all the trouble and difficulties involved in constant returning of bridewealth, let her go with a man of her choice.[24] Evans-Pritchard notes that such women had strong characters, valued their independence and did not desire matrimony.[25]

In conclusion, it must be observed that any social arrangement must have points of flexibility or else it collapses. The point emphasized by several authors,[26] that Nilotic women were much more controlled by their males than Bantu women, cannot be denied. However, our data suggests that perhaps valuable information about institutions can be gained by examining the less obvious options available to different members.

Restless Ganda Women: In rural Buganda men or women who cannot stay in one place for long are referred to as *kirerese*. Informants had quite a lot to say about them: they were transients who could not have a stable relationship with anyone; they were not responsible enough to own homes, and had to stay with relatives, friends and lovers who came to accept their indefinitely prolonged visits. In the Ganda village studied, there were two cases of *men* who had abandoned their homes and just travelled around, occasionally returning home. It was said that *bakirerese* easily get bored, and move on after a year or so in one place.

The *kirerese* usually returned after a few months or years to the same host. If they were women, they helped around with gardening, cooking and even growing and harvesting cash crops like coffee or cotton, while the men helped in building houses, clearing bush or forest, etc. Indeed, I think they were tolerated because they contributed to their upkeep although a pleasant personality would help. For example, I came across cases where male *bakirerese* moved in (*kusenga*) with independent female householders (*banakyeyombekedde*). As lovers (*baganzi*) they were fed and their taxes paid; but as lodgers (*basuze*) they were expected to fulfil certain obligations like treading out bananas for brewing beer, fetching water, working in the garden and performing odd jobs around the homestead. A female *kirerese*, too, could seek a place to stay with a *nakyeyombekedde*. Like the male *kirerese* lodger, she was expected to help with gardening and brewing beer. An old *kirerese* would be allowed to build a house on the same compound. In some cases a young *kirerese* needed some privacy when entertaining lovers and so this necessitated building another house. However, as informants pointed out, owning a house does not mean settling, and *kirerese* have been known to leave houses they had built. The owner of the compound was then obliged to find lodgers or tenants to prevent the house being robbed.

The *bakirerese* were very much dependent upon the social status of their current hosts. At times, of course, a wife might cause a *kirerese* sister-in-law to be expelled (*kugobwa*) because she was not sharing work, or had too many male friends (*baganzi*) or was cantankerous, (*wafujjo*), but this was an extreme measure. Usually just at the time the hosts became weary the *kirerese* would become restless and move on, thus keeping open the option to return.

I was told it was the practice in Buganda for unmarried individuals to spend some time with relatives in different villages and counties in the hope that they would find a marriage partner. If there was any doubt about the friend, then the local relative could do some investigations. But if *kirerese* managed to get married, the marriage was usually short lived. I was told, and I observed it in the various case histories, that the *bakirerese* preferred and often un-wittingly found themselves cohabiting. As 'restless' people, they reserved the right to abandon unsatisfactory relationships. However, men and women believed that the *bakirerese* by and large were out to 'spoil' other people's marriages. As one man put it, 'They are not interested in marriage. They make you believe that they will marry you when your wife leaves or deserts (*kunoba*). You then do all in your power to be discourteous and rude to your wife. When your wife leaves, they also leave for an undisclosed destination, at least until things cool down, which may take years!' Some however stayed with their lovers for indefinite periods.

Single Women and Social Change

The proliferation of literature that deals with female-headed households has led to the term 'matrifocality' (meaning, loosely, 'women-centred') to be accepted as part of the anthropological vocabulary. The term is widely used in three ways mainly to refer to: household composition,[27] this type of kinship bond linking its members, and the relationship between the male members in the household. Gonzalez found matrifocal households to be consanguineal, that is, blood-related women and all their unmarried children lived together. Another typical feature of the consanguineal household was that the men and women in the household were not related by affinal relationships (by marriage).[28] Individuals have extensive knowledge of their female relatives because of the emphasis on family solidarity.

In countries with a capitalist mode of production matrifocal families have been found among people who are marginal to the economic structure.[29] The problems and strategies developed to deal with situations have been termed 'the subculture of poverty' by Oscar Lewis.[30] He listed 70 characteristic economic, social and psychological traits. The critical point is that men are usually unskilled and end up being unemployed or underemployed, and cannot support their families. This results in a high incidence of abandonment by male heads and the establishment of matrifocal families. In cases where the males do not leave, their position in the family is weakened as women become *de facto* household heads[31] by taking on menial low-paying jobs.

In Western societies the assumption has been that men are the household heads by virtue of being breadwinners. Effective domestic power would therefore seem to be in the hands of the family member who works outside the home. According to this kind of thinking, if men are not in control then the mutual affective bonds between husbands and wives never develop strength enough to replace those between each spouse and their consanguineal kin. The result is a high rate of marital instability as has been reported for the U.S. and the West Indies. Elsewhere reports on matrifocal families found that (1) conjugal ties can be strong and yet marriage is unstable,[32] (2) conjugal ties can be strong and yet marriage stable[33] or (3) marriages can be stable but the conjugal ties weak.

The unattached women in this study are examined from the point of view of social change. Through their actions and decisions, they were active agents of change. When they redefined their relationship *vis-a-vis* men, questions about residential practices and the affiliation of children naturally arose. But what comes out most clearly is that, for lasting change, women must have resources such as land, money and the solidarity of other women as a basis for support. For example, the Luo women, existing within the Nilotic type of marriage and family, will not be discussed in this section because the data we have does not show that they have radically challenged the male dominated social structures.

The answer lies in the system of resource distribution and women's access to it. By contrast, the interlacustrine system as represented by the Ganda show that because women could be self-supporting economically, they consequently asserted their rights with regards to sex, motherhood and marriage. Perlman has shown that Toro women achieved social status and some independence from men when they started having children out of wedlock,[34] in other words, when they questioned having children for the man's lineage. Conversely, Parkin has argued that Luo male dominance is based partly on the fact that Luo women never consider not having children for men's lineage.[35]

Richards observed four causes of marriage instability in Buganda: (1) the frequent absence of men doing work in the towns; (2) the easy system of communications provided by the buses; (3) inducements to temporary liaisons with men who can provide clothes sold in the towns; (4) the concept of individual and, in fact romantic, love as presented in European films.[36] Our study suggests that the third reason given by Richards refers specifically to the *bakirerese*, and this also raises the general question of European influence, as suggested by the fourth reason.

There is no evidence to see *bakirerese* as a product of Western influence. There were *bakirerese* in the rural areas who had never seen a European film, but who lived in casual unions. The films may have a great impact upon the behaviour of some urban dwellers and the rural and urban elites but the impact upon the masses seemed minimal in the 1970s.

With the development of towns *bakirerese* became the rural trend setters. They shuttled between the towns and countryside bringing a city atmosphere, fashionable styles of dress, and new ways of cooking. As Leya, a woman in her sixties, put it, 'Fried eggs, meat and beans tasted so much better than just boiling. But people were convinced it was the effect of the charcoal stove. People also started to drink a lot of milk in tea boiled on primus. Married women started asking their husbands to buy charcoal stoves and primus.' Leya should know because she was one of the first people in the area to live in a rented room, behind a shop. By the 1960s there were three shops in the rural centre where she lived. Unlike the first one which had one extra room at the back, the new shops had four extra rooms with doors facing the road. Except for one man all the tenants were women. Some women like Leya continued to work on their farms. Leya moved back on the farm because she felt that women of disrepute were moving into the centre and giving it a bad name. She, however, had a lot to say about the women 'door owners':

> As time went on, the village men started visiting them to eat eggs fried on a charcoal stove, and bananas fried with tomatoes and onions. Men whose wives were constantly away visiting relatives or men who commuted to work in the towns found that it was advantageous to enjoy the friendship of such women. Some men forbade their wives to imitate 'door owners' (*bemizigo*). When village women first started braiding their hair, one man was so angry that he cut off his wife's one-foot-long hair with a sharp garden knife *(panga)*. Again, when women started straightening their hair one man beat his wife senseless. Both men were prosecuted and their wives left them.

It is intriguing to note that the same men who were so eager to enjoy the company of these women so full of exciting new ideas, at the same time discouraged their wives from such dangerous encounters. The informant went on: 'Besides hair styling, I remember that high-heeled shoes, full skirts and *njalayagwa* [literally, famine fell; wide elastic belts that emphasized small waists] became very popular. Hereafter women who had stayed in town for some time returned. Women among the local elite [teachers, clerks, and successful farmers] would threaten to leave if they did not have high-heeled shoes, a full skirt and belt, and a handbag.' Another informant explained the sudden interest in dress: 'When I was growing up in the 1940s, Arabs used to peddle silk and good heavy cotton cloth in the villages. The women would tell them to return at a certain time when the husbands would be home. Woe upon a man who did not buy his wife cloth for making a dress *(busuti)* at Easter *(mazuukira)* and Christmas. This was rather expensive because the ankle length dress took as much as seven yards. The local joke was that the only reason women went to church on Easter and Christmas was to show off their dresses and to see 'who was not well kept by the husband.'

It is my guess that it was this conspicuous consumption, more than the new laws or Christian dogma on monogamy, that effectively curbed the practice of polygamy in Buganda in general and the Ganda village I studied in particular, where I found only three polygamous marriages. At Christmas in 1972 one marriage became monogamous because one woman declared, 'I have not minded for years that he did not buy me clothes on important occasions (*enaku enkulu*), but I will not put up with eating *ntula* (small white or green, yellow or purple, and sometimes sour types of egg plants) at Christmas and when even the Muslims celebrate by dressing and eating well.' Four months later another man found himself monogamous. His second wife had moved off to a village four miles away because, 'I decided that I should be developing my land and not his as long as I was expected to dress and feed myself and the children.' Obviously men could not afford more than one wife in the now expected style. Village women were demanding outings to bars where they would get bottled drinks like Coke or Fanta, and dance to the juke box or band music. Women were demanding that they be dressed decently, elegantly (on important occasions) and fed well, i.e. eating meat at least twice a week. These changes were blamed on the *bakirerese* who were the rural trend setters.

In the urban areas it was difficult to distinguish the *banakyeyombekedde* and the *bakirerese* on the basis of their renting rooms, but one could tell by their life styles. Namuwongo and Wabigalo *banakyeyombekedde* were thrifty and self-employed, while *bakirerese* wore the latest fashions and usually worked in the bottled beer bars. On the whole they preferred paid employment to self-employment. They were also constantly changing residences. One of the Ganda elite who had visited some Namuwongo and Wabigalo bars regularly told me that it was refreshing to be in the area because the barmaids there had a rural air. He contrasted these women with the night club women or those in bars in the city centre, who were aggressive and not at all bashful about asking for money and beer in return for their sexual services. The *bakirerese* at Namuwongo and Wabigalo would come out at the unsophisticated end of any continuum of prostitution. Often, they lived as mistresses of town as well as rural men. This arrangement was known as *mukwano* (friendship cohabitation) if the partner had been introduced to some members of her family who occasionally received gifts of money, meat, clothing or paraffin.

But the anti-urban bias means that all women who rent rooms in urban areas or shuttle between town and country are referred to as *malaya* (prostitute). Even though there is a distinction between *banakyeyomkedde* and *bakirerese* in that the former owned her own house or paid rent for it and did not depend on lovers or relatives, the categories have become blurred. People only bother to point out the finer distinctions when a woman is a relative; and there are many people with such 'itchy footed' relatives. One man told me, 'The *bakirerese* never settle down even in old age. They spend all their lives wandering (*kubunga*) in search of happiness.'

People in both the rural and urban areas were ambivalent about the *bakirerese*; we have already noted the men's interest in both seeing these women themselves and keeping their wives away from their influence. Women did emulate them partly because they were afraid of losing their men to these women. Perhaps it was this anxiety about control of women which was responsible for the word *bakirerese* acquiring a new and derogatory connotation. They became known as the 'urban women' (*abakazi be tawuni*) — mistresses or prostitutes. Since such women could be found in the rural and urban areas as well, 'urban women' really connoted a certain kind of behaviour. But the men and women I talked to made a distinction between, on the one hand, the *mukwano* (friendship) relationships where a woman goes to stay with a lover (*muganzi*) as the *bakirerese* do (both in the rural and urban areas) and prostitution in which case a woman stayed only overnight and her main interest was money. It was the latter behaviour that was associated with urban areas — townships and towns. In other words, cohabitation was regarded as a characteristic of the *bakirerese*.

I have discussed the *bakirerese* at some length because they are an important factor when considering urbanization at least in Buganda. The problems associated with them were topical in both the rural and urban areas. The story-telling and gossip columns of the vernacular newspapers attracted wider readership every time they printed a story depicting 'town women' as shrewd, conniving or vulnerable. This suggests that these women blur the conceptual distinction between town and country. For the *bakirerese*, living in town or the country was not a permanent choice, and they could reside in either when it was convenient.

References

1. A.W. Southall, and P.C. Gutkind, 'Townsmen in the Making: Kampala and Its Suburbs, East African Studies No. 9, (East African Institute of Social Research), 1957, p. 89.
2. A.W. Southall (ed.), *Social Change in Modern Africa: Introduction*,

(Oxford University Press for the International African Institute, London, 1961) p. 51.
3. Southall and Gutkind, *op. cit.*, pp. 79-81.
4. J. Beattie, 'Nyoro Marriage and Affinity' *Africa*, Vol. 28, No. 1, 1958, p. 3.
5. Melvin L. Perlman, 'The Changing Status and Role of Women in Toro (Western Uganda)', *Cahiers d'Etudes Africaines*, Vol. 6, 1966, pp. 568-78.
6. Southall and Gutkind, *op. cit.*, p. 178.
7. L.P. Mair, *Native Marriage in Buganda*, (Oxford University Press, Memorandum No. 19 for International Institute of African Languages and Culture, London, 1940), pp. 23-8.
8. A.I. Richards and Priscilla Reining, 'Report of Fertility Surveys in Buganda and Buhaya, 1952' in Frank Lorimer (ed.), *Culture and Human Fertility: A Study of the Relation of Cultural Conditions to Fertility, Non-Industrial and Transitional Societies*, (UNESCO,Paris, 1954), p. 384.
9. John V. Taylor, *The Growth of the Church in Uganda: An Attempt at Understanding*, (S.C.M. Press, London, 1958), p. 123.
10. Martin Southwold, *Community and State in Buganda*, (Ph.D. Dissertation, Cambridge University, 1959), pp. 208, 338, 342.
11. Margaret Snyder, 'The African Woman in Economic Development – A Regional Perspective', Proceedings of Conference on The African Woman in Economic Development, 8 May 1975.
12. *Employment, Incomes and Equality: A Strategy For Increasing Productive Employment in Kenya*, (International Labour Office, Geneva, 1972), p. 47.
13. Snyder, *op. cit.*
14. Jette Buka, 'Project Paper: Women in Production' (Centre for Development Research, Copenhagen, 1977), p. 3.
15. Southall and Gutkind, *op. cit.*, pp. 51, 223.
16. *Ibid.*, p. 51.
17. Nici Nelson, *Dependence and Independence: Female Household Heads in Mathare Valley, A Squatter Community in Nairobi, Kenya*, (Ph.D. thesis, University of London, School of Oriental and African Studies), 1977.
18. Simeon H. Ominde, *The Luo Girl from Infancy to Marriage*, (Macmillan, Nairobi, 1952), pp. 22, 35.
19. A.B.C. Acholla-Ayayo, *Traditional Ideology and Ethics Among the Southern Luo*, (The Scandinavian Institute of African Studies, Uppsala, 1976), pp. 140, 148.
20. *Ibid.*, pp. 147-8.
21. Gordon Wilson, *Luo Customary Law and Marriage Laws*, (Government Printer, Nairobi, 1961), p. 124.
22. *Ibid.*
23. A.W. Southall, *Lineage Formation Among the Luo*, (Memorandum XXVI, Oxford University Press for International African Institute, 1952).
24. E.E. Evans-Pritchard, *Some Aspects of Marriage Among the Nuer*, Rhodes-Livingstone Paper No. 11, 1945, p. 20.

25. *Ibid.*, p. 21.
26. David J. Parkin, *Neighbours and Nationals in an African City Ward*, (Routledge and Kegan Paul, London, 1969), pp. 43-5; A.W. Southall, 'On Chastity in Africa', *The Uganda Journal*, Vol. 24, No. 2, p. 209.
27. Nancie L. Gonzalez, 'The Consanguineal Household and Matrifocality', *American Anthropologist*, Vol. 67, 1965, pp. 1541-9; M.G. Smith, *West Indian Family Structure*, (University of Washington Press, Seattle, 1962).
28. Gonzalez, *op. cit.*
29. Edith Clarke, *My Mother Who Fathered Me*, (Allen Unwin, London, 1957, reissued 1966); Madeline Kerr, *The People of Ship Street*, (Routledge and Kegan Paul, London, 1958); C.B. Stack, *All Our Kin: Strategies of Survival in A Black Community*, (Harper Torchbook, New York).
30. Oscar Lewis, *Five Families*, (Basic Books, New York, 1959).
31. *Ibid.*
32. Hildred Geertz, 'The Vocabulary of Emotion', *Journal of the Study of Interpersonal Process*, Vol. 22, 1959, p. 225.
33. Michael Young and Peter Willmott, *Family and Kinship in East London*, Penguin, London, 1957).
34. Melvin L. Perlman, 'Children Born Out of Wedlock and the Status of Women in Toro, Uganda', *Rural Africana*, No. 29, Winter, 1975.
35. David Parkin, *The Cultural Definition of Political Response: Lineal Destiny Among the Luo*, (Academic Press, New York/London).
36. Richards and Reining, *op. cit.*, pp. 386-7.

7. Strategies for Urban Survival

'It is up to the woman herself if
she wants to change her situation.'
Rose Mugula (Zambian)[1]

Once migrants have arrived in the towns, they make pragmatic attempts to relate to the urban conditions that they encounter, as individuals, as members of ethnic communities, and as representatives of social groupings and classes (including religious organizations), or simply as women. The strategies are, in nearly all cases, related to economic factors or considerations. Of course there were conflicts between individual goals and societal goals. In this chapter some of the mechanisms used by migrants to deal with the vicissitudes of urban life are presented.

Women and men wanted wealth, status and power. Since men used women as part of their strategies for production and expansion, they found it necessary to control women and the products of their labour, including children. But women realized that they could use their labour to benefit themselves as well. Whenever women perceived it was possible to have a certain amount of economic independence, they were quite prepared to endure drudgery. However, they were weary of having to struggle hard in order to attain their goals. This is a recurring theme in the present study.

Men were very sensitive to pressures and rebellions that resulted from some of the women's strategies because they were dependent upon women's labour to provide them with comfort, wealth and descendants. In most cases women used the legitimate ways offered by the options within their societies, but they often, however, had to resort to manipulation.

Mathiasson has proposed that societies may be categorized as either complementary, ascendant or manipulative.[2] In ascendant societies it may be an advantage to be a woman, and the basis of the advantage is institutionalized,[3] since women are valued for themselves as well as for the contributions they make.[4] In complementary societies women are neither inferior nor superior;[5] the contributions of each sex are essential for the smooth functioning of the societies. In manipulative societies, women see that their position is inferior to that of men and resort to deceit, withdrawal, cunning and circumvention to obtain their own desires and goals.[6] Lamphere has suggested that women's strategies are directly related to the power structure of the family. Where power and authority are in the hands of men, women work to influence the men and this sometimes leads to conflict if 'unseemly' methods are used. However, subtle influence, 'behind the scenes' manipulations and cheating are important components of the actual processes by which life proceeds in manipulative societies.[7]

Generally, *power* is a way of securing compliance with obligations.[8] In a familial decision-making situation, power is the potential ability of one partner to influence the other's behaviour[9] in order to secure favourable outcomes.[10] *Authority* is the right to make a particular decision as well as commanding obedience.[11] This authority is power held by one partner because either or both partners feel it is proper for that person to do so, or because society at large prescribed it.

What society considers the ideal may not be realized in practice. In this study, power and authority do not necessarily coincide. The balance of power is sometimes tipped one way, sometimes the other. Throughout my fieldwork I found that women were very supportive of each other in their marital conflicts, and some would spend several hours a week complaining about the men in their lives, but whenever someone suggested that if their husbands were so bad they should think of leaving them, the atmosphere became much more cautious. Proverbs and songs warned against unquestioning acceptance of advice because the giver may be motivated by envy, frustration or a desire to 'take your place'. Although this did not counteract the collective strength of sharing information and occasionally embarrassing a particular man, the problems of men and women were not perceived as a group phenomenon but in dyadic terms as inter-personal relationships. However, even though the particular strategies of individual women at first appeared to be isolated decisions, on closer examination a clear pattern emerged which suggested they were not unique but prevalent occurrences recognized by both men and women. Knowledge of them was available to anyone although the decision to act was an individual choice that depended upon the social arrangements affecting property rights. The strategies employed most often by the women did not radically differ from those used by the men. However, whereas men used the strategies to compete with everyone in the group or society at large, the women used them specifically against men to acquire whatever they were not getting out of the inter-personal relationships.

Rural women could migrate to the towns or they could turn unrewarded drudgery into remunerated hard work by manipulating resources. Urban women, in order to gain wealth, power and status, not only worked hard but capitalized on the traditional virtues of submission and service and their roles as wives or mothers. In other words, women were changing their situations by means of non-confrontational, non-threatening methods.

Motherhood and Wifehood as Transactional Tools

Women — regardless of the ethnic groups which they came from — on occasion used their reproductive abilities to improve their social status, and sometimes they even manipulated the ethnic and social identity of their children to ensure support by some man. This was possible because, as was commonly said in Namuwongo and Wabigalo, only a mother could tell who was in actual fact the father of her child. This was based on the obvious verity that it is women who possess the womb in which the mysteries of life that result in a child take place. Women can be seen to be pregnant, men can only claim parenthood by association. Unlike paternity, motherhood obviously does not need to be proven by legal recognition on the part of society.

Working in bars or socializing in night clubs or job hunting often brought Namuwongo and Wabigalo women in contact with men on the lookout for sexual pleasure. If children resulted from such affairs, the women were usually advised by old hands to take the men to court. During a period of ten months, four men were ordered by a court to support children they had fathered, as stipulated under the 1964 Affiliation Act. The resident magistrate at the Kampala court frequented by the Namuwongo-Wabigalo women was, in his words, sympathetic to 'poor exploited innocent women', and was very strict, particularly with men in responsible positions who took advantage of 'poor and ignorant' women. A rich man might be required to pay as much as 400 shillings a month to clothe, feed and educate his child, while 100 shillings a month might be demanded of an ordinary middle class man. The denial of responsibility in such cases was never accepted. Aware that they could expect no mercy from the magistrate, men often found the mere threat of court action enough to induce them to support their children, and where this failed their mistresses might threaten to go to the men's wives. Smart women even got the men to find them jobs or build them houses 'for the sake of the secret'. Also, some men supported a mistress not so much because of emotional ties but in order to guarantee a monopoly over the woman's sexual services, and the threat of withdrawing financial support would always be used if the woman seemed to develop an affection for another man. Some men, however, were so flattered to father children that, financial circumstances allowing, they bought land and built houses for their girlfriends in better residential areas.

The strategy of getting the right man flattered or threatened into accepting his paternal duties seems to have worked so well for Namuwongo and Wabigalo women that I never heard any rumours of abortions nor located an abortionist in the area. The clientele of the two local diviner-curers seemed, on the contrary, bent on conceiving children or being lucky in love.

Thus motherhood can be seen as a symbol to be manipulated with children as the trump cards. Through this age-old device it is possible to effect remarkable changes in social status and even ethnicity. One woman told me how she had fared since she became pregnant by a bus conductor while she was still at a private typing school, having failed her high school entrance exams. Afraid to return to her village and deserted by her lover, Kate had moved in with a friend and her husband until the birth of the baby, which was then taken to stay with her mother in the village. She was determined to find a job and get out of Namuwongo; 'I was determined to get out of Namuwongo as soon as possible. In my estimation even the worst rural village in Uganda could not be as filthy as this "town village".' She soon found a job at a cleaners and spent her evenings at night clubs with her friend and the friend's husband, soon acquiring many admirers, one of whom set her up as the assistant to his secretary. She ran a lot of errands but also improved her typing. Her boss was married and lived in the fashionable neighbourhood bordering on Namuwongo. When I met her in 1971 she had borne him three children, two girls and a boy, and he had found her a secretarial job in one of the ministries. 'But my period of monogamy with him was over. We were not married but he was jealous and accused me of seeing other men which was not true. I enjoy dancing in night clubs but that is all.'

In 1971 Kate was living in one of the more attractive and expensive houses in Namuwongo. She was expecting the baby of her latest boyfriend, Miko, a civil servant. At the beginning of 1972 she had a baby boy and Miko was euphoric. He spent a great deal of time in Namuwongo. By mid-1972 she had bought a piece of land in the fashionable neighbourhood and Miko was helping her put up a four-bedroom house. By the end of the year she had moved into the house with her children and been joined by some of her relatives — a nephew, niece and uncle. During 1973 Kate had a second baby boy by Miko, but their relationship became shaky and by 1974 they had ended it. She had her job as a secretary and it paid well. She had risen from being a delinquent schoolgirl earning 80 shillings a month about ($10.00) to earning now over 1,000 shillings. She had this to say about being single: 'I have never married because I have never found an interesting single man after my original misadventure with the bus conductor. I have always lived comfortably. I usually have one boyfriend at a time. You should hear the fantastic stories some of the women I work with tell about the hazards of having many boyfriends all at once!' She knew her strategy involved playing a secondary role but, 'There will be mistresses as long as there are men with a lot of money who are willing to throw it around. It is difficult to find generous men, most of them do not have the long time commitment I have so far been lucky to enjoy. My children are all going to receive a good education so that the girls do not have to play the between-the-leg game to get things they deserve as people. I think the number of men "foolish" enough to throw money around will decrease as time goes on.'

The secret of Kate's success lay in her careful use of the traditional female virtues of modesty and deference. She camouflaged her intelligence and ambition by being extremely docile. One day she told me, 'What men want is a softly spoken woman, who can kneel at their feet while serving them. I have many pairs of stockings torn through kneeling. I do not know why I do it.' But she knew it was one of the traditional female virtues that beguiled men.

Had Kate insisted aggressively that unequal access to opportunities and inequity in income distribution dictated that her lovers share their wealth, she would not have achieved so much.

The following case study shows that, along with having children out of wedlock, issues regarding paternity, kinship and ethnic affiliation could no longer be taken for granted.

Nyakayiru, a beautiful Nkole aged 28, was orphaned in infancy and grew up at her father's brother's home. However, the wife of her guardian mistreated her. When she was only 13 years old, she refused to return to school. She had failed her Standard 6 examinations due to lack of interest in school work. She stayed at home (Ibanda, Ankole), but before the year was out she had eloped with Mukasa, a Ganda employee of Radio Uganda. 'Life was a struggle (i.e. they had little money, food and clothing) but when we "arrived" (i.e. made enough money, bought a plot of land, *kibanja*, at Kireka and built a modern brick house) he started running around with other women and declaring that he wanted to be properly married.' He sent Nyakayiru away, but allowed her to visit her children (aged five, three and two) four times a year. She first stayed at Mulago with two good Nkole friends, later moving to Kibuye but she was forced out of the house for failure to pay the rent which had been raised from 70 to 150 shillings. In 1968 she moved to Namuwongo because it was near the industrial area where she had secured a job with a shirt company, the Uganda Garments Industry. She liked Namuwongo and, 'by this time I had five married, but rich lovers. All my needs were taken care of. They supplied me with money for food, rent and clothing. I had managed to save quite a lot. I met men who wanted to marry me but my first marriage had disillusioned me.' In 1969 she gave birth to a baby girl by one of her rich lovers. He was about 60 years old and married to a woman in her 30s, but they had no children. When Nyakayiru bore 'for him' another baby girl in 1971, he bought her a plot of land and built a modern brick house at Makindye, a prestigious neighbourhood.

In January 1972, she moved into her new house. Her two half-brothers and maternal cousins came to stay with her. Around this time her ex-husband, Mukasa, had decided to get rid of Nyakayiru's children because they had 'bad blood' in them, so she took them in and hired an elderly woman to look after them.

Nyakayiru changed jobs to work as a telephone operator in one of the government departments, a job which she got through her last lover, the chairman of a public board, who even obtained places for her children in two respectable schools (Kitante and Mengo). She wanted her children to have a good education so that they would not suffer like her. Even her former husband was so impressed that he wanted to have his children back. But Nyakayiru refused to part with them.

Nyakayiru was convinced, like so many of the other married and unmarried women I spoke to, that marriage restricted sexual freedom. Nyakayiru maintained sexual and economic relations with different men. If one of them found out about one of her other lovers, he would either talk her out of the relationship or be finished with her. But if they had had a child by her, she knew how to strike bargains with them – she threatened to tell their wives. She did not enjoy doing this, particularly as 'some of the men who visit me are old enough to be my father'. But she made up her mind that, if men wanted to use her, she would use them also. Once in a contemplative mood she confessed, 'I am lucky in that the children resemble me. Those men have no way of knowing whether the children are theirs or not.' Nyakayiru admitted that she had imposed paternity on rich men who were likely to provide handsome financial support. This was not an unusual practice in Namuwongo.

However, when one of the lovers told her blatantly that she was a *malaya* (prostitute), Nyakayiru was extremely upset, and when she got a new job she referred to herself as Mrs. Kanyarutoke (her father's name). This was a conflict typical of many women. While some felt that there was no compelling reason for getting married, others felt that having been married was a better status than not marrying at all. For example, one Ganda woman insisted that marriage was a good thing and told her daughters and granddaughters, 'It is better to go through a marriage ceremony even if the marriage lasts only a week, a month or forever.' Yet a single, rich, but childless Gisu woman asserted that single women who wanted and could afford to have children were saving themselves sleepless nights if they did not bother to marry.

Not all women agreed that it was as simple as this. About half the women interviewed pointed out how difficult it is for women to raise children single-handed, and during a nine month period, I witnessed ten cases of young men, roundabout the age of twenty, who had caused bodily harm to their mothers or their mothers' lovers, fighting over property and sometimes calling their mothers *malayas*.

Although children who stole or fought with other children would be threatened with being sent to the *kampiringusa*, reformatory school, so that they would grow up to be good citizens, when it came down to it, mothers (and fathers) were reluctant to commit their children.

Such problems are particularly acute in the case of the Nubi ethnicity, an essentially urban phenomenon[12] which put great emphasis on the control of women. Boys growing up in such a patriarchal atmosphere are bound to abuse women who are getting out of line. Some women from other ethnic groups solved the problem by giving their children names that would affiliate them with their own clans instead of the fathers' and by sending children to spend time with their brothers or other rural relatives, to make them more disciplined. This was in fact a common practice by all families and not just single mothers. (Richards found it to be widespread in the 1950s.)[13]

The Respectable Married Woman
The strategy of manipulating motherhood did not work for all women. Personal style, beauty and age determined the difference between success and being trapped. Some women ended up in a vicious circle and instead of using the weaknesses of men to obtain fair transactions, they ended up as

either disillusioned wives or as prostitutes. While most women did not regard this as personally desirable, they philosophically recognized it as the price of manipulating men. The following account deals with a woman who felt that she had lost all respect and then used wifehood to regain it. She also lacked the stamina and determination that some of the independent single women had.

I first became interested in this family even before I started my fieldwork in Namuwongo when I spotted a few child traders between the ages of six and ten peddling curried pancakes (*kabalagala*) or a handful of groundnuts. They never sold much and were harassed by mobs of schoolchildren if they went near any of the three local primary schools. One evening after I had settled in the area, I noticed two of the vendors — a boy and a girl — entering a room in a certain house, and I decided to include the owners of the room in my participant observation study. A few weeks later I met Bateresebyabwe, her husband Magulu and her four children.

She was a Rundi women who, though in her early thirties, looked ten years older. In 1955 she had married a Rundi 'circulatory migrant' named Nabenda, who persuaded her to return with him to Uganda. They lived at Kibibi, in the Ssingo County of Buganda where he worked as a farm labourer (*mupakasi*) and life was not easy even though he worked very hard and took five job contracts. Two years after they had migrated, he started beating her, and once even threatened to chop her to pieces with a machete. At about this time he became involved with a rich Ganda 'grass widow' whose husband had migrated to Kampala six years previously and was never heard of again. Her land was near theirs and she invited him to go and live with her. The neighbours did not take any notice of him since most of them had resident labourers, and the 'widow' took great care not to set tongues wagging. But soon he was openly sleeping in her bedroom and another farm hand was hired to relieve him. His lover persuaded him to get rid of his tattered khaki clothes and dress like a respectable Ganda. He decided that the only thing standing in the way of his being a true Ganda was his wife whom everyone knew to be a Rundi and who did not look 'smart like the Ganda women'. In mid-June 1958, he inflicted serious knife wounds on Bate's head, and she was only saved by a Ruandan living in the same compound. Several months later she migrated with him to Namagunga in the Kyagwe County of Buganda, where he was not very successful and so after one year they migrated to Mengo-Kisenyi in Kampala City. By this time they had two children. Between 1962 and 1967 while her husband was in jail for robbery, Bate had several Ruandan lovers and one child. Petero, the lover who fathered her child, denied responsibility. At the same time she met Magulu, a Ruandan who invited her to become his second wife because his first wife was a Luyia and not from his ethnic group. Bate did not want to be a second wife, but in 1970 the Luyia woman packed off her children and left Magulu. Bate went to stay with him. Although he was working as a night security guard for an industrial firm and earning 179 shillings a month, Bate did not know what he did with the money. If she asked to buy food or clothing for his child, a quarrel would result. Later he earned his living through various odd jobs but he invariably spent all his money on drink.

By this time Bate had begun a brewing business and also raised pigs and chickens on the husks that she and other beer brewers threw away. Everyone complained of how terrible her beer and gin were but they kept coming back because her chicken and pork were tasty. She earned 321 shillings a month but this was not all that much once she deducted 50 shillings for the children's school fees, 35 shillings for rent, plus food, supplies for beer and occasionally pigs. The house leaked when it rained which not only interfered with her work and ruined her belongings, but also threatened her health. 'Petero (the lover who had denied the baby) now wants my daughter because she looks so pretty. But I will not allow him to take her away. When I think, before my business got on its feet, I had to sleep with men for money so that my children could survive. Sometimes I made just enough to enable them to eat something. I would starve. The children were constantly ill (*kwashiokor*) but now I can feed them.'

Bate had seen it all. She had been married to a wife beater who scarred her body for life, and a thief who had been thrown in jail. She had to support two children by working in a bar where she acquired several lovers and a child. She realized that 'I am a *malaya*' and was very conscious of public sentiment against this. She then married a drunkard who had lost his job but she stayed with him because she felt that prostituion was more 'rotten' than drinking. She had started a distilling business because she realized that when she grew older she would be unable to make money from sex. Thus, Bate was a prostitute because of economic necessity but she sought marriage as a protection from the lack of self-respect she felt.[14]

Nubinization

Many women in this study were concerned with respectability, and we must now look at women who voluntarily put themselves under male control by joining a uniquely urban ethnic gioup. Unlike other ethnic groups which blamed the decline of their cultures on female migration to the towns, the Nubi culture was itself a result of urban transformations. In fact, anyone could become a Nubi through the process of Nubinization,[15] the assimilation of Nubi culture. When Nubi men married women from other ethnic groups, the children were automatically reared as Nubi because descent was reckoned along patrilineal lines. But even in cases of intermarriage between Nubi *women* and men from other patrilineal societies like the Ganda, Soga and Lugbara, Nubi women still insisted on bringing up their children as Nubi. They taught them the Kinubi language, dressed them in long loose shirts and caps, if they were boys, while girls had to wear ankle length bloomers. If they lived in the rural areas, they would usually travel long distances with the children to join other Nubi in large urban centres to celebrate Islamic holidays.

Although Nubi women were under-represented in my sample, I did talk to many of them, in addition to observations and interviews. I found that there was little difference between Nubi women and those of other ethnic groups, apart from the Luo. For example, three of the four women in the sample had been married three times before their current husbands. Two had migrated as single independent women, and had borne children as unmarried mothers before acquiring their present husbands.

Nubinization was undertaken for a number of reasons, to counteract negative stereotypes or, to escape loneliness. Individuals who for one reason or another find themselves alienated from the rural areas can seek refuge in a small group that increases its membership by an open door policy. The implications are that ethnic identity can be acquired, that symbols are vital for recognition, and that people can learn and unlearn ethnic socialization.[16] In this way provision is made by ethnic associations[17] or ethnic groups to resist 'urban ways' and maintain some kind of morality among individuals, provide for members in times of need and enable individuals to achieve social recognition. Bujra found that when the first women traders in Nairobi suffered status ambiguities within the colonial urban framework they opted to become Swahili Muslims because the Islamic community was conceived in the idiom of kinship. As one woman explained her conversion, 'I wanted *Jamma* (kindred, neighbours, friends). They will bury me.'[18]

The Nubi insist on the respectability of their women, a feature which can be very appealing to women who feel their reputation is in doubt. As one convert explained:

I did not want people to think me that sort of woman. I started attending some of the local (protestant) churches. In some of them the prayers were conducted in Luo and I could not follow. In others I could understand the services conducted in Luganda but the preachers were always condemning thugs and loose women. I felt that I had been damned for life and that there was no hope for me. At the time I was contemplating moving to another neighbourhood, I became friends with an elderly Nubi woman who used to gently tell men that women ultimately are responsible for their morality and no man can actually control them if they should wish to misbehave. Through a lengthy process I became a Nubi. I changed my name from Faith to Fatuma. The rest was easy. The Nubi woman became my 'mother' and instructed me in Nubi ways and I became converted. Although my jobs have not changed, I am a much respected woman. We all need respect, don't we?

Nubi women usually played a large part in the conversion of other women. The whole process of Nubinizing Fatuma took about six months. Her head cover was the flimsiest in Namuwongo but men no longer talked loudly about her being 'loose'. She was a Nubi and her honour would be defended by any Nubi man who overheard insinuations against a Nubi woman, and this had resulted in some nasty quarrels in the area over suggestions that Nubi women were just as 'loose' as women of other ethnic groups. Thus it would seem that the Nubi community offered an attractive option for women willing to place themselves in purdah while at the same time continuing in disreputable ways. Elsewhere it has been reported that Islam was attractive to marginal urban women because, although it did not condone prostitution, or illegitimacy Muslims were in general more tolerant in these matters than Christians.[19]

Nubi women generally voiced agreement with the Namuwongo drunkards' ballad, 'Women control themselves. Don't let anyone deceive you that a man can control a woman. It all depends on what she wants.' All Nubi women engaged in petty trade, and thus found opportunities for having affairs if they wished. Nubi women dressed colourfully and sold food to workers in the industrial area, as well as to travellers at the railway station or at taxi and bus shelters. These sites were public enough for them to attract the interest of some men, but as long as their heads were covered Nubi men were convinced that no one would dare approach them for immoral purposes as this violated Islamic Law. In fact Nubi, Muslim and non-Muslim men did not seem to have much difficulty in approaching Nubi women but the constant lowering of the eyes in public gave the appearance of submission and obedience, and was recognized as an effective strategy that obtained respect for women who thereby appeared to be under proper male control.

Financial Manipulations

While the Nubi were veiling their women, the Luo were attempting to curb women's appetite for money. The most commonly used methods were inducing them to confess during Christian fellowship and keeping them from too much share in their business affairs. It was easy to control women if the weight of custom ('what we have always done!') was evoked.

During the 1950s and 1960s, the Luo Union in Kampala had been an effective instrument in ensuring that women did not disgrace the Luo community. Disgraced women were ordered to return home wearing a jute sack with holes in the lower sections of the back and front. However, even in the 1960s it seems that a few Luo women were migrating alone or separating from their husbands once in town, and deliberately refusing to join the Union so that it could not discipline them. By 1972 the Luo Union had become an underground organization and had very little power over individuals.

It is necessary to explain the decline of this powerful means of controlling women. Parkin has documented how with the coming of political independence Luo dominance in the trade unions was viewed with resentment by Ugandan politicians and non-Luo rank and file in the unions.[20] In an attempt to solve the unemployment problem and curb the drain of foreign exchange from the country, the government ordered unskilled foreign workers to leave Uganda in 1970. Many of those affected were Luo, the majority of whom lived at Namuwongo and Wabigalo. The Luo had originally come in the 1940s to work as labourers on the railway and as porters for the Lake Victoria steamers. Before long the Luo also came to dominate office jobs like clerks, cleaners and security guards. They joined domestic service as cooks, house servants and gardeners. The Luo established themselves as hard working, reliable and loyal. People from other ethnic groups, who were thought by European and Asian employers to be lazy, found it difficult to compete with the Luo. In 1971 with the military coup d'etat, many employers recalled the Luo who had been expelled in 1970, but the next year when the Asians were ordered to leave Uganda, there was an exodus of Luo as well. Some figured that it was better to return home rather than stay unemployed in town. But those who stayed on predicted that their compatriots would soon return to Kampala where the unemployment problem was less acute than in Kenya's Nyanza province, and there were, in particular, more opportunities for self-employment.

When I arrived in the field in 1972, the Luo regarded any mention of politics with suspicion. In fact they refused to participate in any activity that might officially be viewed as political, and some Luo even boycotted the Anglican Church's Christmas party on the grounds that they did not want to get involved in politics. The functions of the Luo Union had been reduced to raising money to help repatriate the disabled and the dead, to run two nursery schools, and to organize beer parties. Most Luo men lamented their lost powers and devised ways to regain the authority the Luo Union had once possessed, in particular control of women. Some churches, such as the Legio Maria (a breakaway from the Catholic Church), attempted to preserve the Luo family and marriages by discouraging women from acquiring independent incomes which would weaken the position of men. The method used was making women confess to such sins as keeping some of the household management money for themselves. What was intriguing was the fact that the confessions were held during prayer fellowships with husbands in attendance.

One such woman was Atieno, and each time she confessed I would wait a week and then ask her whether she had returned the money to her husband. Each of the four times she just smiled sweetly and told me that I should ask other women who confessed too! Her husband was a fisherman who returned from the Ssese Islands every fortnight to sell fish at the Namuwongo market. When departing, he would leave her some money for buying food and for emergencies. Both husband and wife were members of the Legio Maria Church. Their professed religious tenets were: (1) not associating with people belonging to the Church of Rome; (2) not associating with Europeans; and (3) not using European medicines. Prayer time involved dancing and singing until members went into a trance which lasted until they had confessed. During the service they used incense and other herbs, and locked themselves in. Before going in for prayer, each member was required to wash their feet in a communal basin. This water was then kept outside the door and was used by the prayer leader to curse any intruder (on whom it would be splashed).

The Luo in Namuwongo and Wabigalo frowned upon the 40 or so Legio

Maria members whom they regarded as ignorant and inclined to sorcery and dangerous to the Luo people in general. The majority of Luo women who were not members of the Legio Maria Church felt that the leaders were always waiting for a chance to make women members suffer.

One such incident involved a woman who was in labour all day, locked in a small room with ten people chanting prayers in Latin and Dholuo and burning incense. The neighbours became so concerned that they fetched a doctor who was chased away with the dirty water and curses. The neighbours then fetched the police who took the woman by force to a nearby Catholic Mission hospital where a Caesarean delivery was performed. The child was stillborn. Members of Legio Maria did not talk to the neighbours for several weeks because they had violated all three of their religious tenets by taking the woman to the hospital. They were convinced that the power of prayer would have saved the woman and possibly the child. However, when they were assured by the neighbours that the operation had been mechanical and involved no medication, things returned to normal.

There were twelve other fundamentalist churches that practised public confessions during fellowship, although the Catholics and Anglicans did not. 'The saved' (*balokole*), an association within the Anglican Church but which also attracted some Catholics, did practise confessions, but in a sober style. Some of the churches in the area had an almost 99 per cent Luo-Luyia membership. For example, Roho (spirit), Jo Hera (the love of God), Legio Maria, the Israel Nativity Independent Church, the Voice of Healing, and the Church of God. Ten churches had a balanced membership in terms of sex ratio. Legio Maria and two other churches had more men than women. Although Legio Maria had been started in 1973 by a woman named Gaudencia Aoko, the church leadership consisted of men who were either school dropouts or unemployed. They wore long, loose gowns (*kanzu*) and had long, uncombed hair which gave them an aura of devoutness. Going around preaching and organizing prayer meetings in people's homes, they would hear a lot of gossip about things which took place: women who had women friends at the market selling things for them, women who instead of drinking milk in their tea were selling it during their husband's absence, women who sold cooked food to school children, women who had lovers, etc. On Sunday they would induce the women to confess, preferably in front of their husbands. The prayer leader always acted as a medium. For example, he would go into a trance and say, 'I see a woman who is cheating on her husband. She has been trading, but she has not told him. This is bad. It divides the family.' Then he would move and stand near the woman and lay his hands on her head. One day a woman who had lived in Namuwongo for ten years and was a well-known fish trader failed to confess. The prayer leader who had his hands over her head was becoming more and more worked up. Suddenly the woman shrieked and confessed that she had never told her husband the exact income she earned from the market. She lay on the floor, her head covered with blood, for the prayer leader had dug his long sharp nails in her skull — she had been induced to confess. This was not an isolated incident. Thus while the women confessed to wanting to start or having started trading, the men confessed to being angry with the Lord for not dealing satisfactorily with their employment situation, for example. The 1970 government measure to expel the Luo from Kampala was viewed as something that could easily happen again and so the issue was also incorporated in some of the prayers people recited.

Other Luo men gave their wives little or no money at all — because women's financial needs were minimal. But the fact is that there were some women who constantly threatened to divorce their husbands if they were not given money for clothing and food. Even women who had their own sources of income still insisted they had a right to know what their husbands earned and how they spent it. Other women said they would put up with a lot of hardship provided their children were sent to school. Some women were secretly keeping some of the household money for their private use, and generally saving for a rainy day. This bothered many men I talked to and, as an old Luo man declared, 'Everything a married woman earns should be known by the husband who then must decide on what to do. Women today are not content to supplement the family income by trading, or to keep the husband's salary. They insist that they have financial needs too and that some money should be allocated to them. No man can agree to this as a permanent arrangement. I don't know what women need their own money for.' However, not all Luo women accepted such intimidation or humiliation, as the example below illustrates.

Maria had been twice widowed when she decided to migrate to Kampala. She brewed and sold millet beer. She sold mats. She also had an Acholi boyfriend. One day at the beer club someone hinted that Maria was loose and had abandoned their traditional customs by migrating alone. Someone yelled that it was a pity such women could no longer be dressed in a sack and returned home. But apparently Maria had heard this remark once too often and she had decided to lay the matter to rest once and for all. The next day she went to the chief's (*muluka*) meeting and requested that certain individuals be reprimanded publicly for harassing her. The individuals were summoned and they apologized for what they had said but claimed that they had been under the influence of drink. The chief reminded them that a 'drunkard does not skin a dog *(omutamivu tabaaga mbwa)*', a Ganda proverb, meaning that what people do or say under the influence of drink is often related to what they had planned to do or say beforehand. One man told me later that they had had to settle the matter quickly because if they delayed they feared that Maria would tell the chief about the Union. When I told them that the Union was not an illegal association, they laughed and told me, 'What do you know?' This was an obvious reference to the previously mentioned expulsion of foreigners in 1970.

The Luo saw themselves as different from the Ganda and other Interlacustrine groups whose women were supposedly 'loose' and uncontrollable. Luo men and women like to talk about themselves in idealistic terms: 'We Luo do not do this or that.' And one of their ideals was that Luo women

were never dishonest with their husbands in relation to money, and the force
of this ideal probably explains a good deal about why women could be
induced to confess. Nonetheless, there were obvious gaps between ideal
Luo behaviour and women's increasing desire for economic autonomy.

Pooling Resources

Unattached independent women often pooled their resources and invested
in joint ventures. Some of the most successful women distillers had associates
who were either particularly hardworking, or good salespersons, or who had
enough contacts to ensure a steady market. Such women usually lived in
neighbouring rooms or houses and would be on eating and visiting terms.
They borrowed food, clothing, basins, etc. from each other; they babysat and
showed general concern for each other's welfare. The phenomenon is so
striking that some researchers have interpreted this co-operation among women
as an essential element in the lifestyles of the urban poor.[21]

The following example illustrates an arrangement where three Ganda
women preferred to have different economic activities so as to avoid quarrel-
ling over their labour contributions, but co-operated so successfully socially
and economically that they became fictive relatives; on the other hand real
relatives, while helped when in need, were otherwise kept at arm's length
because 'they were not good for business'.

Namu, aged 22, Nankya, aged 35, and Najjingo, aged 46, had not always
lived on the same block as they did in 1972. Namu had been at Kisugu
for only a year, and had at first worked as a barmaid. Her salary of 30
shillings a month was just enough to pay the rent and feed her two small
children. She decided that she would supplement her inadequate salary by
selling curried pancakes and brewing and selling pineapple beer during the day,
while she still worked as a barmaid in the evening. At night she also sold her
sex services for money. After four months of this kind of life, she felt dissatisfied but also felt that she had little option but to go on. She was particularly
distressed at the violence of the men in the bars. By this time she had met
Najjingo who advised her to stop working in the bar if she did not want to
end up every month at the hosptial nursing her injuries. Najjingo had two
large rooms and suggested that Namu come and rent the back one while she
kept the front one that served as a shop.

Najjingo herself had experienced a very unhappy marriage, and used to
visit her married daughter at Kisugu for long periods whenever the daughter
was ill or pregnant, or if one of the grandchildren were ill. Each time she
came, she used to leave the daughter with some money which she had obtained by selling bananas and coffee while her husband was away visiting
friends. Soon the money amounted to 600 shillings, enough to open a shop.
One day in 1968 she came to visit her daughter carrying a large cloth bundle
and a wooden suitcase, and announced that this time she was not returning
to her husband. At first she rented a small room for 35 shillings a month,
and sold soft drinks and cigarettes 'under the bed'. Before long her son-in-
law had found her an old paraffin refrigerator for cooling the drinks. Since

her room was next door to a school, a stand pipe and a church, her drinks were in constant demand, and after two years she was ready to move into two large rooms next-door which a Nubi houseowner had just finished building. Within a few months she realized that the rent was too much for her and this was when she invited Namu to share with her. By this time Namu had borrowed some money from her friends and established herself in the food selling and brewing businesses.

A month later a third woman, Nankya, moved into two large rooms next door. She too was a shopkeeper, but had been born and raised in Namuwongo. Her parents owned some land so she never had to buy food; in fact, sometimes she sold some bananas and sweet potatoes. Meanwhile Namu would sit on Najjingo's verandah every day after work watching the dinner cooking and passersby conversing with Najjingo and the customers at her shop, but above all watching the goings on at Nankya's rooms.

After two months Nankya was a close friend of both Namu and Najjingo. Namu called Najjingo 'mother' (*mama*) and her children called Najjingo 'grandmother' (*jjajja*). Najjingo's own grandchildren, who stayed with her or who occasionally came to visit her, were told to call Namu 'mother'. Namu, on the other hand, addressed Nankya as *senga* (paternal aunt) on account of 'her age' and the fact that they belonged to the same clan (lungfish). But Namu also said that, because Nankya was only in her 30s, they could potentially love the same men. Potential or real rivalry over men between a woman and her father's sister was assumed by my Ganda respondents in the rural areas as well as at Namuwongo and Wabigalo.

Fictive kinship usually developed among people who co-operated intimately in day-to-day activities, paralleling the moral, economic and social support relatives give each other in the rural areas. As one Ganda woman said 'your neighbours are your relatives.' This was not confined to the Ganda only; the Luo too addressed their close associates as 'brother' (*omera*) and 'sister' (*nyamera*). Sometimes both men and women were addressed as *omera* to indicate an even closer relationship. For example, husbands and wives addressed each other as *omera* when expressing affection or anger, depending on the tone of voice. This use of pseudo-kinship was also recorded among other groups, particularly the Nyoro, Soga, Nkole and Toro. Any group of co-workers or neighbours could address each other in kinship terms; this would involve deciding to use either kinship terms from one group or a combination of simple words from different groups. This pseudo-kinship served to distinguish between those who belonged to the 'territory' and those who were strangers.[22]

Namu, Nankya and Najjingo looked after each other's welfare and economic interests. When Nankya's children were ill, which they often were, it was Najjingo and Namu, rather than Nankya's real relatives, who would be asked to look after the shop while she took the children to hospital. Namu often had to leave her pancakes in baskets at Nankya and Najjingo's shop to sell for her while she went to sell food or beer somewhere else and, if she were going to be selling late, they would baby-sit for her. Najjingo always entrusted her shop to her two friends, but never left it open when her brother or nephew were visiting. If one of the three were late, the others would keep some food for her, and during the shortages of cooking oil, butter, milk and sugar in 1972, whoever had the chance to buy any of these commodities bought for all three women. However, unless absolutely necessary, they stayed out of each other's arguments, not interfering even when Namu's ex-husband tried to kidnap one of her sons. But they did defend Namu against the landlord's insinuations, since they could attest to her virtue.

Avoiding Relatives

Few migrants packed up their possessions, jumped on a bus or train, and came to town hoping to cope unaided with whatever they found. Most first-time migrants expected to find support among people they knew, especially relatives, already living in the city. Social scientists have documented how migrants to towns go to known addresses of a relative, acquaintance, or villagemate, age-mate or co-ethnic,[23] in order that accommodation, food, job hunting, and often monetary requirements may be taken care of by someone who knows their way around town.[24] While kinship obligations and other ties are a great help to migrants, these obligations can become a burden for not very prosperous town dwellers, who therefore tend to avoid their relatives, even close ones.

In another part of Kampala, Parkin reported that,even among middle class Luo, conversation was dominated by talk of the need to budget carefully because of the burden of assisting relatives and constantly providing them with tea.[25] This British legacy is so entrenched that in some homes tea is drunk as many as four times a day and those who cannot afford tea and milk usually visit those who can. This in itself represents a financial drain, and was of course just a small part of the obligations imposed by new arrivals.

The Ganda have two revealing sayings: (1) *muna tawuni asanyukira yettise* (a townsperson will welcome someone who arrives carrying something); (2) *ata kwalize nganda, akulaga kifo* (if someone wants to prevent you extending your kinship network, they will not introduce you when someone new is there but wait til they leave and, pointing to their seat, say 'That was so-and-so'). The first saying is used in both town and country to refer to the fact that people in town are less hospitable because they have limited resources and only like the look of someone who will be self-supporting. It is customary for a villager visiting a relative in town for a day to take a bunch of bananas, a basket of potatoes or beans, or whatever is available.

The second saying originated in the villages but assumed greater import in the towns. In the past it may have been an important way of indicating a a need for a real kinship extension as people migrated from their ancestral homes (*butaka*) to escape natural calamities like famines and epidemics or, at the turn of the century, religious persecution; and after 1900 to seek new economic opportunities offered elsewhere by the British-introduced land tenure system and the new towns. By 1972 it referred to the reliance on urban relatives to get government or other salaried jobs, places in school for the children and trading licences, and reflected the habit practised by most low income people of discouraging visitors by not showing friends or even relatives exactly where they lived.

Initially I was impressed by the dedication shown by the Ganda towns-people in finding jobs for recently arrived relatives, but I soon realized that this merely indicated a determination that the relative should be self-supporting in as short a time as possible. Every morning the visitor would be wakened as early as possible, urged to drink a cup of tea or coffee and then taken on a tour of different offices. But in other cases the person being visited would ignore the visitor completely, waking up early and going to work, instructing the children, if they knew where the parents worked, not to direct anyone there. The evening cooking would be accompanied by complaints about food shortages and high prices and pointed remarks to the effect that everything in town had to be slaved for. Most migrants would get the hint and either find ways of contributing to the household budget or would move in with someone else.

The Luo prided themselves on their brotherly ideology, addressing each other as brother (*omera*) or sister (*nyamera*). But they too were operating under a regime of tight budgets and dingy accommodation. When new Luo migrants arrived, they would be taken on a tour of the city and introduced to the important Luo men in the area. If they were men, the next stage would be to help them get a job, through an elaborate network system. When a Luo relative arrived, he was taken to a friend who knew of a vacancy or prospective job. The friend then took the recent migrant to a third party, a Luo or non-Luo, who more often than not asked for their 'tongues to be greased with butter' (*mo dhonge*). The new migrant would usually have no money so he would come home to tell his relative, who would then groan about having no money (sometimes he might be genuinely broke, but often merely pretending), but would promise to get the necessary money for the bribe. The migrant would then be loaned the money for the bribe, thus imparting the first lesson of urban life: 'People should be encouraged to find jobs as soon as they arrive. The loan of money shows them that nothing in town is free and forces them to work hard, and save in order to repay it.' Despite continuing ethnic and kinship obligations, town life taught people economic self-reliance.

Deference, Gifts and Bribes

The only way the unskilled town dweller could get anything from the public services was to show deference and be willing to pay those in charge. Most urbanites felt the need to know someone who 'mattered'. Such an acquaintance would be greeted politely whenever encountered (stiffkneed or fat women made quite a picture trying to kneel on the pavement on such occasions). Sometimes it was necessary to visit the acquaintance's office with gifts of chicken or bunches of bananas, and hang around the office for a day or even a week waiting for the acquaintance to return from errands, journeys or vacations. When they arrived, a tale of woe would be poured out to them in such a way that they would offer to help or steer the visitor to someone else who could. When the request had been granted, the supplicant would expect to be asked to provide 'tea' (*chai*) or 'pepsi-cola' or bananas (*matoke*) or 'lunch' (*kyamisana*) — all euphemisms for a bribe. Namuwongo and Wabigalo residents usually made the initial offer themselves. As one Ganda woman put it, 'Life in town is like a car; some parts have to be greased for it to run.' Thus the habit of 'greasing hands' or 'greasing elbows' was accepted as a normal way of doing business by most people. Those newcomers or non-Ganda who did not know about such customs took forever to get a licence or a job. Each person I talked to had paid a bribe for one service or another and was under no illusion as to the fairness of the practice. But some people believed that they were actually manipulating those in control of the resources and opportunities.

In some cases officials and patrons could be successfully manipulated through the exploitation of their ethnic identity as people were happier to do business with people who attempted to speak their languages. Most business people were either bilingual or trilingual and could 'follow' several other languages. However, language skills had to be supplemented by deference: for example, the most successful business people I knew always called people 'sir' or 'madam' or 'sister' or 'brother' in their own language.

Returning to the Rural Areas

Some migrants would eventually decide to return to the rural areas which were most people's ultimate security against the vicissitudes of urban life. This has been illustrated by the Luo women who shuttled between the towns where their husbands worked and the rural areas where the husbands owned land. Some moderately successful women from Namuwongo invested in rural landholdings, and many elite city people would have houses in the rural areas where they retreated some weekends with their families.

However, the decision to return to the rural areas often meant that a person would have to admit defeat. Even though the rural people heard countless stories about the hardships of urban life, they still expected migrants to have some degree of success, and no urban migrant could make a visit to the rural areas without neighbours and relatives gathering expectantly for some handout such as sugar, salt, clothes, shoes, jewelry, school fees, etc. This was sufficient to scare off migrants in the lowest income brackets from ever visiting the rural areas. In fact, apart from shuttling Luo women, nearly all the rest of the people in the sample only visited their home areas if there were births, marriages, or deaths.

In 1974 when I returned to update my research, I found that 11 of the 33 Ganda direct migrants had left Kampala and returned to the rural areas, giving marriage and employment as some of the causes. I was able to trace only five of the women. Two had married men who commuted daily to work in Kampala (one a clerk and one a taxi driver); one had married a rich farmer, the fourth, a school-leaver, had found a teaching job at a private (unofficial) school; and the fifth, also a school-leaver, had gone to become a hairdresser at a small township. Another woman had returned to the village with her husband who had lost his job in town and they had become pineapple farmers.

The direct migrants, unlike the stage-by-stage migrants, had not invested their money in the urban areas, but had always nurtured hopes of returning to the village some day. Those who had made money in town invested in the rural areas by buying land, building houses and even cultivating, either in the village of origin or elsewhere. During my fieldwork two women invited me on different occasions to visit their rural homes where they had fine houses of corrugated iron with sand plastered walls. One woman had even bought the land before migrating, and while in Namuwongo she managed to build the house, invite her mother to stay in it, and send her children to keep their granny company while they attended the village school.

In another case it had been possible to buy the land and build the house through rural friends who informed the woman in town when they heard of vacant land and supervised the building of her house. They had even hired a Ruandan in his late twenties to caretake. His job was to grow food and keep the place looking like a home. The joke in the village was that even though those two women were never going to return, they had made the village beautiful.

Summary

The mechanisms for dealing with the vicissitudes of urban life had two focuses, the public/communal and the private/personal. Deference, gifts and bribes were used to initiate, speed up and get things done when dealing with city officials or employers, and were such standard practice when dealing with new migrants that Namuwongo and Wabigalo residents had begun to find kinship obligations burdensome.

Among the Luo, the voluntary association, the Luo Union that had been an active regulator of communal welfare, lost its authority in the 1970s due to political pressures. In its place religious movements were used by men as a mechanism for controlling women, inducing them to confess their financial sources of income or holdings. This was obviously an attempt to deal with the threat to male dominance that resulted from women acquiring independent incomes. Like women from other ethnic groups, Luo women not only wanted an independent income, but were willing to seek it through employment or by misappropriating the housekeeping money.

Urban women used their reproductive functions as mothers and wives to improve their social status. Whereas some were aware of the possibilities of this manipulation backfiring, others resignedly hoped for the best. In some instances women gained respectability through submitting to male control. In order to achieve certain goals women sometimes used strategies that do not seem progressive. The Nubi women, however, diluted the effectiveness of the veil so that it became a symbolic shelter that enabled them to do other things.[26] Thus, one way or another women could do something with regard to dominant male ideologies.

Most urban women at one time or another engaged in transactional manipulation, the success of which was due not so much to men's ignorance as to the pragmatic approaches of the women. Women rarely said anything overtly threatening. Deference was the most effective tool women used in manipulating men, and those women seen kneeling in offices and on sidewalks talking to men in low voices were manipulating symbols of the 'obedient woman'. As one elite man explained, 'the women here make men feel like they are still masters.' Men relished the kneeling of women so much that one old man was overheard telling a group of young men, 'Today's women are too much. Controlling them is a waste of time. A woman controls and looks after herself and no one should deceive you otherwise. If you find a woman who obeys you, who respects you, who even kneels before you, thank God.' As a last resort, some people would escape from the pressure of urban life and return to the rural areas.

References

1. Holle Gertner-Hedlund, recounting the experiences of Rose Mugula, 27, of Zambia in *Report from Swedish International Development Authority*, special issue on 'The Woman in the World', 1975, p. 19.
2. Carolyn J. Mathiasson (ed.), *Many Sisters: Women in Cross Cultural Perspective*, (Free Press, New York, 1974), p. xviii.
3. *Ibid.*
4. *Ibid.*
5. Denise Paulme (ed.), *Women in Tropical Africa* (Routledge and Kegan Paul, London, 1963), p. 6.
6. Louise Lamphere and Michelle Rosaldo, 'A Theoretical Overview' in L. Lamphere and M. Z. Rosaldo, *Woman, Culture and Society*, (Stanford University Press, Stanford, Calif., 1974), p. 21.
7. *Ibid.*
8. Marc J. Swartz, Victor W. Turner and Arthur Tuden (eds.), *Political Anthropology*, (Aldine, Chicago, 1966), pp. 4-5.
9. Robert O. Blood, and Donald M. Wolfe, *Husbands and Wives: The Dynamics of Married Living*, (The Free Press, Olencoe, Ill., 1960), pp. 11-12.
10. M.G. Smith, *Government in Zazau*, (Oxford University Press, London, 1960).
11. *Ibid.*
12. A.W. Southall, 'General Amin and the Coup: Great Man or Historical Inevitability', *The Journal of Modern African Studies*, Vol. 13, No. 1, 1975, p. 89.
13. A.I. Richards, 'The Changing Structure of a Ganda Village', *East*

African Studies No. 24, Kampala, 1966, p. 19.

14. Emma Goldman, 'The Traffic in Women' in *Anarchism and Other Essays*, (Mother Earth Publishing Association, New York, 1911), p. 184; *The Female State*, Vol. 4, 1972, p. 22.

15. Barri A. Wanji, 'The Nubi Community, An Islamic Social Structure in East Africa', Makerere University, Dept. of Sociology, Working Paper No. 115, 1971, p. 3.

16. *Ibid.*, p. 7.

17. David Parkin, *Neighbours and Nationals in an African City Ward*, (Routledge and Kegan Paul, London, 1969), p. 150; Kenneth Little, 'Voluntary Associations and Social Mobility Among West African Women', *Canadian Journal of African Studies*, Vol. 6, No. 2; Abner Cohen, *Custom and Politics in Urban Africa*, (Routledge and Kegan Paul, London, 1969).

18. Janet Bujra, 'Women Entrepreneurs of Early Nairobi', *Canadian Journal of African Studies*, Vol. 9, No. 2, p. 266.

19. *Ibid.*

20. Parkin, *op. cit.*

21. Nici Nelson, *Women Must Help Each Other: The Operation of Personal Networks Among Buzaa Beer Brewers in Mathare Valley, Kenya*, Ms., n.d.

22. A.W. Southall and P.C.W. Gutkind, 'Townsmen in the Making', *East African Studies, No. 9*, (Makerere Institute of Social Research), 1957, p. 138.

23. P. Meyer, *Townsmen and Tribesmen: Conservatism and the Process of Urbanisation in a South African City*, (Oxford University Press, London, 1961), p. 101.

24. J.C. Caldwell, *African Rural-Urban Migration: The Movement to Ghana's Towns*, (Australia National University Press, Canberra; C. Hurst and Company, London, 1969), pp. 129-30.

25. David Parkin, *Neighbours and Nationals in an African City Ward*, (University of California Press, Berkeley and Los Angeles, 1969), p. 63.

26. Hanna Papanek, 'Purdah: Separate Worlds and Symbolic Shelter', *Comparative Studies in Society and History*, 1973.

8. Occupations of Migrant Women

Braudel has observed that every town is first and foremost a market[1] where anything can be sold, and Mintz sees marketing systems in 'peasant' societies as major arenas of economic decision-making as well as mechanisms of social articulation.[2] Skinner takes peasant marketing behaviour to be embedded in economic and social systems that are larger than the local community.[3] In this chapter we examine urban women in the process of acquiring financial returns for the products of their labour, and show that market activities of one sort or another were the predominant source of their income.

Women migrated to increase their options and opportunities for self-improvement, even though the unskilled and unschooled had no illusions about their chances of obtaining wage employment in the urban areas. In the rural areas there were many stories about the difficulty of obtaining jobs. Occasionally I met optimistic individuals, usually school-leavers with seven years of education,in the rural areas, who had some hopes of finding urban employment. However, in most cases one week in town was enough for women to realize that they had to rely on their own initiative and skills to create employment for themselves.

Even for women who had migrated for non-economic reasons, economic factors became primary. Since 'everything in town costs money' survival in the urban areas depended upon some form of employment. Even in jobs requiring no great skills, the women found themselves competing with the men who regarded them as a threat. Men regarded towns as a man's world in which they earned wages by right. Female migrants who wanted to work in the towns were an anomaly. While some women spent up to six months trying to get jobs, sooner or later most women came to realize that their greatest assets were their hands and heads. They became engaged in self-employment, performing for money those activities which they had always performed in the rural areas as part of their domestic chores.[4] Often they had to engage in multiple activities to make ends meet.

The important point is this element of women's initiative. Compared to their rural existence, the women had not, for the most part, reduced their working hours but still they expressed positive feelings towards being self-employed. It was not so much the money they made but the fact that they controlled the fruits of their labour which counted.[5]

There were many occupations in Namuwongo and Wabigalo, too many to describe except for the ones in which a significant number of residents were engaged. There were only three women formally employed as workers in the sample: a sorter at a coffee curing plant, a seamstress at a shirt factory and a teacher at a church school. They earned 175, 150 and 300 shillings respectively. In the area generally, there were other women engaged in wage labour — receptionists, nurses, secretaries, newspaper reporters and telephone operators. The rest of the women were self-employed in jobs that required minimal training such as distilling, brewing, shopkeeping, hairdressing and dressmaking; or jobs that utilized already existing skills such as matmaking, cultivation, prostitution, and cooking food; and others such as verandah selling or renting out accommodation.

The women in the latter category belong to what researchers now refer to as the informal sector, which is distinguished from the formal wage-earning sector. These unskilled income earners, who are not defined as employees in official labour statistics, were first described in 1957 in a pioneering study by Southall and Gutkind, who argued, 'In Kisenyi these independent workers and their employees impart to the local community its predominant characteristic'.[6] This was also true of Namuwongo and Wabigalo, and in both instances the official statistics which concentrate solely on wage incomes can tell us little about what was really happening — for example, that the self-employed contributed significantly to public revenue through the licensing and taxation systems.

The self-employed in the informal sector are often illegally employed, either operating without trading licences or stretching and bending the laws a little. For example, the food sellers often operated without licences while officials turned a blind eye; there were those who were licensed to brew but distilled as well, or were distillers licenced to supply the government distilleries with a set amount of gin and who made three times as much selling 'under the bed'. It should also be pointed out, of course, that these illegal activities were being connived at by various government officials, without whose collusion the informal sector would have suffered. People like licensing officers made people pay for services rendered, and the law enforcement officials, for a 'small fee', could overlook illegal building construction or illegal brewing and distilling.

Informal sector activities have been characterized as 'small in scale, limited to simple technologies and little capital (but) economically efficient and profit making'.[7] The success of such ventures may be curtailed abruptly by calling on the law. For example, in 1974 when the Kampala traders in the main shopping areas complained that the informal sector operators were taking away their custom, the army and police engaged in a clearing operation, involving the confiscation of hawkers' merchandise, tailors' sewing machines at the bus station, and the burning of some successful open shack restaurants (*hoteli*) in Namuwongo and Wabigalo.[8]

The International Labour Office Report on Kenya has pointed out that the informal sector lacked links with the formal sector, particularly access to the

formal credit institutions and the main sources of transfer of foreign technology.[9] The report argued for official assistance to the informal sector.[10] But
it is my impression that government involvement in the informal sector would
create further hardship for those who engage in informal opportunities. The
informal sector participants created opportunities for themselves when they
failed to obtain jobs in industry or the government (the largest employer).
Despite legal obstacles, lack of achieved skills, or links with the right people
in important positions, the informal sector grew out of individual initiative.
Increasingly, there is evidence that in the underdeveloped countries most of
those in the informal sector are women.[11] It might be argued that the most
positive step the government could take would be to try to decrease the
difference between urban and rural earning opportunities, since it has been
shown that people are willing to stay in the rural areas if employment opportunities there are expanded.[12] That there is an informal sector at all is
indicative of the employment problems of the economy as a whole. While
the large number of people migrating to escape rural unemployment and
underemployment have created opportunities for earning money in the urban
areas, everyone else feels these people ought to return to their former
situation. This attitude displays an eagerness to cure the effects of asymmetrical development rather than the causes.

Unemployed, Married and 'Kept' Women

At first sight Table 9 seems to confirm the popular suspicion that most female
migrants are indeed unemployed. But this 'unemployment' figure included
women who traded irregularly on the verandah, wives or salaried men who
made mats or practised hairdressing, Luo and Luyia rural homemakers and
managers who sold some millet and groundnuts for a few months a year
while visiting their husbands in the towns, and wives or mistresses of salaried
or self-employed men who gave enough money to provide them with subsistence and even luxury.

This category of 'kept women' needs elaboration because they are the
objects of statements like 'women exchange a life of drudgery in the rural
areas for a life of leisure', or 'urban women are a liability'[13] because they are
non-producing consumers. These women dressed well, ate well, lived in well-
furnished rooms and at weekends were often taken to city bars, night clubs
and cinemas. Some of the women had come to the city upon marriage, others
were educated but regretted not having had some professional training such
as typing or teaching. These women seemed to enjoy being married or 'kept',
both using the title 'Mrs.', and believing themselves to be following the
model of elite women's life styles.

But the unemployed 'kept women' were despised (and envied as well!)
by other women in Namuwongo and Wabigalo, though there was also some
genuine concern for women who depended entirely on their husbands'
incomes. Certainly men were able to control women by giving or denying

Table 9
Occupational Activities of Female Migrants

Occupation	Kakwa	Lango	Acholi	Nubi	Teso	Nyole	Gisu	Ziba	Nyamwezi	Chagga	Kikuyu	Kamba	Luyia	Toro	Ankole	Ruandans	Rundi	Kiga	Luo	Ganda	Soga	Total
Unemployed	1		1							1	1	1	7		1	7		2	27	5		54
Distillers		2				1							1	1				2	4	7		18
Brewers			1													3	1		5	8		18
Teachers																				1		1
Verandah selling																		1	1	2		4
Prostitutes							1	1											1	5		8
Barmaids							2								1					3	1	7
House-owners			2	1											1					5		9
Shopkeepers											1					3			4	3		11
Dressmakers													1			1			1	1		4
Cooked food sellers	1		1												2	2		1		5		12
Cultivators																1				7		8
Market traders										1			1						4			6
Coffee sorters							1															1
Factory workers				1																		1
Matmakers			2																			2
Total	2	2	3	4	2	1	3	1	1	1	2	1	10	2	4	18	1	6	47	52	1	164

them money, and women who made demands or complained about money spent on drink or other women were likely to find themselves with a black eye. Most women took all this without a murmur.

However, some of the women in this category did have economic activities of their own, which they performed while the husbands were away at work and therefore unaware of them. Discovery of such activities usually resulted in sudden complaints of 'bad business'. One Chagga woman, my next-door neighbour, was making as much as 200 shilling a month from selling food, but to her husband and his friends she only admitted to earning 10 shillings. Even so, this seemed enough to upset the normal order of things in which her job was to look after his house and their two children instead of hanging around with 'money-hungry town women'. He claimed that his salary of 600 shillings a month was sufficient to keep the family but she was saving up for a secretarial course, and said, 'Once I am able to earn, I will not be dependent on him.' Thus, not all dependent women intended to stay that way.

Bars, Brewing and Distilling

Brewing was the commonest occupation of those in the sample, which is
not surprising since drinking was a popular recreational activity attracting
outsiders nearly every evening as well as the local people at the weekend.
The licensing rules distinguished three types of bars: bottled and unbottled
liquor bars and Native Beer bars.

Bottled Liquor Bars

The highly and moderately successful bars in this category were owned by
men who had been in town for a long time. The bars represented substantial
investments, with about 150 shillings a month needed for the salaries of three
or four barmaids, between 200 and 400 shillings to stock up every month, and
about 800 shillings to furnish the bar with counters, chairs, tables, pictures
and glassware. Bar licences cost 300 shillings under the 1964 Liquor Act, and
a liquor licence cost an additional 900 shillings.

Needless to say, there was a high casualty rate in this business and the
successful owners needed a good accounting system. Prices were usually
posted on the wall and the bar owners handled all the cash themselves or
occasionally left trusted barmaids in charge for a few minutes. These bottled
liquor bar owners made monthly net incomes averaging 400 to 1,000 shillings.
They lived in big houses whose large front rooms were the bars, but which
also had more comfortably furnished rooms at the back for the better clientele.
The stock of drinks was geared towards a clientele that demanded imported
liquor such as Cinzano, Black Label and other whiskies, or good locally
refined liquor like *waragi* (gin). Although a handful of local people regularly
went to these bars to drink beer, Guinness, and soft drinks such as Fanta,
Sprite, Pepsi Cola, etc, the bars depended for survival on elite men and their
sophisticated women from outside the area. These bars offered hideaways
for the businessmen, executives, and politicians, who wished to entertain
their girlfriends discreetly after work. Despite the number of such discreet
bars and the men's habit of circulating among them, in a small country
like Uganda it was difficult for the elites to achieve the anonymity they
sought, although they did at least avoid the confrontations which might
have occurred in the prestigious bars in the city centre frequented by their
wives.

For local and nearby customers, the most popular drinking days were
at the middle and end of the month, corresponding to the fortnightly pay
days of the lower-scale employees. Some of the clients were Muslims from
the neighbouring Kibuli area, who wanted to keep their drinking a secret
because Islamic law prohibits drinking. Groups of men patronized particular
bars and bought drinks in rotation, so that whether or not one of them had
any money at a given time, he was still expected to show up at the bar. Men
who worked together usually drank together because as one said, 'We find a
lot to talk about and we know when we have money.' But, more important,
drinking together seemed a solution to the fact that these bars did not permit

drinks on credit. The bar owners claimed that people were always moving
house, or simply objected to paying their debts.

Unbottled Liquor Bars

These bars sold *enguli* (unrefined local gin), bottled soft drinks, beer and
chibuku (a thick, sweet, creamy drink made from maize and imported from
Zambia in lorry tankers). A licence costing 300 shillings a year was required
to run such a bar, and although there were many men and women licensed
to sell *enguli*, there were also many more 'under the bed' sellers. There were
six *chibuku* bars: two of them owned by local women and four by two
businessmen and two civil servants who did not live in the area, and who
were reluctant to talk about the money they made. In fact, their businesses
were running at a loss but they still continued to operate, and the secret
lay in the fact that they obtained the licences at half the normal price and
had found ways to avoid custom duties on imported liquor. It was easy to
get away with a lot of other things as well, for example, inadequate furnishings
and lack of washing facilities for drinking containers.

However, the *chibuku* bars were popular because the ones owned by men
had juke boxes (bought second-hand from the city bars) which provided music
for dancing. Even though the bars allowed credit on *chibuku*, already only 30
cents a pint, even this did not seem to make this drink popular; *chibuku* bars
were only a cover for the sale of illegal gin, particularly in the two bars
owned by women.

Barmaids

Although these two kinds of bars were mainly owned by men, the employees
were all women. Men enjoyed hanging around bottled liquor bars because the
girls were ever so polite. They sometimes knelt when serving drinks and
listened to customers' problems. The majority of barmaids were school-
leavers who looked for jobs in the formal sector during the day and worked
in the bars during the afternoon and evening. The job was something to tide
them over until they found a job that justified their having been to school.
Six girls from the area did acquire jobs as telephone operators, typists and
receptionists, but the majority were not so lucky. There were also some
newly acquired illiterate women who had come directly to the city and were
naive about urban employment opportunities. They, too, said the bars were
good places for earning money or finding husbands, or both. These women
usually knelt before men because this was a sign of politeness in Buganda,
particularly in the rural areas.

Whether they worked in bars where the business was intermittent or in
the exclusive bars with a regular and lucrative clientele, barmaids were
always underpaid. They got 25 to 30 shillings a month, just enough to rent
a small room. The inadequate salaries were usually supplemented by brewing
and selling pineapple beer or banana beer. The advantage was that these
types of beer required little investment and minimal attention, and could
mean an extra 60 shillings a month in income. Still this was not enough if a

woman had children. So some barmaids fried spiced banana bread (*kabalagala*) and simsim balls and groundnuts which they sold on verandahs, either their own or those of shops. Namuwongo-Wabigalo children loved such snacks, and such business usually fetched about 80 shillings a month. However, their income was still less than 200 shillings, the minimum one could live on. Some barmaids further supplemented their incomes by acquiring lovers who would help them pay for food, rent, hospital bills and clothing. In six cases I knew of outside the sample, the women had 'rich' boyfriends, usually referring to them by pseudonyms.

Women employed in the *chibuku* bars earned 50 shillings, slightly more than other barmaids. But this was still not enough to provide for minimum food, housing and clothing requirements. The *chibuku* bar girls were notorious for the lack of subtlety in their relationships with men, and were regarded as prostitutes by nearly everyone in the area. However, they did not seem to mind, for 'if there are men who have enough money to throw around, why should I not take it.'

The barmaids working in *chibuku* bars owned by non-residents or in the less respectable bottled beer bars usually sold other beers they had brewed themselves. But this was risky because, if discovered (usually through a disgruntled customer or jealous barmaid), the culprit inevitably lost her job.

Native Beer Bars

To brew native beers also required a licence costing 100 shillings, but to sell the beer in bars meant additional licences costing 160 shillings. Most houseowners were building bars for their tenants consisting of corrugated iron or papyrus roofs, with open walls. The tenants who wished to make use of the facilities to sell beer paid an extra 10 to 25 shillings a month, while nontenants were charged a monthly fee of 40 shillings. Some women had worked out an ingenious way of co-operating. Each woman brought her beer and sold it, but claimed that she was hired to work for the woman who had paid the rental fee.

Beer brewing was usually a one-woman operation, the size of her capital determining the type of beer and the income indicating how hard a particular individual worked.

Pineapple beer (*munanansi*) was generally brewed by people with very little capital, perhaps 20 shillings. With only 15 shillings needed to purchase saucepans, cheese cloth for straining, pineapples, sugar and tea leaves, women could get started. The supplies had to be purchased every month, and their average income was 50 shillings a month. Some brewers produced only two gallons, others as much as eight. Thus through hard work and care to produce better tasting beer, some women could make it a profitable venture. However, in the area pineapple beer was regarded as a business for only new arrivals or barmaids. Almost half of the 53 Ganda respondents said that their first occupation had been pineapple beer brewing and selling.

Kwete was beer made from roasted maize or cassava flour, often sold in open air bars for 60 cents a pint, measured by glass, tin cup or aluminium bowl. With an investment of about 50 shillings, brewers could make between 50 and 200 shillings a month, depending again on how hard they worked. *Mwenge* is *kiganda* beer made by mashing together particular bananas (*mbidde* or *kisubi*) and a special grass (*lusenke*) or banana leaves. The resulting sweet juice (*mubisi*) is preferred by non-drinkers. Fermentation or 'souring' can be prevented by boiling the juice for about an hour, and then storing it in tightly closed bottles for several months or even a year.

Competition existed between migrant and non-migrant brewers. Migrant brewers made their beer from banana skins which they purchased from the cooked food sellers and restaurant owners at 50 cents a tin, and they usually made 21 shillings from beer brewed with five shillings worth of skin. Non-migrant brewers were cultivators who had a steady supply of their own bananas which they grew or bought cheaply from 20 cents to two shillings a bunch from their neighbours. For them, five shillings worth of bananas yielded at least 200 shillings worth of beer. Although the standard price for a pint of beer was 60 cents, the price for large quantities above three gallons varied according to individual brewers. Some sold a four gallon tin of beer for between 15 and 20 shillings. Others would sell a calabash (*kita*) containing 12 gallons of beer at 35 shillings to Namuwongo-Wabigalo people, but 65 shillings to outsiders. Smaller three gallon calabashes cost 10 shillings, or 25, depending again on whether the purchaser looked prosperous or 'ignorant' — in other words, an outsider.

One of the reasons for the success of the banana beer business was an upsurge of traditional Ganda religious activities throughout the city of Kampala and its suburbs.[14] Diviners demanded that clients bring beer which was the customary present for the medium before consultation. Another stimulus for banana beer was the fact that the government distilleries bought gin from distillers for purification. Although people were required to have licences allowing them to distil, gin made from bananas was so special and popular nationally because of its flavour that illegal distillers openly sold their unrefined gin to the distillery without difficulty. The brewers claimed that if they sold gin to the distilleries they made 50 shillings more than if they sold beer.[15]

There were six millet beer (*malwa, kong'o*) bars in the area, including the 'Club', and each had regular customers drinking in groups. Millet beer drinking in the urban areas was just as much a social acitivity as it was in the country-side.

The Acholi and Luo women had the reputation of making the best *malwa*. This is hardly surprising: it is a skill migrant women from millet growing areas would have mastered. Once the beer had been served, the job of the brewers was to constantly add hot water to the beer pots and bring more beer when the original became too diluted. After the drinking was over, they cleaned the pots and straws. The dregs were fed to the chickens to 'fatten them up to lay more eggs'.

The 'Club' belonged to a rich entrepreneur who in 1972 had built the largest open air bar which was used by the *Malwa* Drinkers Association. The 'club' licence cost him 40 shillings. The Association consisted of 20 Luo women who brewed millet beer on a weekly basis. Each woman paid a monthly membership fee of 30 shillings which enabled her to brew and sell on the premises. Once, when the City Council Law Enforcement Unit raided the 'Club' for alleged licensing violations, the owner managed to convince them that the customers who were drinking were the club members and that the brewers were their wives who regularly contributed beer. Initially each brewer realized net incomes of 150 shillings a month, but after five months these rose to as much as 250 shillings, which was what other successful brewers in the area made. It is likely that the 'Club' women would have made less if they had operated individually at their houses or at other open air bars.

Distillers

Brewing is closely connected to another economic activity, distilling. Any beer that goes 'bad' can be distilled, as can anything that ferments. For example, sugar cane and honey beer were distilled into gin by Kikuyu and Ruandan women respectively. In fact, successful brewers usually became distillers. The gin that was distilled in the area and other parts of Buganda was referred to as *enguli*. Elsewhere in Ugandan and East African small urban areas it was known as Nubian gin because it allegedly was first brewed by the Nubi. Gin distilled from maize flour was most popular because of its strength and lack of hangover. It was in great demand locally, and in other suburbs like Kisenyi, Mulago, Kamwokya, Kireka and Kibuli. This gin was popularly known as the 'Kisumu brand' or 'Namuwongo brand', since it was first brewed by the Luo living in the Namuwongo area most of whom were presumed to have migrated from Kisumu, the largest town in Luoland (Nyanza Province, Kenya). It was more expensive than the other brands: an eight ounce glass cost one shilling, as opposed to sixty cents.

Since distilling involves a substantial initial investment of over 200 shillings, it was thus a reflection of the distiller's economic success. To produce four gallons of gin one needs 20 kilos of maize flour, 10 gallons of water, 20 kilos of sugar, several saucepans, four faggots of firewood, two empty oil drums, and copper pipes half an inch in diameter and 7 to 12 feet long.

It was illegal to distil without a licence to sell it to the East African Distilleries for purification and eventually to be sold as *Uganda Waragi*. Twenty or so distillers of banana gin illegally supplied the E.A. Distilleries, but all of the 34 distillers in the area were illegal anyway. In fact, so widespread was illicit distilling that by 1972 the Uganda Amalgamated Brewers and Distillers petitioned the government to crack down on illegal brewing, claiming that although they were the licensed distillers, they had difficulty keeping up standards because the business was flooded with less meticulous illegal distillers. They also claimed that a number of deaths had resulted from the illegal gin because of its high 'crudity and acidity,'[16] a euphemistic way of describing wood alcohol. While the officials were not aware that the licensed distillers often produced twice the authorized amount, and sold the excess gin illegally, resentment was directed towards the unlicensed distillers who were a threat to this illicit market.

The various illegalities involved exposed distillers to all sorts of blackmail, and made them suspicious of strangers who came into the area because they were constantly having to pay bribes of 200 to 500 shillings to people who claimed to be City Council officials. The problem of unauthorized persons posing as City Council staff had become so widespread that in 1972 the acting Town Clerk found it necessary to issue a series of notices in newspapers and on radio warning the public in Kampala to beware of bogus City Council officials.

Excuses for not having a licence ranged from claims that applications had been caught in the two year licence processing backlog at the City Council which could be speeded up only with the right connections, to the fact that they lacked the money to pay off the officials. The only licences issued for Namuwongo belonged to two women who came in every morning from the suburbs of Makindye and Kibuye, 5 or 6 miles away.

Namuwongo, situated in the valley, was much more important for distilling than Wabigalo on the slopes of Kisugu hill. The neighbouring swamps, poor state of the roads, superior technology for distilling and the attitudes and activities of chiefs made Namuwongo an attractive area for local distillers.

For a long time the area had been inaccessible by car because the roads were badly potholed and rarely repaired. During the research period the roads were better taken care of than previously and Police and City Council patrols in the area were quick to deal with tax absconders, thieves and illegal brewers and distillers. The distillers were the most vulnerable, but they could acquire the patronage of the chief by paying him 25 shillings every month. However, the situation could become complicated when all four sub-chiefs, in addition to the ward chief, demanded payment from one distiller. Although the sub-chiefs settled disputes, arrested thieves, appeared in court, collected taxes and generally ensured that municipal regulations were observed, they were not paid officials. Bribes secured from illegal distillers and builders, etc. were their main sources of income. In 1973 the reorganization of the Local Administration framework included, among other things, salaries for the sub-chiefs, in the hope that with assured incomes chiefs would carry out their duties more efficiently.[17] But this did not change the patronage system. Even in 1974 the chiefs were still protecting illegal brewers by warning them when there was to be a raid or, if the raid was unexpected, diverting the patrol party from sites where their clients distilled. Consequently, most of the gin trade was 'in the bush' or 'under the bed' where it could be hidden without much fuss if a City Council official was sighted.

The difference between success and failure depended upon the size of the distiller's market, the frequency of distilling and type of ingredients used. A successful business required distilling every day, at least 40 gallons. In six cases a group of women formed work co-operatives to distil and market the gin. They took turns fetching water, obtaining firewood, attending the fires

and the distillery. The nucleus of such associations was usually a very successful woman who had built up her business by working alone and later employing men to do all the odd jobs. The monthly net profit of a successful distiller
reached 700 shillings or more.

As distilling was a hazardous operation, this description would be incom-
plete without the mention of technology. The method of gluing saucepans
on top of drums was considered too slow for large quantities and frequent
distilling. It was tiresome to change the cooling water every 10 to 20 minutes.
The new technology using pipes and Namuwongo swamps as condensers was
an improvement. Copper pipes 7 to 12 feet long and one-half inch in diameter
were connected to the drum at one end and at the other to the vapour
connector. The middle part of the pipes was placed in water-filled ditches or
streams. Some parts of the swamps were cleared by Acholi boys who grew
sugarcane to sell in the city where a large demand existed. The papyrus and
sugarcane plants usually grew very tall and thus prevented spirals of smoke
from betraying the distillers to the authorities. The life of a distilling drum
was less than four months, and if used for longer was liable to burst and
cause serious burns to the distillers. One retired doctor who lived at Kisugu
told me that he suspected that 80 per cent of all the people admitted to
Mulago Hospital with severe burns were victims of burst drums.

The brewing and distilling industries generated other secondary businesses.
For example, there were special shops downtown that specialized in oil
drums, copper pipes and crude sugar. Locally, the survival or failure of most
shops was directly related to their volume of maize trade. Firewood sellers
and water carriers also benefited from the liquor business, as did pig and
chicken raisers.

Services, Selling and Trading

Gin drinkers claimed that roasted pork cooled their throats and prevented
the gin from scorching their stomachs. Pig raising was a speciality of the Kasanvu
area of Namuwongo which was a Ruandan colony. The pigs required little care
except for shelter at night. They roamed around scavenging on vegetable and
human waste, which performed a useful cleaning service since the city garbage
collectors sometimes came only once a fortnight and the area had poor latrine
facilities. The pigs were regarded as disgusting by most residents, the Muslims
for religious reasons and the rest for sanitary reasons. One Christian Luo non-
drinker told me what he had observed: 'By the time people start asking for
meat they are already very drunk and they don't seem to care about what
they eat. A few weeks ago, two men brought a case before the chief. They
claimed that a named man had made them eat dog's meat during the evening,
but by next morning everyone was calling them dog eaters. They received
100 shillings from the defendant and changed their drinking place.' The same
informant quickly pointed out that the people who frowned upon 'pig eaters'
did not hesitate to eat the chickens which fed on the same waste materials.

Firewood and Charcoal Sellers

Long-time residents could remember the time, in the 1950s, when a few
Acholi women and teenage Luo girls supplied most of the firewood needed
for making millet beer and distilling. By 1972, while the Acholi women
continued to engage in the business, the great demand for wood had attracted
outside entrepreneurs. Firewood was delivered by about 10 lorries to different
agents in the area once a week. Each lorry carried a load of about 100 large
faggots. The price per faggot varied from two to four shillings depending on
the size of the bundle.

Individual firewood sellers depended upon the nearby forest reserves,
where every six months the trees were pruned and the cuttings sold off.
Because builders always acquired the largest share of wood, firewood sellers
had to resort to poaching in order to make a reasonable income from firewood.
Forest rangers never arrested anyone but they were always threatening to
do so.

In the rainy season the nearby forest became swampy and impenetrable,
forcing the women to look for firewood in more distant places. Their favourite
spot was Namanve Forest on Jinja Road which at eight miles from Namuwongo-
Wabigalo was 'within easy walking distance'. The women firewood sellers
preferred medium-sized sticks about one or two inches in diameter, but the
distillers preferred large pieces of chopped wood. Having located a log, the
women immediately set to work, sometimes taking a week to chop a large
log. The chopped wood was tied in bundles of 50 to 100 pounds, which, if
wet, weighed much more. Increasingly, the women were hiring pick-up trucks
to transport the wood, but a few women still could be seen balancing heavy
faggots on their heads and carrying sleeping babies on their backs. Not
surprisingly, the firewood sellers had the reputation of being tough and they
admitted themselves that firewood collecting was really as back-breaking as
digging. But as one woman put it, 'What a poor person does out of necessity
is termed strength by onlookers.' Firewood sellers usually gave up this
occupation in the end and tended to become millet beer (*malwa*) brewers and
sellers.

Firewood was not really important for cooking since every household
owned one or two charcoal stoves (*si giri*), and did most of their cooking
outdoors partly because of lack of kitchen facilities and partly for social
reasons. For women who worked all day, the only time they had to catch
up on local news and share their various experiences was when they were
preparing dinner. The popularity of charcoal as the major source of fuel was
to some extent due to its being regarded as an urban phenomenon. As one
woman put it, 'In the town we do not have to kneel before three stones
while cooking, or weep from the smoke of firewood.' Charcoal was delivered
daily to stores in Namuwongo and Wabigalo by lorries carrying between 65
and 70 charcoal sacks. One sack consisted of six tins (*malebe*) of charcoal.
The store owners bought the sack for eight shillings and divided it into tins
which sold for two shillings each, thus making a 50 per cent profit on every
sack.

Besides the stores, women also sold charcoal on the verandahs of their rooms. This was delivered on bicycles by Ruandans and Luo who peddled it from rural areas as far as 20 miles away. The verandah charcoal trade flourished because it was flexible, allowing people to buy small amounts of charcoal if they did not have money to buy a tin or time to go to the market or stores. At the same time they could also buy tomatoes and onions, or a few bananas. However, most of the verandah traders were losing their charcoal businesses to a multi-ethnic group of 35 teenage boys who delivered charcoal direct on bicycles or wheelbarrows, and charged a uniform price, unlike the verandah sellers.

Cooked Food Sellers

Selling cooked food was one of the activities popular with new arrivals at Namuwongo and Wabigalo, as 50 shillings savings or credit from a friend was enough to launch the business right away. Many women in the area had sold cooked food at one time. The women focused on the industrial area with its labourers and office clerks but still could not supply the demands of all the workers by themselves.

Most women could reconnoitre an area first, making arrangements with a group of workers for particular kinds of dishes. Other women just appeared at places and, if the workers liked the food, they would come again. As for the type of food a particular woman supplied, this would in most cases reflect the staple diet or ethnic cooking of the vendor. For example, Ganda women supplied bananas, sweet potatoes, groundnuts and spinach sauce. The Nubi sold fried flat bread (*chapatis*) and triangular breads (*samosas*) stuffed with curried vegetables or mincemeat. Ruandan, Acholi, Lugbara and Kakwa women supplied cassava, potatoes, beans and fish; while the Luo concentrated on supplying roasted and cooked maize.

Most food sellers bought their supplies every two or three days from suppliers outside the big retail markets at Nakivubo and Katwe, thus paying, I would estimate, 25 per cent less than inside the market. They would have to get there before 6.30 a.m. and be prepared to bargain but, as Table 10 shows, quite a number of Kampala traders conducted their business this way. This did present the problem of getting large quantities of food back to Namuwongo and Wabigalo, and the women would either club together and hire a pickup truck for 10 or 15 shillings or go individually, using a combination of wheelbarrow boys and taxi. One way or the other, each round trip to market cost at least 5 shillings. Some Ruandan, Acholi and Luo women would carry the food supplies balanced on their heads all the way to Wabigalo. The 'almost trot' which this necessitates was referred to as a 'Luo walk' because the Luo women's calf-length dresses permitted a faster movement than the ankle-length wraps of the Ganda and other women.

Arriving home by 9 or 10 a.m. the woman would set about the day's business — preparing the food, cleaning the house (while she drank her morning tea) and fetching water, a laborious business if one could not get back from market before the queue had formed. The cooking was done

Table 10
Traders Transacting Business Outside Official Market Places

Name of Market	Traders Outside Official Market Place
Nakasero*	569
Bwaise*	39
Kibuye and Katwe area*	128
Bakuli (incl. Old Kampala)	74
Mulago	18
Kiswa	4
Mengo (Namirembe)	6
Nakawa	40
Nakulabye	52
Wandegeya	85
Others	200
Total	*1,215*

*Markets where Namuwongo and Wabigalo residents shopped.
Source: J.J. Oloya and T.T. Poleman, *The Food Supply of Kampala*, (Makerere Institute of Social Research, Kampala, 1972), p. 42.

outside which was much safer from the point of view of starting fires but more dangerous for children playing roundabout.

Having fed the children and transferred the food into suitable receptacles, the woman would set off for her destination, getting there by 12:30 or 1 p.m. in time for the 30-minute lunch breaks. Plates were scarce and customers would sometimes bring their own. Food was sold for cash only, at prices determined by the vendors.

The prices depended upon the food served and the vendors. A plateful of bananas (*matooke*) or two large sweet potatoes served with meat sauce (consisting of four 2-inch pieces of meat), or chicken sauce with an 8 ounce piece of chicken, or fish sauce with a 2 inch slice of fish cost between 2 and 2½ shillings. However, bananas or sweet potatoes served with beans, greens and groundnut sauce cost only 1½ shillings a plate. Cassava mixed with beans (*katogo* or *nyoyo*) cost the same but plain cassava with salt cost as little as one shilling a plate. The cost of *chapati* varied according to the width: 9, 7, 6 and 5 inches cost 100, 70, 50 or 30 cents respectively. *Samosas* stuffed with cowpeas and Irish potatoes cost 10 or 20 cents; those stuffed with mince-meat, garlic and herbs cost 60 to 80 cents. Four thin slices of fried cassava cost 10 cents. The price variations depended on size and popularity of the particular vendor's food. If the clients felt they were being overcharged or that the vendor did not maintain some minimum standards of cleanliness, they would just abandon her for another vendor.

Food sellers made monthly net profits of between 50 and 300 shillings.

Like most Namuwongo businesses, success depended upon hard work. Although the food business did not appear competitive because there were more workers than the women could feed, some women constantly expanded their market while others did not and even lost customers.

In 1970 a Food Sellers Association was formed by seven Wabigalo women including Ganda, Nyoro, Toro and Nkole, who had been co-operating for two years. The Association had a three-fold aim: to try and secure trade licences for members, to request managers to allow them to sell food in the firms' or factories' premises, and finally to give financial help to members. A yearly subscription of 15 shillings was to be paid by all members. The Association lasted only six months, when the members realized that food could be sold without a licence or capital loan, and that demand was such that if the sellers were refused entry into work premises the workers would simply come and buy food on the pavement.

The City Council licensing and law enforcement officers were aware that none of the women food sellers had the necessary 30 shillings hawker's licence but, as the licensing officer told me, they had decided to close their eyes to the practice, first of all because the women were servicing government employees including the law enforcers themselves. Secondly, unlike the snack vendors selling roasted groundnuts, and maize and fried bread (*mandazi*) who would often establish themselves for long periods on the pavements or corners of buildings or under the trees, the women usually came at specific times, sold their food, and left. The women were also careful to pick up the banana leaves or papers they may have brought with them, unlike the roast maize and cassava sellers who placed their charcoal stoves in strategic positions and produced a general aura of husks, peelings, and smoke which was regarded as a blemish on Uganda's image in the eyes of the tourists who often had a full view of these traders even from their hotel rooms. As a consequence, the women food sellers were left alone while snack and soft drink vendors were frequently prosecuted for littering the city and trading in the wrong places.

In the Namuwongo-Wabigalo area, there were six licensed eating houses, known in Uganda as *hoteli*, which could seat as many as 15 people. These *hoteli* were usually two papyrus curtain shaded rooms, furnished with long tables with benches on either side. Some of the furniture was old and creaky but no one seemed to mind. The *hoteli* business had been male-dominated until May 1972 when three women opened a restaurant at a strategic point situated 300 yards from the nearest 'go-downs' and the terminal for Namu-wongo taxis. There was a constant flow of people who stopped in to eat from 10:30 a.m. to about 10 p.m. in the evening. They were an instant success because customers claimed that they prepared excellent sauces to go with their main dishes.

These Namuwongo restaurants were patronized by white collar workers (although they were not always willing to tell their colleagues where they ate) and ordinary labourers who claimed that they preferred the *hotelis* because they could 'get water to wash the hands and face'. It should be added that Namuwongo and Wabigalo *hotelis* served only food, sauce and water whereas the other *hotelis* in Uganda served tea (black and white), milk, sliced bread (buttered and unbuttered), small cakes and various snacks of fried and stuffed breads.

It was commonly known that fish and meat were cheap in the evenings. Most sellers preferred to get rid of them before they 'went bad'. Housewives would buy some, but the bulk was taken by *hoteli* owners. Toward the end of my fieldwork, I noticed that even cheaper food became available at the markets around sunset everyday, and this affected the *hotelis* who were losing most of their evening customers to traders in the market who had started frying fish or meat and serving them with cooked food. In other words, some market traders were functioning as *hoteliers* as well. There was a disparaging joke in Namuwongo and Wabigalo that people who lived on *hoteli* food looked healthier than most people who subsisted on the usual carbohydrates, and this was in fact supported by my calculations on food expenditures for Namuwongo and Wabigalo in 1972. Fifty per cent of the total income spent on food went on starch staples. This can be compared with figures for Kampala as a whole between 1950 and 1964 as Table 11 shows.

Table 11
Food Expenditure Patterns, Kampala

Date of Survey	Total Expenditure per Household	% Spent on Food	Expenditure on Starchy Staples as % of Total Food Expenditure			
			Maize Flour	Matoke	Cassava	Bread
Sept. 1950	41.34	57.3	2.7	15.8	11.7	2.2
Sept. 1951	38.41	61.8	4.5	17.4	14.7	4.1
Sept. 1952	43.50	64.9	5.5	24.2	9.7	3.7
Sept. 1953	55.13	64.9	22.6	8.9	6.3	3.6
Feb. 1957	77.39	58.3	15.0	21.1	2.3	2.3
Feb. 1964	158.17	50.1	12.6	17.0	1.0	2.6

Source: Oloya and Poleman, op. cit, p. 17.

Market Trading

Trading in foodstuffs was a common activity amongst women in Namuwongo and Wabigalo. Although there were three markets in the area, at every third house something was being sold in small quantities. This I have called 'verandah trading' and I recorded monthly incomes of 30 to 200 shillings. Most residents, however, preferred to buy their food at the markets where they got 'a fair price' (compared to other parts of the city). Food in Namuwongo and Wabigalo was cheaper by about 30 cents or more partly due to the fact that the women obtained the foodstuffs directly from the growers, and partly because most local residents would rather live on maize porridge (*posho*) and dried beans than pay excessive prices.

The three markets in the area served noticeably different ethnic groups corresponding to the ethnic affiliations of the predominant traders. This practice was justified with elaborate rationalizations. The Ganda who patronized the Kisugu market claimed that the other two had dubious sanitary standards. The Namuwongo market was said to 'be full of flies and Luo women who spat everywhere'. The Wabigalo market was suspect because of an old story: the Toro and Nyoro had started a meat and fish market in the village during the 1920s, but the Ganda Muslims who lived in nearby Kibuli were disdainful of buying meat from uncircumcized Christians and non-Christians, and as the market expanded they 'discovered' that the 'foreigners who were trading handled the meat with dirty hands (*bigalo*)'. The market and later the whole neighbourhood where these foreigners lived came to be known as Wabigalo (place of dirty hands). Even with the multi-ethnic composition of the area in 1972, some Ganda still regarded the Wabigalo market with disgust (*kwenyinyala*) unless, of course, they knew a Ganda trader there. On the other hand, the people from Western Uganda – the Toro, Nyoro, Nkole and Kiga – claimed that they preferred Wabigalo market to Kisugu market because things there were cheaper. They claimed that the Ganda traders always tried to cheat them by overcharging or selling old potatoes or cassava (*biwutta*) and stale fish. If they went to Kisugu market they said they avoided Ganda traders, but bought from any others. The Luo also claimed that the Ganda traders overcharged them. Those who lived in Wabigalo would walk the two and a half miles or so to visit the Namuwongo market every three days ostensibly to obtain a special cabbage spinach known as *sukuma wiiki* (Swahili for 'push the week' implying that even when people have no money to buy meat or fish, they can subsist satisfactorily on this spinach). The Luo claimed to have popularized it in the Kenyan cities of Mombasa and Nairobi.

There might have been some truth in the reasons people gave for frequenting particular markets. However, the markets also seemed to be the primary sites of various communication networks, filling in the news individuals failed to get while conversing with neighbours or acquaintances in other places such as the water taps. The Luo particularly were known to have an efficient system of communication through gossip. Just as Luo men gossiped at the *malwa* bars, the Luo women gossiped at the markets. As one man told me, 'It takes my wife three hours to buy three tomatoes.'

There were 30 market traders in the research area, 18 of whom were women making monthly profits of between 80 and 300 shillings. In the Namuwongo market, nine Luo couples worked together but by the end of 1972 four Luo women had their own market stalls. The men said they were flabbergasted, but the women said that it was about time.

In order to protect their businesses, market traders scared away anyone who tried to establish a new stall. At the Namuwongo market a newly arrived Luyia woman found a skinned rat on her stall, and accused the Luo women of trying to use sorcery on her. She was so scared that she abandoned market trading and became a *kwete* brewer. After a few months she claimed that Ganda women were putting salt in her brew and thus sabotaging her business. Essentially what was required before doing any trade in Namuwongo and

Wabigalo was to befriend the existing traders and extract their blessing before joining them. At the Kisugu market, a Ganda fish trader found the head of a fish put in the middle of her stall, and medicines and one-cent coins sprinkled all around it. She left the area. Gutkind has reported similar threats among traders at Mulago.[18]

Shopkeeping and House-owning

Shopkeeping and house-owning were regarded by Namuwongo and Wabigalo residents as a sign of arrival at the top of the economic ladder. They represented reward for hard work, shrewdness and saving money. There were 20 female shopkeepers in the area and almost half of them were in their late 30s or early 40s. One Ganda woman had obtained her shop by inheriting it; another had a rich boyfriend. Of the remaining 10 Ganda women who were shopkeepers, three had pinched money over the years from their husbands; three had previously had successful *enguli* businesses and the shops were the result of their savings; three had influential lovers who gave them financial backing; and one had been accused of witchcraft in the village and her husband had sent her away with all the things in his shop.

There were houses in the area specially built for shops, consisting of a family room in the back and a double doored front room that served as a shop, and was usually rented out for 140 shillings. One such shop was stocked with small bags of wheat flour, a four gallon tin of cooking oil, matches, cigarettes, bathing and washing soap, a small bag of beans, dried tobacco, mugs, bread, buns, pancakes, milk, sugar and soft drinks. All this represented 250 shillings of investment, but Lusi, the owner, enjoyed telling her friends that business was bad. However, while her neighbours stocked up only once a month, she stocked up every week. Any doubts that I had about the success of Lusi's businesses vanished when I discovered that she also owned four old mud and wattle grass thatch-roofed houses with two or three rooms. She rented each room for 20 shillings, making 280 shillings overall in a month. She also had built a four-roomed house of brick with a corrugated iron roof, from which she made another 400 shillings a month (not a great deal compared to the 1,000 shillings other houseowners were making).

The shop next door was one of the few businesses that specialized in selling maize flour and sugar. Maize flour was the main food for most Namuwongo-Wabigalo residents. It took only 15 minutes to prepare the thick maize porridge (*posho*), a task which even single men could undertake without much trouble. In addition, maize flour was cheap and easy to store. A single tin of maize flour would feed a family of four for a week, whereas one tin of sweet potatoes or a bunch of bananas would last only two days. So it was much cheaper to live on *posho* than on bananas or potatoes.

The second reason that made maize flour profitable for shopkeepers was the fact that it was an important ingredient in the distilling of gin. As we have seen earlier, Namuwongo was one of the most important areas in the city for gin production.

Lusi had built up a sizeable clientele by extending credit and hoarding cooking oil, milk and sugar for them during shortages. At least half of her customers were Ruandan or members of her church. Although there was a shop on nearly every second block, individuals would walk to shops further away from where they lived to buy a kilo of sugar from a fellow ethnic. As one Ruandan told me, 'It is fine to buy small things like milk or tomatoes from any shop, but you should not buy expensive things from outsiders.' It is not surprising then that whenever armed thieves (*kondos*) broke into a shop, the shopkeeper was most likely to accuse people from other ethnic groups of having hired them. This happened seven times during a six month period.

Women shopkeepers were usually single women, but even in cases where the women were married, they distrusted men and did not allow them to serve in the shop. In nine cases it was observed that women never told their partners how much they made, and this distrust between the sexes over money matters was mutual. In a discussion with a Ruandan, Kikuyu and Nkole, a Ganda man put it this way, 'The quickest way to go bankrupt is to entrust a woman with a shop'. In the town a woman could drain a shop in six months to a year, he said, and told several stories in which women either took the merchandise from the shops for personal use or to give to relatives or lovers, and hoarded any money from sales for themselves. Thus, when men went away for a short time, they always checked the money and shop articles as soon as they came back. When men left for prolonged periods, i.e. to buy new stock, the shops would remain closed.

In detailed discussions with 40 men in the Namuwongo-Wabigalo area they unanimously agreed that whenever a shop failed the cause was most likely to be a woman. In the group there were 10 men who had been shop-keepers: six who regarded themselves as victims of the 'greedy town women' who had caused their shops to collapse, and four who had never allowed women 'to mix themselves in my shop business,' i.e., handle the cash box. They felt women should not know how much they made or be allowed to handle the cash box.

Although most people insisted that it was the 'town women who were greedy for money', the same distrust existed in the rural areas. Certainly several cases I encountered in a Ganda village confirmed this mistrust.

The exception to this were the Luo men who did trust their wives with businesses. Luo couples usually assisted each other with the running of the shops, and in my sample the four Luo women shopkeepers sold the goods while the men took care of the stocking and the money. Some Luo men who had shops also had other businesses or were engaged in wage employment. For example, one of the richest Luo men had shops in Namuwongo and Kisenyi run by his wives, while at the same time he operated an under-the-bed one in Kikubamutwe. When Luo women were interviewed over the ownership of the shops, they would say 'ours', whereas the women from other groups specified the shops either as 'mine' or as 'my husband's' shop.

Summary

In this chapter employment has been categorized in terms of those occupations that brought in the maximum income for each woman, but the categories are, in fact, overlapping since most women had more than one source of income. For example, of those listed as cultivators, one was also a distiller, one was a house owner and the other a banana beer brewer, but they were listed as cultivators because most of their incomes came from selling agricultural produce. Other cases of multiple occupations included two prostitutes who were brewers and one who sold pancakes and owned her own home. One distiller was also a barmaid and a pineapple beer seller; another sold cooked food; one millet beer brewer owned houses for rent; a cooked food seller was also a house owner; one unemployed woman owned her own house; a dressmaker was also a verandah trader and owned her house. And, as mentioned above, most distillers found it safer to be brewers as well.

The fact of multiple occupations reflects the struggle to make as much money as possible. Sometimes the women over-extended themselves and did not make enough money in all their multiple employments put together. But as one woman put it, 'I would probably starve if I did not do all these things. There is little money in either one of them.' One woman who had become very successful in distilling, food selling and house owning, nonchalantly said, 'If people who are employed by the government and paid well are still trying to get rich quickly by grabbing every business opportunity, and having their hands, tongues and elbows greased for doing their duty, surely we the poor have more need to have several sources of income.'

Thus, although many different types of people migrated to Namuwongo and Wabigalo, the ones who succeeded in occupational activities were also entrepreneurially aggressive, and had often demonstrated this in the rural areas before migrating. For example, the most desirable form of employment was shopkeeping, but it was also difficult to keep from going bankrupt. It turned out that the veterans whose shops succeeded had had their beginnings in the villages before migrating. This meant that individuals who were not willing to work hard and chase money wherever it appeared were least likely to stay in the urban areas.

I also found that the rural areas were well connected to the urban areas by communication networks. While the young were prone to exaggerate the virtues of town life, particularly if they were men talking to young girls they hoped to marry, the older migrants gave a more modest appraisal. In fact most of the stories I heard in the rural areas concerned the 'rogues' in the urban areas and how one had to deal with them whether in trying to obtain jobs, houses, merchandise or even asking for directions. While some migrants confessed they did not realize what they were getting into when they migrated, others admitted they had hoped to be lucky in manipulating the urban structure. As one woman succinctly put it, 'There is work here if you look for it and if you are not afraid to work hard and get dirty.' The statement stresses initiative in creating employment by identifying need areas. It is no accident that most businesses in this informal sector were interdependent, with the distillers depending upon the wood sellers, the shopkeepers depending upon the brewers and distillers, the labourers depending upon the food sellers for a balanced diet, and the house owners depending upon the constant stream of migrants.

References

1. Fernand Braudel, *Capitalism and Material Life, 1400-1800*, (Weidenfeld and Nicholson, London, 1973), p. 389.
2. S.W. Mintz, 'Men, Women and Trade', *Comparative Studies of Society and History*, No. 12, 1971.
3. G.W. Skinner, 'Chinese Peasants and the Closed Community: An Open and Shut Case,' *Comparative Studies of Society and History*, No. 13, 1971.
4. Christine Obbo, *Women in a low income situation: Namuwongo-Wabigalo, Kampala*, M.A. dissertation, Makerere University, Kampala, 1973.
5. Karen Sacks, 'Engels Revisited: Women: the Organisation of Production' and 'Private Property', in M.Z. Rosaldo and L. Lamphere (eds.), *Woman, Culture and Society*, (Stanford University Press, Stanford, Calif., 1974).
6. A.W. Southall, and P.C.W. Gutkind, 'Townsmen in the Making: Kampala and its Suburbs', *East African Studies No. 9*, East African Institute of Social Research, 1957, p. 51.
7. Keith Hart, 'Informal Income Opportunties and Urban Employment in Ghana', *Journal of Modern African Studies*, No. 11, 1973.
8. *Voice of Uganda* (Kampala), 28 April, 1974.
9. ILO.
10. *Ibid.*
11. Lourdes Arizpe, 'Women in the Informal Sector: The Case of Mexico City,' *Signs: Journal of Women in Culture and Society*, No. 3, 1977.
12. Caroline Hutton, *Reluctant Farmers*, (East African Publishing House, Nairobi, 1971).
13. M.J.B. Molohan, *Detribalization*, (Government Printers, Dar es Salaam, 1957), p. 42.
14. Peter Rigby, *Continuity and Change in Kiganda Religion in Urban and Peri-Urban Kampala* (forthcoming).
15. Some old people were scandalized by the fact that good beer was being distilled. Traditionally only beer that had 'gone bad', i.e. too sweet and not dry, known as *nkenku* was distilled. However, for the brewers the important thing was that they could raise their incomes from 90 to 200 shillings a month.
16. *The People* (Kampala), 26 February, 1972.
17. *Munno* (Kampala), 8 February, 1973.
18. A.W. Southall, and P.G. Gutkind, 'Townsmen in the Making: Kampala and Its Suburbs', op. cit., pp. 138-9.

9. Conflict and Ambivalence

Our purpose has been to find out how and why women migrate to urban areas, what they do there, and how this affects relationships between men and women. The dominant stereotypes assumed that most women were migrating alone and supporting themselves by becoming prostitutes or 'kept' women. This was supplemented by a contradictory concern that the influx of women contributed to already severe urban unemployment by competing for jobs with men whose labour was assumed to be more valuable. Women were valued in their traditional and 'proper' place — in the rural areas and cultivating food crops for their families or cash crops to provide second incomes for families of migrant men.

This study has indicated that various economic, political and social considerations in East Africa are fundamental in determining the extent to which women participate in economic activity. There are wider lessons to be learnt from the struggle of both urban migrant women and rural women. Rural women were given great responsibilities as managers of families and farms, but at the same time they were excluded from the modern sector. These women, who constituted almost 80 per cent of the agricultural work force, continued to labour, untrained and illiterate or semi-literate, with the most outmoded methods and tools. Yet, as producers and reproducers, their assistance was required if the planners and policy-makers were to solve the great problems of overpopulation, starvation, underdevelopment and illiteracy.[1]

Even though the world is changing all about them, it seems that women's own attempts to cope with the new situations they find themselves in are regarded as a 'problem' by men, and a betrayal of traditions which are often confused with women's roles. Women must act as mediators between the past and the present, while men see themselves as mediators between the present and the future.[2] This seems to be part of the reason behind opposition to female migration. The forces of urbanization and international influences have imposed rapid changes upon East African societies, yet men expect women to be politically conservative and non-innovative. Socially, women were accused of 'going too far' when they adopted new practices usually emanating ultimately from the capitals of the metropolitan countries. Yet women who did not keep up with social change rendered themselves

143

socially and economically vulnerable. Women, therefore, found themselves in a double bind: improving their individual positions in relation to men in the rural areas was considered to be against the interests of the local community; yet if they tried to migrate to the towns, the centres of social change and hence the possibilities of achieving individual autonomy, public sentiment decreed that this was not good for women. They were exhorted to eradicate 'ignorance, poverty and disease' in the name of national development, yet when they attempted to do something about these things in their own lives, they were regarded as threatening economic development.

Women wanted power, status and wealth, just as men did. The men regarded any attempt by women to seek more opportunities for acquiring these goals as their 'getting out of control'. To the extent that women have always been an important prop of male success, so has been the need to control them. Although the women in this study were not engaging in direct confrontation with men, their strategies made men uncomfortable and insecure, particularly if they tried to repudiate wifely duties.

Both single and married women felt that economic independence was a basic requirement if they were to improve their social conditions. In order to achieve economic autonomy, the women employed three main strategies: hard work, transactional manipulation and urban migration. To the extent that these were used by men as well, they were general strategies. The difference was in style: the men, backed by societal authority, could act openly whereas women had to resort to deceit, withdrawal, cunning and circumvention. In this chapter a wider range of instances will be called upon to highlight the picture of women we have so far studied in terms of Namuwongo and Wabigalo.

Ploys for Power

All kinds of manipulative techniques have been employed by women at various times and places. In this section we will examine one technique significantly rejected by the women in this study — spirit possession — to emphasize that they were by and large option seekers who insisted on being active in changes taking place in their lives. The actual strategies they employed will then be reviewed and summarized.

Spirit Possession
Anthropological literature has provided and analysed a great deal of material showing that women play a prominent role in such spirit possession activities in many societies. According to many of my own informants, women who became mediums command attention and respect, as well as gaining wealth and power. Indeed, during the period of my research, a woman from one of the Kampala suburbs had become famous throughout the country for her accurate divinations and effective cures. Her enemies accused her of practising sorcery and selling the most powerful of sorcery medicines. She was known as

Mwambalampale (one who wears the trousers), a nickname given to her by a male rival. She advertised on the radio and people travelled many miles for often costly consultations. In 1974 she died in a hit and run accident.

Examples of the way in which women relate to their social environment by means of spirit possession can be found in many parts of Africa. Mernissi has described how Moroccan women mediated their place in the material world by visiting the saints' tombs regularly. Women would gather around any one of their number who was distressed or suffering, but try to build hope in them of regaining their rights.[3] A woman would come in and tell the saints her family problems, naming those responsible and describing their attitudes. The women present would ask for more detail. Eventually the woman broke down, falling to the floor and screaming, only to recover soon as the other women massaged her head and helped her to regain her composure and leave the stage for another woman.[4] Such 'therapy' was soothing and made life bearable for a while.

Lewis has distinguished between central cults, which uphold the moral codes of society by providing an idiom in which men compete for power and authority, and peripheral cults which provide therapeutic aid to the powerless — women, the poor, etc.[5] These therapeutic functions, it seems, mask the cults' real aim of protesting against the dominant sex, protecting women from male demands and providing an effective vehicle for manipulating husbands and other male relatives. Lewis argues that this was particularly so in male-dominated societies,[6] and he associates spirit possession with sexual antagonism.[7] According to him, Somali women who failed to conform to the idea of Somali womanhood — for example, childless women or women who did not wish to have a co-wife — would become possessed with spirits that demanded expensive parties. Unsympathetic to the substantive but allegedly 'trivial' complaints, the men still obeyed the man-hating spirits by financing the parties.[8]

However, Wilson disagrees with Lewis's arguments and proposes instead that spirit possession is associated with 'conflict, competition, tension and rivalry or jealousy between members of the *same* sex, rather than between members of opposite sexes.'[9] For example, women marrying into the lineage try to solve the 'status ambiguity' among themselves and the other women of the lineage.[10]

An attempt to reconcile the arguments of Lewis and Wilson was made by Curley who found that among the Lango of Uganda spirit possession was a symbolic expression of hostility between the sexes *and* an attempt to resolve the status ambiguity that resulted when women went to live with the husbands' people as required by the customary rules of residence. Thus spirit possession was an expression of the resentment women felt at the social and economic changes which benefited men, already possessing a monopoly of judicial and political power. The women, thus reasserted their identity as mothers to the children of the husbands' lineages.[11]

Lindblom reported similar 'deceitful feminine tactics' among the Akamba of Kenya. Under the influence of possession women would demand things from their husbands, originally Masai spears and red cloth, but with the coming of the cities, they started to be possessed by spirits that demanded European goods such as shoes, etc.[12]

Harris found that, among the Taita of Kenya, women were not allowed to engage in wage labour or large-scale trading activity in the urban areas. The men explained that they opposed female migration because unaccompanied women in the towns became prostitutes. Women could, however, trade locally with the consent of their brothers, husbands or fathers, and could occasionally visit their husbands in town.[13] These women, too, were being afflicted by spirits that demanded the foreign things found in the urban areas.[14]

Both in the societies mentioned above and amongst the Tonga of Zambia[15] and the Zaramo[16] and Kaguru[17] of Tanzania, spirit possession is an attempt to do something about women's lack of participation in the things their societies offer.[18] While the social dynamics of spirit possession have been stressed, this does not mean that there were no women who were genuinely psychologically afflicted. But even Chesler's study of American and English female mental patients revealed that only a minority of these women had experienced what she would call genuine states of madness.[19] Most were simply unhappy and self-destructive in typically female ways (tacitly approved by patriarchal culture) such as turning to drink or attempting suicide. Chesler further asserted that this kind of 'mad' behaviour is not particularly valued or understood in Western culture. On the other hand, she was also concerned that we should not romanticize madness, even as a manipulative strategy, because usually it is the women who get hurt.[20] Overall, it is significant that the women in this study chose other means of achieving some control over their situations.

Manipulating Motherhood and Respectability

Visiting the saints, being possessed by spirits or madness involving 'crying out for help' will never bring about cultural or political or economic change in the positions of women. In other societies women have attempted what seemed to be radical behaviour, and it has been claimed that some of the women who participated in the 1929 Aba Riots in Nigeria were in actual fact reasserting their powers as reproducers[21] when they stripped and wore leaves.[22] Whether or not they were really 'sitting on a man' to reclaim their lost political powers,[23] these 'possessors of wombs' certainly did not want their rights to be infringed through increased taxation. But, as a tactic, it can be doubted whether stripping and singing lewd songs was very successful.

The women in this study also made use of their reproductive powers (albeit in a very different way) in order to try and improve their social status. They would manipulate their children's ethnic and social identity so as to get the money necessary to feed and educate them. Women had learned that even reluctant men could be persuaded to accept paternal responsibility by threats of one sort or another (some men were, of course, pleased to be fathers and offered to help voluntarily).

This was a popular strategy in Namuwongo and Wabigalo but, needless to say, the strategy did not work for some women due to their style, age or physical appearance, while some would-be manipulators ended up as prostitutes. But even prostitutes could gain respectability by marrying and thereafter 'putting up with a lot of nonsense' from husbands or, by changing their identity and joining ethnic groups of people perceived as respectable, these women could put themselves beyond social reproach.

Other women were 'lucky' in marriage. Their marriages 'worked' and they had devoted husbands. In fact, the majority of marriages in this study belonged to this category, although some of the women attributed this to sheer hard work, that is, manipulation by them of the traditional virtues. So the Ganda women lowered their eyes, knelt and talked softly when greeting or serving their husbands. In many cases it was a habit that most women had never thought about. However, we have seen how deference was not simply polite behaviour, but also a way of getting things done. Since the Ganda men in the study were obsessed about women cheating them financially or sexually, or deserting without warning, kneeling seems to have lessened the threat and made them, in the words of several men, 'feel that we are in control of women who are no longer controllable'.

The same strategy has been reported elsewhere in Africa. Yoruba women feigned ignorance and obedience when approaching their husbands, and knelt to serve them as they sat. Yet these women actually controlled the family's food supply and were responsible for accumulating wealth by trading.[24] Frontal attack is not the only means to achieve power over decision making. The submissive wife stereotype was publicly maintained despite the fact that women could plead in court, own and dispose of property, carry on independent trade, and often have sufficient wealth for their husbands to borrow from them when in difficulty.[25] A Zambian woman asserted, 'Sometimes husbands forbid their wives to take jobs outside the home. I believe that this is because many women become so stubborn when they have jobs. They think that they, too, are "masters of the house". Many men do not like this attitude . . . . Men don't want to have pressure put on them by a woman.'[26] Korda's study of American male chauvinism pinpoints the central issue. He claims that what American men wanted in marriage was not power so much as 'face'. A woman might be dominant in many ways pertaining to the domestic sphere and the spending of her husband's money, provided she allowed him to play the dominant role in public.[27] A man lost prestige among his peers if he lost an argument with his wife in public.[28] This was certainly true in Namuwongo and Wabigalo as well.

Hard Work
The introduction of a cash economy that required either male migration from the rural areas or the growing of cash crops greatly increased women's work, but her new economic tasks continued to be regarded as part and parcel of domestic work. Yet the women in this study were doing something about their position. By growing more on their husbands' land, some rural women

were able to trade and reinvest the proceeds in the production of still more crops, or goats, cows or mules and in other cases even to buy land themselves.

It is evident that the strategy of hard work was fruitful for women who could own land in their own right as in Buganda, or where animal ploughs and grain mills were available as in Luoland and Ukambani. Even within those areas there were differences among women depending upon their resourcefulness and the amount of farm labour they could muster. For example, at planting and harvest time Luo women who had extended their acreage could rely on the pooled labour of their neighbours as long as they reciprocated whereas the Ganda women in some cases used the husband's hired Ruandan or Rundi labourers or hired their own.

However, factors such as infertile land or low productivity often made hard work a frustrating and unrewarding exercise. Agricultural educationists ignored women, even though in some parts of Buganda they had shown themselves capable of improving food, vegetable and cash crop production. In Western Kenya it was found that farms managed by women had considerably less access to services than farms jointly managed by men and women. Despite these inequalities, women farm managers adopted new crops and husbandry practices at the same rate as male-operated farms. In both areas communication networks through visiting friends and relatives or neighbours facilitated the flow of information.[29] Where land was available and women could own some legally in their own right, where rainfall was plentiful and the soils fertile, migration within the rural areas became a viable alternative. Where all these were lacking, urban migration was the perceived alternative.

'Town Migration Is Not For Women'

Opposition to female migration in East Africa is partly a result of the urban policies that governed the migration of Africans in general and not just in East Africa. There was great concern in the colonial era over detribalization as shown by a survey of the literature on urbanization in Africa. Mitchell has lucidly reported that official perception of Copperbelt towns as areas 'in which Europeans lived by right and followed their way of life . . . , in which Africans were by definition temporary sojourners in the same way that Africans in the tribal area lived their own lives and white men in those areas were but temporary visitors. This thinking was incorporated into the legal and administrative structure from the earliest days of settlement.'[30] If this sounds like an apartheid manifesto, it certainly was intended to separate Western culture from the African cultures. This assumption was shared by many administrators living in the colonial towns and cities of Africa. Africans were to be spared the ravages of urbanization that 'dispossessed' them.[31] However, in East Africa as elsewhere, a few porters, clerks and house servants were needed to provide essential urban services. But to make doubly sure that these workers remained mere 'visitors', irrespective of how long they resided in the towns, they were provided with cramped one-room houses. As a result, the labourers were not certain about urban life and so they left their wives and children in the villages, thus in turn necessitating visits to the rural areas.

As has been pointed out, the fact that wage employment in East Africa began on the basis of male labour has meant that the towns have always been full of men. Since men were not bringing their wives, it is likely that the first women in the towns were prostitutes. Elsewhere, in Northern Rhodesia during the 1950s, Europeans prevented single women from going alone to find work in the Copperbelt.[32] In both Central and West Africa, women who were living alone and not under the authority of a male relative were expelled from the towns.[33] In South Africa women are not allowed to migrate (with or without their husbands) unless their services were required as domestic servants.[34] Caldwell found that, in post-independence Ghana too, strong emotional pressure was exerted on girls and young women to stay in the villages.[35] While five-sixths of the Ghanaian male population he surveyed approved of young men going to towns for a while, only half felt the same way about young women. They argued that men migrated to earn money and acquire skills, while female migrants were simply liable to become prostitutes;[36] shopkeeping was seen as more 'respectable' than trading.[37]

Most of the opposition to female migration is strongest among groups whose homes are not near the towns, whereas the groups indigenous to the towns are usually resigned to accepting the forces that overtake them. However, in East Africa both the host groups and migrants opposed female migration on the grounds of its damage to cultural traditions and the family. But letters to the press indicated that at the heart of the outcry was the fear of losing the vital work force of women in the countryside.

The women in this study were vocal about why they migrated. They were 'tired of rural life': being unpaid labourers on the farms, using outmoded farm tools — the short hoes that 'broke the back' — and the lack of farm produce surpluses for trade. In the urban areas, on the other hand, they could obtain incomes from their labour. Migration thus changed the women's economic position by increasing their personal responsibility and self-reliance.

Except in a few cases most female migrants were self-employed. They created jobs for themselves in accordance with the opportunities they perceived. And these women, for example those who sold cooked food, were contributing directly to economic development. They contributed in many other ways. If they were living alone, they had to pay poll tax from what they earned. Also by feeding men cheaply who could not afford restaurant prices (because their pay was too low or they were saving) they helped out — as they did men who had no family of their own to cook for them and who therefore ate poorly. Indeed in the 1950s, when the authorities tried to discourage women from migrating to the urban areas, employers were faced with poorly fed and lethargic workers who never ate properly at lunch-time.

Of course, not all migrant women's activities contributed positively to development. In fact, the most dubious activities were also the most financially rewarding, such as distilling and brewing.

Although in most cases women were putting in the same working hours as before, they expressed positive feelings towards being their own boss. Married women, however, still had problems asserting control over their own labour, and we have seen the contradictions involved, where women are regarded on the one hand as valuable producers, and on the other as not worthy of being rewarded for their efforts. There are rural areas in which the effects of such contradictions are highly visible. Vansina found that Tio women in Zaire were bitter towards men partly because the division of labour and spatial separation of work places estranged couples and partly because the work load was unequally distributed and required a woman to work long hours daily right from her early youth. The men, on the other hand, were allowed to enjoy their youth and marry late; only then would they start farming and stop caring only 'for their toilet'.[38]

Schneider has reported that in Tanzania Turu women grumbled about the amount of energy they had to spend in comparison to men.[39] Divorce was common, for women knew that a sure way of being divorced was through laziness. This method of eating into a man's wealth seemed to be preferred if a woman wished to erode his power.[40] And, without wealth and power, a man's status would not be very high in the community.

Cohen claimed that in Nigeria Kanuri men repeatedly gave the burdens of cooking, food producing and childbearing as the reasons for marrying, and in calculating factors affecting annual increase or decrease in crop yield they would refer among other things to the loss or gain of a wife. Women, however, showed a desire for wealth and more freedom and power in marriage than what was allowed by the cultural expectations.[41] Indeed the many discrepancies in everyday life weakened the traditional dominant position of men. Women could leave their husband's compound against his wishes and men commonly joked in conversation about their role in making many of the women unfaithful sexually. Men allowed women to have their way in order to avoid the exposure of their lack of authority by having wives walk out on them.[42] Kanuri men also mentioned causes of divorce similar to those of the Ganda. They complained that their wives cooked badly, or not on time or not enough, that their wives visited relatives and friends unnecessarily, committed adultery and were disobedient. In contrast, Kanuri women cited a husband's intolerance, stinginess, lack of sexual attention or skill, or his extra-marital affairs, his lack of appreciation of their services especially their cooking, and the presence or imminence of co-wives.[43]

When the case histories of the various women in this study are set in the broader framework of social history and ethnic traditions, it is clear that the women are struggling for autonomy and individuality. Although there are ethnic variations in the extent of female assertiveness, the common goal women are striving for is dignity, which they maintain has as its minimum condition economic independence from men. Some women were living examples of the fact that, with economic independence, social and sexual independence were possibilities too. Hard work, urban migration and manipulation of men were perceived by the women as essentially the means to achieve these goals.

Controlling Women

By their utterances and life styles the majority of women in this study demonstrated the importance of their own integrity in doing what they thought was good for them individually and not what men dictated. However, even in societies with an urban tradition like the Yoruba, men were still concerned about women getting out of control. The economic emancipation which broadens the scope of a woman's decision-making power seems to take a psychological toll on men.

Yoruba women in West Africa often sued for divorce in order to marry lovers whom they had met in the course of business and who usually paid for the divorce proceedings.[44] Married Yoruba men, as a result, were reported to experience and fear impotence, talking about it and seeking cures.[45] Ganda men in East Africa reacted in similar ways.[46] In the 1930s Nadel found that Nupe men were enslaved to their wives who lent them money acquired through trading and adulterous liaisons. The women also used contraceptives to avoid pregnancy. Finding their position unbearable, the men escaped into fantasies of witchcraft in which women figured as evil witches and men as benevolent wizards.[47] The men protested against female economic emancipation and sexual freedom by avidly consuming Onitsha Market literature that protrayed women as money-loving, adulterous killers.[48]

The central issue is economic autonomy. The men viewed this as a zero sum situation in which the women acquired economic autonomy while the men lost control over the women. If a man cannot control a woman's money directly, he can at least devise all sorts of ways to spend the money that women earn, pretending to be short of money all the time or making a wife feel that any money earned is indirectly due to the husband who brought them to town and allowed her to work in the first place.

Men have used all sorts of other devices to try and perpetuate their waning authority over women in town. We looked at the Luo Union, which had been an important association for helping and controlling members in the urban areas, but which by 1971 had lost its authority — and this meant that only an insignificant number of Luo woman in Kampala could be controlled in this way. We have also singled out the Legio Maria as a Namuwongo church which used confessions to control women — the women being made to feel guilty about trying to acquire an independent source of income (which allegedly demonstrated both greed and a departure from the Luo ideal of a good wife). Such women were seen as anti-social by the church leaders, as 'not decent' — with the connotation, it must be remembered, that traditionally decent women have been those who have submitted to control by men.

Wallace has suggested, though not proved, that religious movements originate in situations of social and cultural stress in an effort by those weighed down by such tensions to revitalize the group or community by creating new dogma, myths and ritual.[49] In the case of the Legio Maria Church the men were under pressure of periodic unemployment and the effects of the 1970 government measure which led most unskilled Luo in the area to lose their jobs in the formal sector. In this context, the endeavours of Luo women to acquire money of their own exacerbated the men's sense of insecurity and caused marital friction.

Thus both Ganda and Luo women reacted in similar ways to changed circumstances. For example, even as early as 1948, rural Luo women were engaged in selling foodstuffs to obtain money for household necessities.[50] And some women refused to work in the gardens of their migrant husbands so that they could devote a large portion of their energy to producing for trade. This in turn became a threat to the security of the rural second income which Luo men in the urban areas have always enjoyed.

The Luo were not the only ethnic group attempting to control members through ethnic organization or religion. In Kenya the Rift Valley Agikuyu Union, that was formed in 1948, dealt with the welfare of its members by repatriating prostitutes, 'loose' girls and errant wives so as to maintain ethnic purity and dignity.[51] The Nubi, too, were concerned over the morality of women, using Islamic law to justify everything from the covering of women's heads to their keeping out of the public sphere. In fact, Nubi men had so successfully convinced everyone of their moral superiority and control over their women that not only were many people from other groups abandoning their ethnic affiliations to become Nubi, but women in particular were being converted mainly to ensure that they appeared respectable. The Nubi seemed to have found the most effective ways of dealing with the vicissitudes of urban life, and have been associated with the Ugandan urban centres almost from the beginning. Thus, like the Xhosa who lived in the immediate surroundings of certain towns in South Africa and who differentiated themselves from the Xhosa who came from far afield, the Nubi encapsulated themselves in a culture centred on Islam which they claimed set them apart from the other groups that were losing their good 'old ways' to foreign practices and had no effective way of solving the problem.[52] The Nubi further distinguished themselves by conspicuously avoiding manual jobs although in fact, while the Nubi men asserted that their women were not strong enough to dig like women from other ethnic groups, the women told me how they had always cultivated food for their families.

For most groups, however, hard dirty work was the main means by which they supported themselves. This work ethic resulted from the fact that in town 'everything costs money — even firewood and water which are free in the villages.' The upshot was that newly arrived migrants in Namuwongo and Wabigalo were discouraged from living off relatives and friends and were pushed towards self-reliance, sometimes by being completely shunned by their relatives or contacts in town.

Creating Options

The women in this study wanted a share in society's wealth, status and power but this did not come very easily. Although these women had never heard of the women's liberation movement in the West, their assertions about equal pay for equal work and economic independence were not very different.

In some parts of Africa, certain women have succeeded in keeping their finances separate from their husbands'. And in one such case, among Ghanaian senior civil servants, it was found that segregated financial management allowed a couple some security and helped avoid conflicts resulting from social change.[53] Women aimed at having separate incomes and keeping their spouses ignorant of it, while the men did the same. The women claimed that this gave them security in the event of bad times and it also reduced the conflict over whether or not the man was being stingy or wasting money on other women or drinking. But the men were greatly concerned that, once women had independent sources of income, they were uncontrollable. In some cases the conflict between individual goals and societal expectations led women to reject marriage as their destiny as long as such a relationship rested upon that economic and social subordination otherwise referred to as femininity.[54] Although most women migrated as wives, there was nonetheless significant migration of single women, whose presence in the urban areas has alarmed many people.

Single Women

Women were not only using their labour to achieve desired goals, but traditional options as well. Among the Ganda the traditional unmarried statuses were being used more and more by women who had gained or hoped to gain economic independence from men, and therefore, had no further use for marriage. The *banakyeyombekedde* would set themselves up as independent householders and dictate the kind of relationships they wanted to have with men. These unattached independent women can be referred to as *femmes libres*.

Femmes libres, a term originally coined in the colonial Congo (now Zaire), referred to women who were legally qualified for residence in African townships *(centres extra-coutumiers)* in their own right by virtue of having an identity card. These women were independent and sexually choosy.[55] Studies in Zairean cities such as Kinshasa and Kisangani suggest that they were a female 'elite' whose company was sought by men with high social aspirations. However, whereas the Kisangani *femmes libres* were urban trend setters, the independent women in this study were to be found in both the rural and urban areas. In both places they enjoyed high visibility, and were agents of social change by virtue of individual achievement.

Independent female householders have been reported among the Nyoro[56] and the Toro[57] in Western Uganda, and among the Toro in particular the status of women rose considerably from the 19th Century to 1960. During this period more women were having children out of wedlock and thus assuming responsibility for their own sexuality, and reducing men's control over women's virginity and the children they bore.[58] But even among the Nyoro, men were concerned about women's increased economic independence as a result of growing and selling cash crops, which meant that a woman could, if she wished, repay her own bridewealth and leave her husband more or less as she chose.[59]

If independent women did not stay in the rural areas, they would migrate in stages. This style of migration occurred in the Belgian Congo during the 1950s,[60] and contrasts sharply with the direct migration or leap from the small village to a large and distant urban centre. Among the Luo the examples of the few widows and divorcees were not lost on the rest of the women: these female independent householders were pioneers.

The dependent women (*bakirerese*), on the other hand, were by definition supposed to be restless. In most cases they used marriage, sexual affairs and children to gain economic goals from men. These women had no particular commitment to either the rural or urban areas, living anywhere that opportunities for self-realization existed.

Concern over the unattached woman was expressed in many quarters. The Ugandan and East African public associated them with marital instability, premarital sex, pregnancy, illegitimacy, prostitution and violent crimes. The usual problems of urbanization and social change were attributed to the fact that women in particular were leaving the countryside. As one official put it, 'The problem of unemployment is caused by these unmarried women who come to town with their children. Single women are also responsible for violent crimes because they have illegitimate children whom they cannot control. Their sons turn into beggars, thieves and armed robbers (*kondos*). The daughters cannot stick to marriage just like their mothers and so turn to prostitution.' These are all problems of the increased expectations and changing ideals that resulted from the political rhetoric of the early 1960s.

Social scientists have also concerned themselves with matrifocal families that are actually headed by women. In the Western industrialized countries these kinds of families are found among the poor who have no hope of ever getting out of the situation.[61] In conjunction with arguments about the asymmetrical patterns of resource and opportunity distribution in many countries, this had led to the presumption that women, such as the ones in this study, will be trapped in perpetual poverty. However, if there is going to be poverty, being married does not solve it. It almost goes without saying that there were poor married people in Wabigalo and Namuwongo. As one woman put it, 'The worst thing is to be weighed down by poverty and to have a man who is also poor, struggling to keep you there. My husband used to drink all my meagre savings and earnings and whenever I had no money he would beat me. The scars on my body made me leave him, not the poverty.' This view is definitely startling since poor women are thought to be submissive. Some questions need to be answered, though, before we fully understand the women who abandon marriage. For example, are they more sensitive to physical and psychological abuse than the majority of women? How does it happen that, even when they are materially the same or worse off than they were, they think they are better off single than married?

More recently social scientists have tended to view the matrifocal family as a distinct traditional family type in which the mother occupies an effective central role,[62] and may serve as a model for thinking about women left in the rural areas when men migrate to work in the mines or the urban areas. Traditional institutions like polygyny have always resulted in matrifocal families. Among the Ganda, where some rich men had several wives, they would settle them on different pieces of land and officially keep only one wife as far as their employers and church leaders were concerned. Save for periodic visits to bring school fees and clothes, the other women would have to cope on their own. Interestingly, these women were not regarded as independent householders and I doubt that they would show up in the census figures. Above all, they did not have the self-reliant attitudes of the unattached women, although in fact they were self-supporting.

Other social scientists view the unattached single women as strategists dealing with the everyday problems of poverty, unemployment, and oppression,[63] and this survivalist perspective corresponds to the attitude taken by the single women in this study. The women told me repeatedly how difficult it was to improve one's lifestyle by challenging social norms.

In other places, historical social arrangements have allowed women much more latitude for leading unattached lives. For example, Robertson has documented the history of the Ga people, the original population of the city of Accra, Ghana. Each patrilineal clan was centred upon its focal compound which contained a war shrine whose strength was believed to be destroyed by the contaminating menstrual blood of women. The husbands, therefore, resided in separate compounds, at night visiting their wives who lived with their mothers and children. The system worked well as men fished and farmed while the wives sold the surplus. However, with the growth of urban occupations in the modern city, men had no surplus, and their support for their wives and children dwindled. The women still derive their income from trade.[64] It is my impression that the Ga women are no better or worse off then the women in this study.

Coping With Social Change

Women who had acquired substantial sums of money found the traditional power relationships between the sexes unacceptable and the threat to the changed power and authority relationships was often felt first in the domestic sphere. However, men found that, just as they could not 'control' women at home, so they could not stop them by exerting moral pressure in public. They tried to reverse or curb changes in power and authority relationships by dividing women into 'good' and 'loose' women. However, women had come to accept the fact that their assertions of individuality were bound to be met with such stereotypes. After all, the division between the good and the bad

155

woman has been used all over the world when women are deemed to be gettin out of control. The ridiculing of women in the West for bra burning is comparable to the myth of prostitution in East Africa since both are aimed at perpetuating the social control of women.

The findings of this study, despite the small size of the sample, are relevant to current women's issues. They show what happens when women take action to bring about change in their personal circumstances and hence, indirectly, wider social change. It has been shown that East African women are doing something about their situations by tackling the specific problems of poverty, ignorance and unsatisfactory personal relationships. The women were convinced that, if they dealt with poverty and acquired independent sources of incomes, then dealing with the other areas of their lives would be relatively easy. With this end in mind, the rural women traded, invested in land and ploughs and expanded their crop acreages; as a last resort they migrated to the urban areas where they hoped to make their lives better. In their personal relationships, some manipulated the sources of cash income for their benefit, others used their reproductive ability to improve their status or used traditional courtesy, preferring to get their way by quiet manipulation. The wome knew what they wanted and they were willing to achieve these goals by hook or by crook.

In their non-economic as well as their economic aspirations, the women's demands paralleled the rhetoric of Western feminists. They, too, wanted fair and equal treatment in the homes, particularly with regard to the products of their labour. Some, too, asserted their individuality through the decisions the took regarding their sexuality and childbearing, and often resulting in the tota rejection of marriage.

In Namuwongo and Wabigalo women tended not to organize formal associ tions or groups. True, the Food Sellers Association was formed while I was there, but it soon disbanded when the members found that they could manipulate the bureaucrats much more efficiently as individuals than as a group, and this attitude may explain why no formal women's groups existed in the area despite the great potential for women to form a movement and harness their collective energy to improve their conditions. The symbolic patterns of activities and behaviour were public knowledge, yet their articulation was on an individual basis.

Much has been said on this question in other contexts. Sullerot has argued that ties of affection between wives and husbands, mothers and sons, sisters and brothers, girlfriends and boyfriends cut across generalized relationships of sexual domination and submission. The interdependent personal relationships between members of the sexes minimize the potential conflict between them as groups because any violence, however mild, would imply a negation of these relationships.[65] John Stuart Mill made a similar point when he claimed that social and natural causes (like affection between the sexes) undermine the collective rebellion of women against the publicly sanctioned domination of men; the wife is entirely dependent on the husband, in a way an extension of him socially, economically and legally and dependin entirely on his will. Unlike other kinds of subordinate relationships that are based on fear, men not only want obedience from the women in their lives, they want their affection as well.[66]

These factors make it difficult for women to identify themselves primarily with other women. According to Simmel, 'the fact that a group called women' exists, easily identified and classified on a sex basis, actually militates against the formation of strong groups and the attainment of solidarity with other women.[67] He further stated that male culture denies the autonomy of female identity by asserting that women, unlike men, are more earthbound, more whole and natural than men.[68]

Certainly, the women in this study, while they provided moral and emotional support for their female friends, acquaintances and relatives in need, could not form any coherent basis for struggling together. Even where they discussed possible strategies and solutions, their implementation finally depended upon the individuals concerned. These women who constantly quoted the proverb that 'the teeth that are close together bite the meat' (*agali awamu gegaluma enyama*) failed to extend the analogy to their own struggles and were more comfortable with strategies that did not antagonize men.

Opposition to Change

Very often it is women themselves who resist change even when it is sweeping them along unwittingly. This is graphically illustrated by Betty Friedan, whose book, *The Feminine Mystique*,[69] was an important statement of women's submerged discontent and exposed the emptiness of the lives of middle-class women supposedly liberated by technology, education and science. She had to hide her writing from her suburban neighbours when they dropped in for coffee, and, once the secret was out, she was snubbed by these same neighbours who stopped inviting her to dinner and excluded her children from the car pool arranged to take them to dancing classes.[70] She had threatened the tranquility of restless wives who had spent their lives being nice and reasonable.[71] Women who saw their own dissatisfaction as a sign of personal failure viewed her writing as a personal attack. In other words, dissatisfaction with life, and particularly with marriage, must not spill out into the public sphere. As one American woman put it to me during a conversation, 'Some women are over-sensitive over the question of Women's Rights. No woman with a happy marriage goes around complaining about male domination and injustice.' According to this way of thinking, an itch becomes oversensitized by constant scratching. But Namuwongo and Wabigalo residents would say that it is also possible that some people are good at controlling itches by keeping a stiff upper lip — and sometimes collapsing eventually as a result. Even Betty Friedan herself felt so guilty, fearful and pained at having incurred the hostility of her husband that she clung on desperately to her marriage,[72] but the marriage did in the end break down.

However, even when women's consciousness has been raised to form actual groups, there are usually other fears with regard to other aspects of social life.

A study of the American Women's Liberation Movement by Cassel has shown that it is divided into the conservative and radical branches: women's rights and women's liberation. The former tended to be older, more likely to be married, well educated, established in their life patterns as professional women or housewives with older children, with higher incomes in their own right or through their husbands — and they indicated more positive and fewer negative feelings about marriage. As members of upper and middle class families they had a stake in the system. The women's liberationists, on the other hand, were more likely to be students or hold low-paying clerical jobs. They were less likely to be married or have children and more likely to be separated or divorced. Many expressed extreme views on marriage, the family, childrearing, careers, and the need to overthrow the establishment.[73]

The tasks of coping with the male world makes divisions between women more visible than what unites them. For example, in America it did not take long for the mainly male employers to realize that there were two kinds of women's movement. According to Korda, this is the difference between the struggles of young, better educated women to define themselves as individuals in a work situation, and the concerns of mainly older women over salaries, promotions and respect for work done.[74] Neither struggle could really change the structure of the work situation. The former were found to be irritating because they were not talking about work itself and the latter were threatening because their deep involvement in the system meant that they were just as interested in the profits as the men.[75] In support of this distinction, Korda cites two cases. The first one, of presumably an older woman, is a very common occurrence in my experience. She complained that women's liberation was about issues and not about work. She worked hard, kept a low profile and did not associate with the Women's Movement. Her male supervisor thought that she was terrific, hardworking and rational. But in her words, she was still treated like a faithful dog.[76] Another case concerned a militant woman organizer who tried to change the situation of women in the work place instead of just talking privately about male attitudes. When she had made such substantial gains for women that even the timid non-joiners were in sympathy with her, the management promoted her because she was talented. They gave her an overload of work to keep her from the others, and when there was a decline in the business she was quietly fired along with many others.[77] Women soon learned to 'shut up and go on with the job.'[78] The claims of feminists are further neutralized by the fact that anyone can mouth feminist rhetoric without being committed.

We noted previously that most African women are reluctant to enter into public discussion of the important issues affecting them. Those who do write or talk make very little impact. The causes are many but they are all rooted in the fear of not playing the right game in a man's world. At the 1972 All-Africa Women's Organisation week-long conference in Dar es Salaam, 200 leading women from 41 countries did meet together but they spent a great deal of their time discussing the 'menace of miniskirts and hot pants' that were foreign and unsuitable for African women.[79]

The main political speech was delivered by Julius Nyerere, the President of Tanzania, who called upon women to become more involved in public affairs because both men and women were needed to develop the Continent. He pointed out that the rejection of class exploitation must be accompanied by an end to viewing women as the servant of the species.[80] He further stressed that women would only fully participate in the struggle against political colonialism, 'when they themselves are liberated from all obstacles put in their way by their male counterparts.'[81] This was an enlightening speech but a predominantly women's conference was really the wrong audience for it. Of course everyone, male and female, must be liberated from their colonial roles, but, as one newspaper editorial pointed out, a free and independent Africa is no guarantee in itself that women will enjoy the same freedoms as men: 'African leaders who by and large are men, are not at the moment particularly anxious to extend the philosophy of equality to women.'[82] The sphere of politics provides a striking example of this, for one male journalist could write in a magazine: 'To most educated African women politics is anathema, and that springs from the fact that most of them are terribly inhibited, humorless and inward-looking. Most of our women graduates are plain bores who leave one with the impression that they believe it is a crime to talk politics, let alone engage in political activities. Theirs, they seem to think, is only to minister to the emotional and sexual needs of their men; to be seen but not to be heard.'[83]

But newspaper stories and correspondence, novels and casual remarks tell a different story. A Zambian woman, who was discouraged from entering politics but who believed that it was only when women entered Parliament and participated in the legislative process that the ills of society would be corrected, aptly sums up the situation and experiences of East African women: 'A progressive and intelligent woman who participates in politics is regarded as a hooligan. She is said to have every possible fault, bad behaviour, and so on. She isn't worth anything; she is finished.'[84] Even in university circles men will yawn or smirk when a woman is discussing political or emotionally charged social issues, while other men will tell the woman that she talks too much. This leads some ambitious women to hush other women in discussions with the men!

Another method of getting on is, of course, an affair with those (men) in power. But this issue has provoked surprising comments from women. For example, during a meeting of the Kenya women's organization, Maendeleo ya Wanawake, its president condemned the men who exploited poor, defenceless, innocent girls, but she reserved her most scathing comments for these working women who had 'affairs' and she declared that it was the women who 'should be sacked immediately' on discovery. She even suggested that there should be a law limiting the purchase of contraceptives by married women,[85] presumably to discourage evils like prostitution by making sex less easy and safe for women.[86] Clearly the boss's power is taken for granted even by national women's leaders.

Certainly this problem is not peculiar to Uganda or East Africa. A study at

the University of Texas-San Antonio by Professor Sandra Carey revealed
that sexual harassment at work was ubiquitous in the United States. In a
sample of 401 working women, the sexual advances mentioned included
leering or ogling (mentioned by 36 per cent), hints and verbal pressures (37
per cent), and touching and brushing against, grabbing and pinching (30 per
cent). Male superiors asked 18 per cent of the women away for a weekend,
and 6 per cent said they were promised rewards for their 'other business
activities.'[87]

The difference is that in East Africa, it would be futile to protest whereas,
in America, the Women's Movement has created a climate that makes public
protest and favourable results possible. In fact, East African women are
usually reluctant to support measures that would protect them by controlling
the behaviour of men. It is worth examining the abortive 1976 Marriage Bill
in Kenya which was to apply to all ethnic and religious groups in the regu-
lation of marriage, property rights, separation and child maintenance. It aimed
at the mandatory maintenance of the children by the father; the wife's right
to own and sell property in her own name; punishment for anyone forcing a
man or woman to marry against their will; and adultery duly constituted as
an offence with a prison term of up to six months. The last section on adultery
resulted in a lot of discussion and editorials. The Bill was only supported by
the Roman Catholic Bishop of Eldoret, John Njenga, who analysed it and
urged that the baby be not thrown out with the bathwater because of the
clause on adultery.[88] Opposition from a mainly male Parliament was expected
and so was that of the Nairobi branch president of GEMA (Gikuyu, Embu,
Meru,Akamba Association) who declared, 'African culture is bound to
perish if the population does not see the danger behind having such a bill
passed. There cannot be two masters in the house' (referring to the property
clause).[89]

The most startling opposing arguments, however, came from the women.
This is understandable in the light of all we have mentioned in this chapter.
One woman declared, 'An African man is born polygamist; let's face it.'[90]
Another objected to the bill because 'Once you jail a spouse you have already
wrecked his or her future life. And who looks after the family while the
husband is in jail?'[91] The President of the Maendeleo ya Wanawake organization, the national women's group we have already mentioned, also the
wife of a minister, spoke at a meeting of women from 20 districts, and
advised them to study the bill carefully before endorsing it. To the press
she said that the women of Kenya faced a grim future if Parliament were to
pass the bill, and added, 'As a housewife, I would not like my husband going
to jail merely because he has gone to bed with another woman.'[92]

Given this situation in which elite women are the most vocal opponents
of concrete measures to improve the lot of women, changes are going to continue to come not from the top but from the bottom of the social strata
where women have nothing to lose. In fact, the Namuwongo and Wabigalo
women told me that the elite women were so attached to status, particularly
with regard to their marriages, that their lifes were 'hollow in the middle'. All

form, but little substance, to put it strongly. It remains to be seen whether the situation changes with the increase in female graduates. Currently they are too busy stressing publicly that there is equal pay and access to opportunities between men and women, while privately moaning about sexism and lack of promotions. But it is the unskilled, unschooled women of this study who have demonstrated that, 'We must be worthy of our demands for emancipation.'[93]

References

1. Evelyne Sullerot, *Woman, Society and Change*, World University Library, London, 1971), p. 248.
2. *Ibid.*, p. 88.
3. Fatuma Mernissi, 'Women, Saints and Sanctuaries', *Signs: Journal of Women in Culture and Society*, special issue on 'Women and National Development', Vol. 3, No. 1, 1977, p. 104.
4. *Ibid.*, p. 105.
5. I.M. Lewis, *Ecstatic Religion: An Anthropological Study of Spirit Possession and Shamanism*, (Penguin, Harmondsworth, 1971).
6. I.M. Lewis, Spirit Possession and Deprivation Cults', *Man*, Vol. 1, 1966, p. 309.
7. *Ibid.*, p. 314-6.
8. *Ibid.*
9. Peter J. Wilson, 'Status Ambiguity and Spirit Possession', *Man*, Vol. 3, 1967, p. 316.
10. *Ibid.*, p. 373.
11. Richard Curley, *Elders, Shades and Women: Ceremonial Change in Lango, Uganda*, (Stanford University Press, Stanford, Calif., 1973), p. 190.
12. Gerhard Lindblom, *The Akamba in British East Africa, An Ethnological Monograph*, Archives d'Etudes Orientales, Uppsala, Vol. 17, 1920, pp. 230-40.
13. Grace Harris, 'Possession "Hysteria" in a Kenya Tribe', *American Anthropologist*, Vol. 59, 1957.
14. *Ibid.*, p. 1051.
15. Elizabeth Colson, 'Spirit Possession Among the Tonga of Zambia' in John Beattie and John Middleton (eds.), *Spirit Mediumship and Society in Africa*, (Routledge and Kegan Paul, London, 1969).
16. Marja-Liisa Swantz, 'Ritual and Symbol in Transitional Zaramo Society', *Studia Missionala Upsaliensia*, Vol. XVI, Uppsala: Gleesup, 1970.
17. T.O. Beidelman, *The Kaguru: A Matrilineal People of East Africa*, (Holt, Rinehart and Winston, New York, 1971).
18. Edwin Ardener, 'Belief and the Problem of Women' in Jean S. La Fontaine (ed.), *The Interpretation of Ritual: Essays in Honour of A.I. Richards*, (Tavistock Publications, London, 1972).
19. Phyllis Chesler, *Women and Madness,* (Avon Books, New York, 1972), pp. xxii-xxiii.
20. *Ibid.*

21. Caroline Ifeka Moller, 'Female Militancy and Colonial Revolt: The Women's War of 1929, Eastern Nigeria' in S. Ardener (ed.) *Perceiving Women*, (Malaby Press, London, 1975).
22. *Ibid.*
23. Judith Van Allen, 'Sitting on a Man: Colonialism and the Lost Institutions of Igbo Women', *Canadian Journal of African Studies*, Vol. 6, No. 2, 1972.
24. Peter Lloyd, 'The Yoruba of Nigeria', in James L. Gibbs, Jr.,(ed.), *Peoples of Africa*, (Holt, Rinehart and Sons, New York, 1965).
25. Janheinz Jahn, 'A Yoruba Market-Woman's Life' in Alan Dundes (ed.), *Every Man His Way*, (Prentice Hall, Englewood Cliffs, N.J., 1968).
26. Holle Gertner-Hedlund, 'Recounting the Experiences of Rosa Mugula, 27, of Zambia', in *Report from SIDA* Special Issue: 'The Woman in the World', 1975, pp. 20-21.
27. Michael Korda, *Male Chauvinism: How It Works and How To Get Free of It*, (Medallion Books, Berkeley, 1972), p. 162.
28. *Ibid.*
29. Kathleen Staudt, 'Agricultural Productivity Gaps: A Case Study of Male Preference in Government Policy Implementation', *Development and Change*, Vol. 9, 1978.
30. Mitchell, 1969, p. 161.
31. E. Hellman, 'Rooiyard: A Sociological Survey of an Urban Native Slum Yard', International African Institute, *Social Implications of Industrialization and Urbanization in Africa South of the Sahara*, UNESCO, Paris, 1956).
32. William Watson, *Tribal Cohesion in a Money Economy*, (Manchester University Press for Rhodes Livingstone Institute, 1958).
33. A.W. Southall, 'Kinship and Friendship in Kisenyi' in A.W. Southall (ed.), *Social Change in Modern Africa*, (Oxford University Press for the International African Institute, London, 1961), p. 223.
34. Sheila Van der Horst, *African Workers in Town*, (Capetown, 1964), p. 35; Elizabeth S. Landis, *Apartheid and the Disabilities of Women*, (UN Department of Political and Security Council Affairs, New York, 1975).
35. Julius Caldwell, *African Rural Migration: The Movement To Ghana's Towns*, (Australian National University Press, Canberra, 1969), p. 103.
36. *Ibid.*, pp. 106-7.
37. A.W. Southall, (ed.), *op. cit.*, p. 51.
38. Jan Vansina, *The Tio Kingdom of the Middle Congo, 1880-1892*, (Oxford University Press for The International African Institute, London, 1972), pp. 161-3, 166.
39. Harold   Schneider, *The Wahi Wanyaturu: Economics in an African Society*, (Aldine, Chicago, 1976), p. 24.
40. *Ibid.*, pp. 64-5.
41. Ronald Cohen, *The Kanuri of Bornu*, (Holt, Rinehart and Winston, New York, 1967), p. 41.
42. *Ibid.*, p. 44.
43. *Ibid.*
44. *Ibid.*
45. Robert A. Le Vine, 'Sex Roles and Economic Change in Africa' in

John Middleton (ed.), *Black Africa: Its Peoples and Their Cultures Today*, (MacMillan Co., Toronto, 1970), p. 179.

46. John H. Orley, *Culture and Mental Illness*, (East African Publishing House for Makerere Institute of Social Research, Nairobi, 1976), pp. 13-14.

47. Cited in Abner Cohen, *Custom and Politics in Urban Africa*, (Routledge and Kegan Paul, London, 1969), p. 68.

48. Robert A. Le Vine, *op. cit.*, pp. 178-9.

49. Anthony Wallace, *Religion: An Anthropological View*, (Random House, New York).

50. Simeon H. Ominde, *The Luo Girl from Infancy to Marriage*, (MacMillan, Nairobi, 1952), p. 55.

51. M. Tamarkin, 'Tribal Association, Tribal Solidarity and Tribal Chauvinism in a Kenya Town', *Journal of African History*, Vol. 14, No. 2, 1973, pp. 259-61.

52. Philip Mayer, *Townsmen or Tribesmen*, (Oxford University Press, Capetown, 1961).

53. Christine Oppong, *Marriage Among a Matrilineal Elite*, (Cambridge University Press, Cambridge, 1974), p. 85.

54. See Simone de Beauvoir, *Le Deuxième Sex*, (Editions Gallimard, Paris, 1949), Introduction.

55. Georges Balandier, *Sociologie des Brazzaville Noires*, (Colin, Paris, 1955).

56. John Beattie, 'Nyoro Marriage and Affinity', *Africa*, 1959, p. 1-2.

57. M. Perlman, 'The Changing Status and Role of Women in Toro (Western Uganda)', *Cahiers d'Etudes Africaines*, 1966, p. 618.

58. M. Perlman, 'Children Born Out of Wedlock and the Status of Women in Toro, Uganda', in *Rural Africana*, No. 29, Winter 1975-76, pp. 95-119; S. Comhaire-Sylvain, *Femmes de Kinshasa*, (Mouton, Paris, 1968), pp. 162-3; J.S. La Fontaine, *City Politics: A Study of Leopoldville, 1962-1963*, (Cambridge University Press, 1970), p. 204; Valdo Pons, *Stanleyville: An African Urban Community Under Belgian Administration*, (Oxford University Press, 1969); Kenneth Little, *African Women in Towns: An Aspect of Social Revolution*, (Cambridge University Press, 1973), pp. 113-20.

59. John Beattie, *op. cit.*, pp. 57-8.

60. A. Doucy and P. Feldheim, 'Some Effects of Industrialization in Two Districts of Equatoria Province (Belgian Congo) 1956' in D. Forde (ed.) *Social Implications of Industrialization and Urbanization in Africa South of the Sahara*, (UNESCO, Paris).

61. Oscar Lewis, *Five Families: Mexican Case Studies in the Culture of Poverty*, (Basic Books, New York, 1959); Raymond Thomas Smith, *The Negro Family in British Guiana: Family Structure and Social Status in the Villages*, (Routledge and Kegan Paul, London, 1956).

62. Nancy Tanner, 'Matrifocality in Indonesia and Africa and Among Black Americans' in Michelle Zimbalist Rosaldo and Louise Lamphere (eds.), *Women, Culture and Society*, (Stanford University Press, California, 1974), pp. 129-36.

63. Helen Safa, 'The Female-Based Household in Public Housing: A Case Study of Puerto Rico', *Human Organisation*, No. 24, 1965; Carol B. Stack, 'Sex Roles and Survival Strategies in an Urban Black Community',

in Rosaldo and Lamphere, *op. cit.*, pp. 113-28.
64. Claire Robertson, 'Social and Economic Change in Twentieth Century Accra: Ga Women', Ph.D. Dissertation, University of Wisconsin, Madison.
65. Evelyne Sullerot, *Women, Society and Change: 1971*, (World University, London, 1971), p. 70.
66. John Stuart Mill, 'The Subjection of Women, 1869' in John Stuart Mill and Harriet Taylor Mill, *Essays on Sex Equality*, (Chicago University Press, Chicago, 1970), p. 141.
67. George Simmel, *Philosophische Kultur*, (Werner Klinkhard, Leipzig, 1911).
68. *Ibid.*
69. Betty Friedan, *The Feminine Mystique*, (Dell Publishing Co., New York, 1963).
70. Betty Friedan, *It Changed My Life*, (Dell Publishing Co., New York, 1977), p. 89.
71. See Sheila Rowbotham, *Woman's Consciousness, Man's World*, (Penguin Books, Middlesex, 1974), p. 5.
72. Betty Friedan, *op. cit.*, 1977, p. 90.
73. Joan Cassel, *op. cit.*, pp. 103-5.
74. Michael Korda, *op. cit.*, p. 80.
75. *Ibid.*
76. *Ibid.*, p. 83.
77. *Ibid.*, pp. 82-5.
78. Sheila Rowbotham, *op. cit.*, p. 81.
79. 'Our Women in Politics', *Africa* (London), No. 16, 1972, p. 23.
80. *Ibid.*
81. *Daily Nation* (Nairobi), 26 July 1972.
82. *Ibid.*, 24 July 1972.
83. *Africa, op. cit.*, p. 20.
84. Holle Gertner-Hedlung, *Report from SIDA*, Special Issue on 'The Woman in the World', 1975, p. 21.
85. *Sunday Nation*, 14 August 1971.
86. *Sunday Nation*, 22 August 1971.
87. *The Capital Times*, 20 April 1977 (Madison, Wisconsin).
88. *African Woman* (London) 1976, p. 55.
89. *Ibid.*
90. *Ibid.*, p. 54.
91. *Ibid.*
92. *Ibid.*, p. 55.
93. Teresia Elad, *African Woman* (London) No. 15, May-June, 1978.

Relevant Reading

Ardener, Edwin, 'Belief and the Problem of Women', in J.S. LaFontaine (ed.), *The Interpretation of Ritual*, London: Tavistock, 1972; also published in Shirley Ardener (ed.), *Perceiving Women*, London: Malaby Press, 1975.

Basch, Francoise, *Relative Creatures*, New York: Schocken Books, 1974.

Beauvoir, Simone de, *The Second Sex*, New York: Bantam Books, 1968.

Boserup, Esther, *Woman's Role in Economic Development*, London: George Allen and Unwin, Ltd, 1970.

Brain, James L., 'Down to Gentility: Women in Tanzania', *Sex Roles*, Vol. 4, No. 5, 1978.

Cohen, Ronald, *Dominance and Defiance: A Study of Marital Instability in an Islamic African Society*, Anthropological Studies No. 6, Washington: American Anthropological Association, 1971.

Elkan, Walter. The Employment of Women in Uganda, (mimeo); also published in *Bulletin de l'Institut Inter-Africain du Travail*, Vol. IV, No. 4, 1957.

Hafkin, Nancy J. and Edna G. Bay (eds.), *Women in Africa*, Stanford: Stanford University Press, 1976.

Little, Kenneth, 'Some Methodological Considerations in the Study of African Women's Urban Roles', *Urban Anthropology*, Vol. 4, No. 2, 1975.

Mernissi, Fatima, *Beyond the Veil*, Cambridge (Mass.): Schen Kaman Publishing Co., 1975.

Mill, John Stuart, *The Subjection of Women*, New York: Frederick A. Stokes, 1911.

Nyerere, Julius K., *Man and Development*, Dar es Salaam. Oxford University Press, 1974.

Parkin, David, *Town and Country in Central and Eastern Africa*, Plymouth: International African Institute, 1975.

Parkin, David. *Neighbours and Nationals in an African City Ward*, London: Routledge and Kegan Paul, 1969.

Paulme, Denise (ed.), *Women of Tropical Africa*, trans. by H.M. Wright, London: Routledge and Kegan Paul, 1963.

p'Bitek, Okot, *Song of Lawino*, Nairobi: East African Publishing House, 1966.

Pellow, Deborah, *Women of Accra: A Study of Options*, Reference Publications, 1977.

Richards, A.I., F. Sturrock and J.M. Fortt, *Subsistence to Commercial Farming in Present Day Buganda*, Cambridge University Press, 1973.

Rosaldo, Michelle Zimbalist and Louise Lamphere, *Woman, Culture and Society*, California: Stanford University Press, 1974.

Rowbotham, Sheila, *Woman's Consciousness, Man's World*, London: Pelican Books, 1973.

Schuster, Ilsa, *New Women of Lusaka*, Mayfield Publishing Co., 1979.

Southall, A.W. (ed. and intro.), *Social Change in Modern Africa*, London: Oxford University Press for the International African Institute, 1961.

Sudarkasa, Niara, *Where Women Work: A Study of Yoruba Women in the Market Place and in the Home*, Ann Arbor: University of Michigan, Museum of Anthropology, 1973.

Relevant Reading

Sullerot, Evelyne, *Woman, Society and Change,* London: World University
    Library, 1971.